District Gazetteers of India Series 26

BENGAL DISTRICT GAZETTEERS

DACCA

Owing to the antiquity and rarity of this book, certain pages are regrettably absent, and readability is compromised due to the blurring of the original text. If you possess any insights regarding the availability of these missing sections, kindly inform us. Your assistance is crucial in ensuring the completion of this significant work for the benefit of future generations.

District Gazetteers of India Series 26

BENGAL DISTRICT GAZETTEERS

DACCA

B. C. ALLEN

52 VOLUMES

(VOL. 15th)

GYAN

Published by

Gyan Publishing House
5, Ansari Road
Daryaganj, New Delhi-110002
Phone: 011-47034999, 9811692060
E-mail: books@gyanbooks.com

Distribution Network
gyanbooks.com
India, USA, Canada, UK, Australia, France

ISBN: 978-93-6208-915-1 (Set) 52 Volumes
978-81-212-6135-7 (PB)
First Published, 1912

2nd Impression 2024

Printed at: Gyan Press, Delhi.

BENGAL DISTRICT GAZETTEERS (VOL. 15th)
Author: B. C. Allen

LIST OF VOLUMES

S. NO.	ISBN NO.	VOLUME	TITLE	AUTHOR	PRICE	PAGES
			ASSAM DISTRICT GAZETTEERS			
1	9788121285926	1st	Cachar	B. C. Allen	600	300
2	9788121285919	2nd	Sylhet	B. C. Allen	750	378
3	9788121285902	3rd	Goalpara	B. C. Allen	400	203
4	9788121285896	4th	Kamrup	B. C. Allen	675	344
5	9788121285889	5th	Darrang	B. C. Allen	725	364
6	9788121285872	6th	Nowgong	B. C. Allen	560	280
7	9788121285865	7th	Sibsagar	B. C. Allen	675	343
8	9788121285858	8th	Lakhimpur	B. C. Allen	690	347
9	9788121285841	9th	Naga Hills and Manipur	B. C. Allen	580	294
10	9788121285834	10th	The Khasi And Jaintia Hills, The Garo Hills And The Lushai Hills	B. C. Allen	675	363
11	9788121285827	11th	The Sadiya and Balipara Frontier Tract	B. C. Allen	375	190
			BENGAL DISTRICT GAZETTEERS			
12	9788121218672	1st	Angul	L. S. S. O'Malley	340	168
13	9788121259637	2nd	Bakarganj	J. C. JACK	970	194
14	9788121218696	3rd	Balasore	L. S. S. O'Malley	450	228
15	9788121259590	4th	Bankura	L. S. S. O'Malley	1000	199
16	9788121218375	5th	Bhagalpur	J. Byrne	390	194
17	9788121218290	6th	Birbhum	L. S. S. O'Malley	300	150
18	9788121259651	7th	Eastern Bengal and Assam - Bogra	J. N. Gupta	940	188
19	9788121218351	8th	Burdwan	J. C. K. Peterson	450	227
20	9788121259538	9th	Calcutta District Gazetteer - Statistics, 1901 - 02		340	68
21	9788121218313	10th	Champaran	L. S. S. O'Malley	410	205
22	9788121259613	11th	Eastern Bengal District Gazetters - Chittagong	L. S. S. O'Malley	1080	216
23	9788121259552	12th	Chota Nagpur Tributary		130	26
24	9788121259415	13th	The Cooch Behar Gazette: Statistics		1460	292
25	9788121218412	14th	Cuttack	L. S. S. O'Malley	490	248
26	9788121261357	15th	Eastern Bengal District Gazetteers Dacca	B. C. Allen	400	207
27	9788121218436	16th	Darbhanga	L. S. S. O'Malley	360	180
28	9789362089335	17th	Darjeeling	L. S. S. O'Malley	500	248
29	9788121259453	18th	Eastern Bengal District Gazetteers - Dinajpur	F. W. Strong	890	178
30	9788121259392	19th	Faridpur	L. S. S. O'Malley	700	140
31	9788121218474	20th	Gaya	L. S. S. O'Malley	540	270
32	9788121214032	21st	Bihar and Orissa District Gazetteer: Hazaribagh	E. Lister	715	234
33	9788121218337	22nd	Hooghly	L. S. S. O'Malley	680	340
34	9788121218191	23rd	Bengal District Gazetteer Howrah	L. S. S. O'Malley	390	199
35	9788121259293	24th	Eastern Bengal and Assam - Jalpaiguri	John F. Gruning	890	178
36	9788121259279	25th	Jessore	L. S. S. O'Malley	960	192
37	9788121259231	26th	Khulna	L. S. S. O'Malley	1100	220
38	9788121259217	27th	Malda	G. E. Lambourn	670	134
39	9788121267854	28th	Manbhum	H. Coupland	600	313
40	9788121218498	29th	Midnapore	L. S. S. O'Malley	500	252
41	9788121218597	30th	Monghyr	L. S. S. O'Malley	560	280
42	9788121259156	31st	Murshidabad	L. S. S. O'Malley	1250	250
43	9788121259576	32nd	Bengal District Gazetteers - Muzaffarpur	L. S. S. O'Malley	940	188
44	9788121259132	33rd	Mymensingh	F. A. Sachse	960	192
45	9788121259118	34th	Nadia	J. H. E. Garrett	1070	214
46	9788121259095	35th	Eastern Bengal and Assam - Noakhali	J. E. Webster	580	115
47	9788121218450	36th	Feudatory States of Orissa	L. E. B. Cobdenramsay	790	395
48	9788121259071	37th	Pabna	L. S. S. O'Malley	710	142
49	9788121218511	38th	Palamau	L. S. S. O'Malley	380	190
50	9788121218634	39th	Patna	L. S. S. O'Malley	500	250
51	9788121218535	40th	Puri	L. S. S. O'Malley	650	328
52	9788121218757	41st	Purnea	L. S. S. O'Malley	440	220
53	9788121258937	42nd	Rajshahi	L. S. S. O'Malley	1080	216
54	9788121256681	43rd	Bihar and Orissa District Gazetteers: Ranchi	M. G. Hallett	1350	278
55	9788121258913	44th	Eastern Bengal and assam - Rangpur	J. A. Vas	890	178
56	9788121218559	45th	Sambalpur	L. S. S. O'Malley	480	242
57	9788121214056	46th	Santal Parganas	L. S. S. O'Malley	940	308
58	9788121218610	47th	Saran	L. S. S. O'Malley	380	190
59	9788121218658	48th	Shahabad	L. S. S. O'Malley	380	190
60	9788121256704	49th	The Gazetteer of Sikhim	H. H. Risley	960	481
61	9788121218573	50th	Singhbhum, Saraikela And Kharsawan	L. S. S. O'Malley	560	280
62	9788121259439	51st	Eastern Bengal District Gazetteers - Tippera	J. E. Webster	730	146
63	9788121259033	52nd	24 Parganas	L. S. S. O'Malley	1420	284

S. NO.	ISBN NO.	VOLUME	TITLE	AUTHOR	PRICE	PAGES
			CENTRAL PROVINCES DISTRICT GAZETTEERS			
64	9789362081728	1st, Vol. A	Akola (Descriptive)	A. E. Nelson, C. Brown	870	436
65	9789362085481	2nd, Vol. A	Amraoti (Descriptive)	S. V. Fitzgerald, A. E. Nelson	1050	524
66	9789362089267	3rd,Vol. A	Balaghat (Descriptive)	R. V. RUSSELL	430	216
67	9789362083494	4th, Vol. A	Betul (Descriptive)	R. V. RUSSELL	610	306
68	9789362085146	5th, Vol. A	Bhandara (Descriptive)	R. V. RUSSELL	580	292
69	9789362088390	6th, Vol. A	Bilaspur (Descriptive)	R. V. RUSSELL	870	434
70	9789362086044	7th, Vol. A	Buldana (Descriptive)	A. E. Nelson	1090	543
71	9789362089014	8th, Vol. B	Chanda (Descriptive)	R. V. RUSSELL	470	234
72	9789362086938	9th	Chhattisgarch Feudatory State	E. A. De Brett	880	440
73	9789362082961	10th	Chhindwara (Descriptive)	R. V. RUSSELL	550	274
74	9789362089342	11th, Vol. A & B	Damoh (Descriptive and Statistical Tables 1891-1901)	R. V. RUSSELL	830	414
75	9789362081230	12th, Vol. A	Durg (Descriptive)	A. E. Nelson	460	232
76	9789362086037	13th, Vol. A	Hoshangabad (Descriptive)	R. V. RUSSELL	860	430
77	9789362086792	14th, Vol. A	Jubbulpore (Descriptive)	A. E. Nelson	950	474
78	9789362089663	15th, Vol. A & B	Mandla (Descriptive and Statistical Tables 1891-1901)	R. V. RUSSELL	370	186
79	9789362086419	16th, Vol. A	Nagpur (Descriptive)	R. V. RUSSELL	790	394
80	9789362080646	17th, Vol. A	Narsinghpur (Descriptive)	R. V. RUSSELL	510	257
81	9789362084835	18th, Vol. A	Nimar (Descriptive)	R. V. RUSSELL	600	299
82	9789362087737	19th, Vol. A	Raipur (Descriptive)	A. E. Nelson	790	396
83	9789362080264	20th, Vol. A	Saugor (Descriptive)	R. V. RUSSELL	570	285
84	9789362081117	21st, Vol. A	Seoni (Descriptive)	R. V. RUSSELL	460	232
85	9789362084965	22nd, Vol. A	Wardha (Descriptive)	R. V. RUSSELL	600	302
86	9789362083401	23rd, Vol. A	Yeotmal (Descriptive)	R. V. RUSSELL	550	277
87	9789362080325	24th, Vol. I, Pt. I	Gwalior (Text and Tables)	R. V. RUSSELL	980	489
88	9789362087133	24th, Vol. I, Pt. II	Gwalior (Maps)	R. V. RUSSELL	400	198
89	9789362086341	24th, Vol. I, Pt. III	Gwalior (Village List)	R. V. RUSSELL	810	406
90	9789362085467	24th, Vol. I, Pt. IV	Gwalior (Photos)	R. V. RUSSELL	1400	698
91	9789362087393	25th, Vol. II	Indore (Text and Tables)	C. E. Luard	1050	524
92	9789362084422	26th, Vol. III	Bhopal (Text and Tables)	C. E. Luard	540	272
93	9789362086815	27th, Vol. IV	Rewah (Text and Tables)	C. E. Luard	500	250
94	9789362087584	28th, Vol. V, Pt. A	Western States - Malwa (Text)	C. E. Luard	1520	762
95	9789362087300	29th, Vol. VI, Pt. A	Eastern States - Bundelkhand (Text)	C. E. Luard	930	463
96	9789362082169	30th, Vol. VI, Pt. B	Eastern States - Bundelkhand (Tables)	C. E. Luard	830	417
			GAZETTEER OF THE BOMBAY PRESIDENCY:			
97	9788121283441	1st, Part I	History of Gujarat	Ed.: James M. Campbell	3220	644
98	9788121285582	1st, Part II	History of the Konkan Dakhan and Southern Maratha Country	Ed.: James M. Campbell	4200	840
99	9788121285568	2nd	Gujarat, Surat and Broach	Ed.: James M. Campbell	2990	598
100	9788121285544	3rd	Kaira and Panch Mahals	Ed.: James M. Campbell	1690	339
101	9788121285520	4th	Ahmedabad	Ed.: James M. Campbell	1860	372
102	9788121285506	5th	Cutch, Palanpur, and Mahi Kantha	Ed.: James M. Campbell	2390	478
103	9788121285483	6th	Rewa Kantha, Narukot, Cambay, and Surat States	Ed.: James M. Campbell	1450	290
104	9788121285469	7th	Baroda	Ed.: James M. Campbell	3260	652
105	9788121285445	8th	Kathiawar	Ed.: James M. Campbell	3790	758
106	9788121285421	9th, Part I	Gujarat Population - Hindus	Ed.: James M. Campbell	3170	636
107	9788121285407	9th, Part II	Gujarat Population - Musalmans and Parsis	Ed.: James M. Campbell	1520	304
108	9788121285384	10th	Ratnagiri and Savantvadi	Ed.: James M. Campbell	2500	501
109	9788121285360	11th	Kolaba and Janjira	Ed.: James M. Campbell	2550	513
110	9788121285346	12th	Khandesh	Ed.: James M. Campbell	3190	638
111	9788121285322	13th Part I	Thana	Ed.: James M. Campbell	2050	413
112	9788121285308	13th Part II	Thana	Ed.: James M. Campbell	1770	357
113	9788121285285	14th	Thana - Places of Interest	Ed.: James M. Campbell	3290	659
114	9788121285261	15th Part I	Kanara	Ed.: James M. Campbell	2340	348
115	9788121285247	15th Part II	Kanara	Ed.: James M. Campbell	1740	348
116	9788121285223	16th	Nasik	Ed.: James M. Campbell	3490	698
117	9788121285209	17th	Ahmadnagar	Ed.: James M. Campbell	3860	772
118	9788121285186	18th Part I	Poona	Ed.: James M. Campbell	2930	586
119	9788121285162	18th Part II	Poona	Ed.: James M. Campbell	2680	537
120	9788121285148	18th Part III	Poona	Ed.: James M. Campbell	2500	503
121	9788121285124	19th	Satara	Ed.: James M. Campbell	3450	692
122	9788121285100	20th	Sholapur	Ed.: James M. Campbell	2730	547
123	9788121285087	21st	Gazetteer of the Bomaby Presidency: Belgaum	Ed.: James M. Campbell	2570	514
124	9788121285063	22nd	Dharwar	Ed.: James M. Campbell	4200	841
125	9788121285049	23rd	Gazetteer of the Bombay Presidency:Bijapur	Ed.: James M. Campbell	3550	712
126	9788121285025	24th	Kolhapur	Ed.: James M. Campbell	2250	450

S. NO.	ISBN NO.	VOLUME	TITLE	AUTHOR	PRICE	PAGES
127	9788121285001	25th	Botany	Ed.: James M. Campbell	2040	408
128	9788121284981	26th, Part I	Materials Towards a Statistical Account of the Town and Island of Bombay - History	Ed.: James M. Campbell	2500	504
129	9788121284967	26th, Part II	Materials Towards a Statistical Account of the Town and Island of Bombay - Trade and Fortifications	Ed.: James M. Campbell	2690	538
130	9788121284943	26th, Part III	Materials Towards a Statistical Account of the Town And Island of Bombay - Administration	Ed.: James M. Campbell	2450	702
131	9788121284929	27th	General Index	Ed.:R. E. Enthoven	2190	428
			MADRAS DISTRICT GAZETTEERS			
132	9788121258814	1st	Anantapur	W. Francis	1140	227
133	9788121258555	2nd	Malabar	C. A Innes & F. B Evans	3010	602
134	9788121258791	3rd	Bellary	W. Francis	1890	377
135	9788121258777	4th	Statistical Appendix For Chingleput		280	56
136	9788121258753	5th	Coimbatore	K. N. Krishnaswami Ayyar	3420	628
137	9788121232814	6th	Madras District Gazetteers District Gazetteer Cuddapah	C. F. Brackenbury	1120	285
138	9788121258715	7th	Statistical Appendix For Ganjam		370	73
139	9788121256766	8th, Vol. 1st	Godavari District Gazetteer	F. R. Hemingway	650	320
140	9788121256803	8th, Vol. 2nd	Godavari District Gazetteer	F. R. Hemingway	160	83
141	9788121258678	9th	Statistical Appendix For Kistna		640	127
142	9788121258654	10th	Statistical Appendix For Kurnool		270	54
143	9788121258616	11th	Madura	W. Francis	1900	379
144	9788121258579	12th	Statistical Appendix For Madura		740	148
145	9788121258630	13th	The Nilgiris	W. Francis	2190	437
146	9788121234276	14th	Madras District Gazetteers Gazetteer Of The Nellore District Brought Upto 1938		1150	386
147	9788121258517	15th	North Arcot		590	118
148	9788121258494	16th, Vol. 1, Part I	Salem	F. J. Richards	1710	343
149	9788121258593	16th, Vol. 1, Part II	Salem	F. J. Richards	1800	360
150	9788121258456	17th	South Arcot	W. Francis	2400	480
151	9788121258470	18th	Statistical Appendix For South Canara		400	80
152	9788121258432	19th, Vol. 1st & 2nd	Tanjore: Main Volume and Statistical Appendix		2070	401
153	9788121258395	20th	Tinnevelly	H. R. Pate	2740	547
154	9788121258418	21st	Statistical Appendix For Tinnevelly		320	64
155	9788121258371	22nd, 1st & 2nd	Trichinopoly: Main Volume and Statistical Appendix	F. R. Hemingway	2440	487
156	9788121241953	23rd	Vizagapatam District Gazetteer	W. Francis	760	385
			PUNJAB DISTRICT GAZETTEERS			
157	9788121255943	1st	Ambala District 1883-84		620	124
158	9788121255967	2nd	Amritsar		1180	236
159	9788121255981	3rd	Delhi		1300	260
160	9788121256001	4th	Ferozepore		950	188
161	9788121256025	5th	Faridkot		350	70
162	9788121256049	6th	Gujranwala 1893-94		1270	254
163	9788121256063	7th	Gujrat	C. E. Luard	1140	228
164	9788121256087	8th	Gurdaspur 1891-92		1260	252
165	9788121256100	9th	Gurgaon 1883-4		1020	203
166	9788121256124	10th	Hazara	H. D. Watson	2290	458
167	9788121256148	11th	Hissar district and Lohar State		1840	367
168	9788121256162	12th	Hoshiarpur		1420	283
169	9788121256186	13th	Jhang		1070	213
170	9788121256209	14th	Jhelam		1010	202
171	9788121256223	15th	Jalandhar District 1883-84		540	108
172	9788121256247	16th, Vol. XIV-A	Jullundur District, with maps and Kapurthala		1990	398
173	9788121256261	17th, Pt. I	Kangra (Proper)		1450	290
174	9788121256285	17th, Pt. II	Kangra (Kulu, Lahual, Spiti)		1800	357
175	9788121256308	18th	Karnal		1930	386
176	9788121256322	19th	Kohat		1540	307
177	9788121256346	20th	The Lahore District 1883-84		1220	244
178	9788121256384	21st	Ludhiana and Maler Kotla		1680	335
179	9788121256407	22nd	Lyallpur		735	147
180	9788121256421	23rd	Mianwali		1170	234
181	9788121256445	24th	Montgomery	P. J. Fagan	1590	318
182	9788121258364	25th	Multan (1901-02)	E. D. Maclagan	2400	480
183	9788121258708	26th	The Rohtak District 1883-84		980	196
184	9788121258746	27th, Vol. III A	Dujana State 1904		500	16
185	9788121256483	28th	Shahpur District		1780	356
186	9788121256506	29th	Simla District		800	159

S. NO.	ISBN NO.	VOLUME	TITLE	AUTHOR	PRICE	PAGES
187	9788121256520	30th	The Chamba State		2040	408
188	9788121256544	31st	The Chenab Colony 1904		1550	310
189	9788121256568	32nd	Kalsia State		270	53
190	9788121256582	33rd	Suket and Mandi		770	154
191	9788121256605	34th	Phulkian States, Patiala Jind And Nabha 1904		2070	414
192	9788121256643	35th	Simla Hill States		2220	443
193	9788121256667	36th	Sirmur		920	183
			RAJPUTANA DISTRICT GAZETTEERS			
194	9789362088994	1st, Vol. I-A & B	Ajmer-merwara (Text and Statistics Tables)	C. C. Watson	1230	246
195	9789362080882	2nd. Vol. II-A & B	Mewar Residency (Text and Statistics Tables)	K.D. Erskine	1700	339
196	9789362088444	3rd, Vol. III-A & B	The Western Rajputana States Residency And The Bikaner Agency	K.D. Erskine	3590	718
			UNITED PROVINCES OF AGRA AND OUDH DISTRICT GAZETTEERS			
197	9789362087560	Vol. I	Agra	H. R. Nevill	2260	452
198	9789362082466	Vol. II	Aligarh	H. R. Nevill	1300	260
199	9789362089779	Vol. III	Allahabad	H. R. Nevill	2050	409
200	9789362081346	Vol. IV	Almora	H. G. Walton	1670	333
201	9789362085658	Vol. V	Azamgarh	D. L. Drake Brockman	1750	349
202	9789362080547	Vol. VI	Bahraich	H. R. Nevill	1410	281
203	9789362085214	Vol. VII	Ballia	H. R. Nevill	1750	350
204	9789362084668	Vol. VIII	Banda	D. L. Drake Brockman	1750	349
205	9789362086518	Vol. IX	Bara Banki	H. R. Nevill	1720	344
206	9789362084101	Vol. X	Bareilly	H. R. Nevill	1640	327
207	9789362086631	Vol. XI	Basti	H. R. Nevill	1610	321
208	9789362083814	Vol. XII	Benares	H. R. Nevill	2290	458
209	9789362086105	Vol. XIII	Bijnor	H. R. Nevill	1820	363
210	9789362081674	Vol. XIV	Budaun	H. R. Nevill	1890	378
211	9789362086891	Vol. XV	Bulandshahr	H. R. Nevill	2100	419
212	9789362081520	Vol. XVI	Cawnpore	H. R. Nevill	2210	442
213	9789362088031	Vol. XVII	Dehra Dun	H. G. Walton	1710	342
214	9789362088710	Vol. XVIII	Etah	E. R. Neave	1600	320
215	9789362082992	Vol. XIX	Etawah	D. L. Drake Brockman	1390	277
216	9789362082220	Vol. XX	Farrukhabad	E. R. Neave	1620	324
217	9789362083869	Vol. XXI	Fatehpur	H. R. Nevill	1890	377
218	9789362085962	Vol. XXII	Fyzabad	H. R. Nevill	1700	339
219	9789362087997	Vol. XXIII	Garhwal	H. G. Walton	1270	254
220	9789362089892	Vol. XXIV	Ghazipur	H. R. Nevill	1600	320
221	9789362085436	Vol. XXV	Gonda	H. R. Nevill	1650	330
222	9789362080271	Vol. XXVI	Gorakhpur	H. R. Nevill	1890	378
223	9789362086129	Vol. XXVII	Hamirpur	D. L. Drake Brockman	1390	277
224	9789362087638	Vol. XXVIII	Hardoi	H. R. Nevill	1680	336
225	9789362081636	Vol. XXIX	Jalaun	D. L. Drake Brockman	1180	236
226	9789362084309	Vol. XXX	Jaunpur	H. R. Nevill	1750	350
227	9789362084187	Vol. XXXI	Jhansi	D. L. Drake Brockman	1960	391
228	9789362089168	Vol. XXXII	Kheri	H. R. Nevill	1650	330
229	9789362086778	Vol. XXXIII	Lucknow	H. R. Nevill	1760	352
230	9789362088635	Vol. XXXIV	Mainpuri	H. R. Nevill	1740	348
231	9789362080424	Vol. XXXV	Meerut	H. R. Nevill	2170	434
232	9789362081087	Vol. XXXVI	Mirzapur	D. L. Drake Brockman	2430	486
233	9789362085443	Vol. XXXVII	Moradabad	H. R. Nevill	1900	380
234	9789362082763	Vol. XXXVIII	Muttra	D. L. Drake Brockman	2140	428
235	9789362089915	Vol. XXXIX	Muzaffarnagar	H. R. Nevill	2260	451
236	9789362086143	Vol. XL	Naini Tal	H. R. Nevill	1890	377
237	9789362086761	Vol. XLI	Partabgarh	H. R. Nevill	1560	312
238	9789362081124	Vol. XLII	Pilibhit	H. R. Nevill	1570	314
239	9789362084453	Vol. XLIII	Rai Bareli	H. R. Nevill	1610	322
240	9789362088284	Vol. XLIV	Rampur	H. R. Nevill	1170	234
241	9789362083654	Vol. XLV	Saharanpur	H. R. Nevill	2190	438
242	9789362083142	Vol. XLVI	Shahjahanpur	H. R. Nevill	1510	302
243	9789362083623	Vol. XLVII	Sitapur	H. R. Nevill	1590	317
244	9789362089939	Vol. XLVIII	Sultanpur	H. R. Nevill	1330	266
245	9789362080851	Vol. XLIX	Unnao	H. R. Nevill	1530	305

EASTERN BENGAL DISTRICT GAZETTEERS

DACCA

BY

B. C. ALLEN

1912

PLAN OF CONTENTS.

PREFACE.

THE history chapter of this Gazetteer was written by Mr. J. T. Rankin, I.C.S. Exigencies of space necessitated its compression but to him entirely is due whatever merit it possesses. I desire to acknowledge with gratitude the assistance rendered by Colonel Hall, I.M.S., who examined the chapter on Public Health, Nawāb Khwaja Muhammad Yusuf, Chairman of the Dacca Municipality, Khān Bahadur Saiyid Aulad Husain, Babu Shoshi Bhusan Mitra, late District Engineer, and the staff of the Collectorate.

B. C. ALLEN.

TABLE OF CONTENTS.

CHAPTER I.

PHYSICAL ASPECTS.

CHAPTER II.

HISTORY.

CHAPTER III.

THE PEOPLE.

CHAPTER IV.

PUBLIC HEALTH.

CHAPTER V.

ECONOMIC CONDITION OF THE PEOPLE.

CHAPTER VI.

AGRICULTURE.

CHAPTER VII.

TRADE AND INDUSTRIES.

CHAPTER VIII.

NATURAL CALAMITIES.

CHAPTER IX.

MEANS OF COMMUNICATION.

CHAPTER X.

GENERAL ADMINISTRATION.

PAGE

CHAPTER XI.

LAND REVENUE.

CHAPTER XII.

LOCAL SELF-GOVERNMENT.

CHAPTER XIII.

EDUCATION.

CHAPTER XIV.

GAZETTEER

OF THE

DACCA DISTRICT.

CHAPTER I.

PHYSICAL ASPECTS.

THE district of Dacca is situated between 23° 14′ and 24° 20′ north and 89° 45′ and 90° 59′ east about the centre of the Province of Eastern Bengal. It covers an area of 3,250 square miles* and in 1911 contained a population of 2,960,402. The principal town, Dacca, is situated in 23° 43′ north and 90° 24′ east on the north bank of the Buri Ganga river, and is not only the head-quarters of the division that bears its name, but was for a time the capital of the Province of Eastern Bengal and Assam. GENERAL DESCRIPTION

Several explanations have been offered of the origin of the name Dacca (Dhākā). Some derive it from *dhak*† the name of a tree (*Butea frondosa*), others connect it with the goddess Dhakeswari (*lit.* the concealed goddess) whose shrine is situated in the western part of Dacca city. The famous Ballāl Sen is said to have been the son of one of the wives of Adisura by the river Brahmaputra who visited his mother in the guise of a Brahman. The woman and her child were banished to the jungle lying north of the Buri Ganga river, and here Ballāl Sen discovered an image of Durga for whom, on his succession to his father's throne, he built a temple, the goddess taking the name of Dhakeswari in consequence of the seclusion of the site.‡ A third account derives the name Dacca from *dhak* the Bengali for a drum. It is stated that in 1608 A.D. when Alāuddīn Islām Khān thought it expedient to move his capital eastwards from Rajmahal, he anchored on the Burī Gangā at the spot where Dacca now stands. Impressed by the advantages of the site he determined to make the place the head-quarters of the Province and fixed the Origin of name.

* This area is calculated from a survey made in 1859-1866. Since that date there have been considerable modifications in the boundaries of the district due to fluvial action. An unusually large proportion of the total area is permanently under water, and until a new survey has been completed it would be difficult to give even an approximate estimate of the number of square miles of land.

† One objection to this derivation is the fact that *dhak* trees are not at the present day common in Dacca.

‡ Taylor's Topography and Statistics of Dacca, Calcutta, 1839, p. 66.

boundaries of the city by sending men to the north, east and west. They were ordered to walk to the point where the drums beaten in the Governor's camp first became inaudible, and all the land where the sound of the *dhak* could be heard became the city of Dacca.*

Boundaries.

The district has the shape of a triangle with its apex to the south and a considerable protrusion towards the western end of the base. On the east and west it is bounded by great rivers. To the east by the Meghnā which separates it from the district of Tippera; to the west by the Brahmaputra or Jamunā which, after its junction with the Ganges, is known as the Padmā or Kīrtināsā and separates it from the districts of Pabna, Faridpur, and Bakarganj. To the north lies the district of Mymensingh.

Natural divisions.

Dacca falls into two natural divisions very dissimilar from one another both in appearance and geological formation. From the centre of the base of the triangle a wedge of elevated land is driven into the low alluvial flats which form the greater portion of the district. This high land is known as the Madhupur jungle and is roughly bounded on the west by the river Bansi, on the south by the river Buri Ganga as far as Dacca city, on the east by a line drawn from Dacca city to Rūpganj, thence by the Lakshya river to Kāliganj and thence by a line drawn from Kāliganj to Belābo on the old Brahmaputra. The remainder of the district consists of low land inundated to a greater or less depth during the rainy season but yielding fine crops of rice and jute. This low land is intersected by numerous creeks and minor streams and is watered by four main rivers, the Meghnā and the Padmā which enclose it and the Dhaleswari and the Lakshya which intersect it. The Dhaleswari is an offshoot from the Jamunā and flows parallel to it till it joins the Meghnā opposite Munshīganj town, their united waters joining the Padmā near Rājābāri police station. The Dhaleswari and the Padmā thus form a great island, the whole of which lies very low and which is subject to heavy inundations in the rains. The Lakshya enters the district from Mymensingh near Naonda Sagar and flowing parallel to the Meghnā falls into the Dhaleswari at Madanganj

SCENERY. The lower levels.

In the lower parts of the district the scenery is very tame and dull. The density of the population and the high floods alike forbid the growth of woods or jungle and the dead level of the plain is only broken by the groves of fruit trees which surround the houses of the villagers. In the lowest parts of all the eye is not afforded even this small measure of relief, as the depth of the flood is such that the houses have to be perched on hillocks on which there is barely room for a cowshed and none for anything so pleasant as a garden. This dismal country is really least unattractive in the rains. It is then covered with water which is green with jute and rice and all the creeks and channels are full. These minor streams flow between banks which

* Notes on the Antiquities of Dacca, 1904, by Khān Bahadur Saiyid Aulad Husain, p. 1.

are higher than the neighbouring country and are generally fringed with trees, and thus form much more attractive waterways than the great rivers from which little can be seen but a dreary waste of waters with here and there a few huts rising precariously above the flood which threatens to engulf them. The people who live in these tracts have become almost amphibious in their habits. In the height of the inundation no land is to be seen and all travelling has to be done by boat, a state of affairs which is not unfavourable to commerce, but, as will be afterwards seen, adds largely to the difficulty of the administration of the district. To say that travelling has to be done by boat gives, however, but an inadequate idea of the real condition of affairs. Half a dozen huts are clustered together on a little hillock a few yards square and the inhabitants cannot proceed beyond that hillock whether to visit their neighbours or their fields, to go to market or to school without wading, swimming or travelling in or on something that can float. This expression is used advisedly for the people by no means confine themselves to boats. For minor excursions rafts made of plantain trees are much in vogue or circular earthenware pipkens, more difficult of navigation than a coracle. A visitor to one of these hamlets in the rains may see a grey-bearded patriarch swimming towards him from the fields and may be asked for alms by an old woman standing in water breast high amongst the jute plants.

The Madhopur jungle. The Madhopur jungle is a tableland with an average elevation of about 40 feet above the alluvial flats. It is intersected by long winding depressions called *baids* in which rice is grown and contains within its area depressions and marshes of considerable size. The higher land is sown with jute or winter crops but much of it is still covered with forest, the staple tree being the *gajari*, an inferior kind of *sāl* (*shorea robusta*). There are few streams and a general dearth of water in this tract and this has proved a serious impediment to the extension of cultivation. The country is considered to be unhealthy and has been left almost entirely to poor Muhammadans and aboriginal tribes like the Rājbansis and the Bunas, but for any lover of the picturesque it possesses many charms. In place of the dead level of the alluvial plain there are rolling uplands covered with short grass or dark green forest which dip towards the basins where the people grow their rice; and even where the high ground has been cleared for cultivation the view is broken by fine forest trees which have been left standing on the peasants' holdings. Carts have taken the place of boats as a means of communication and roads, which in the lower parts of the district are not merely superfluous but may be positively harmful, have here become absolutely necessary.

Hills. There are no mountains or hills in the district and the only elevated tracts are the ridges in the Madhopur jungle, none of which exceed fifty or sixty feet in height. These ridges have, however, exercised an influence upon the formation of the district out of all proportion to their actual size, as the hard tenacious clay of which they are formed has successfully opposed the movements of the great rivers and has compelled them to seek a course through the low land to the south-east. On the west of the Bansi the flourishing village of Dhāmrāi is situated on a hillock high enough to raise it above the level of the floods and there is land at Sonārgāo in the south of the Nārāyanganj subdivision, and near Munshīganj town which is raised a little above the surrounding swamps.

River System. The district is much subject to fluvial action both from the two great rivers which bound it on the east and west and from the various distributaries which intersect it. All these rivers are heavily charged with silt and sand and the fall is sufficiently slight to admit of their having a depositing rather than an excavating tendency. As long as the current is fairly swift this silt is carried on towards the sea, but it is rapidly deposited in the slack water on the banks where it is caught by high grass or other vegetable growth. When the banks have been raised above flood level the silt is deposited in the river-bed which thus gradually rises above the level of the surrounding country and when once the bank gives way the river falls into the lower land lying at the back and shifts its course. In addition to these pronounced changes of course, the standard instance of which is the shifting of the Brahmaputra, the great rivers are continually eating away one bank and making deposits of silt upon the other, while islands, some of considerable size, rise from their beds, sometimes to disappear as quickly as they came. The surface of the country in the neighbourhood of the great rivers is thus subject to continual change and instances are known of a spot of land being twice washed away and twice reformed within twenty years. The rivers are subject to tidal action, and it was found that a float thrown into the Buri Ganga opposite Dacca in the dry season was carried nearly five miles up-stream. This is a factor which has to be taken into serious consideration when formulating any sewage system of drainage for Dacca city.

The largest river, any portion of which falls within the boundary of the district, is the Padmā which is formed by the confluence of the Brahmaputra, known here as the Jamunā, and the Ganges. In the lower part of its course it is known as the Kīrtināsā or 'destroyer of memorable works' from the ravages it wrought amongst the monuments and buildings of Rājā Rāj Ballabh at Rājnagar in the Faridpur district. The Brahmaputra is generally supposed to be identical with the Tsanpo and to rise in Tibet in 31° 30′ north and 82° east near the upper waters of the Indus and the Sutlej. In 1779 A.D., when Rennell published his map of 'The Low Countries beyond the Ganges,' the Brahmaputra flowed round the western face of the Garo Hills past

Shirpur, Toke, and Kātiadi till it joined the Meghnā near Bhairab Bāzār. It is many years since the main volume of the mighty Brahmaputra flowed by this route, but even this is not the oldest channel that can be traced through the district. There can be little doubt that the river originally turned south at Agarasinda and flowed past Simulea, Pānchdona, Nāngalband, across the present channel of the Dhaleswari past Munshīganj, finally falling into the Ganges near Rājābāri. The small creek on which the famous bathing festival of Nāngalband is still held and the creek that runs from Munshīganj to Rājābāri are still dignified by the high sounding title of Brahmaputra. At the beginning of the nineteenth century the great river changed its course to the westward and it is now but a small stream that flows along the north of the district to Bhairab Bāzār.

The Brahmaputra reaches the western frontier of the district at a place about six miles north-west of Nathpur in the Manikganj subdivision and about 14 miles lower down is joined by the Ganges. Their united waters form the south-western boundary as far as Rājābāri. The main channel of this enormous river forms the boundary between Dacca and the adjoining districts, but this, though the only one that is feasible, is a somewhat unsatisfactory boundary as the main stream will flow in one year on one side of the great strath over which it spreads its waters, and the next year on the other so that the islands in its course fall sometimes in one district, sometimes in another. Even in the dry season it has a breadth of from three to four miles, and it is perpetually throwing up islands in its bed and washing them away again. It cuts away and adds accretions to its banks with equal impartiality and these continual changes are a source of much litigation and no little violence. At the time of Rennell's survey the lower course of the Padmā was more to the south than it is at the present day, and joined the Meghnā near Dakhin Shābāzpur island instead of at Rājābāri. There are three main creeks which branch off from the Padmā in this district, the Hilsāmāri, the Srīnagar, and the Tāltala Khal. The Hilsāmāri was originally a considerable river, but its bed has been much silted up and its lower reaches have been swallowed up by the encroachments of the Padmā. It unites with the Ichhāmati at Husnābād whence the Tulsikhal connects the Padmā again with the Dhaleswari.

The Dhaleswari.

A river which is of great importance in the economy of the district is the Dhaleswari which takes off by several channels from the Jamunā. The most southerly head is known as the Gajahata which is now but an insignificant stream in the dry season. Next comes the Selimabād channel which flows past Ghior and for long was the principal source of the Dhaleswari but is now so silted up that only the smallest boats can pass by it when the river is low. The principal channel is now about ten miles to the north of Selimabād in Mymensingh and is known as the Elashin channel, but even this is unfortunately silting up and is only open to launches drawing five feet of water during the rains. It flows a tortuous course past Elashin, Kedarpur, Kustia and Sābhār, and after receiving the waters of the Lakshya falls into the Meghnā a little below Munshiganj. The total length of the Dhaleswari is about one hundred miles and in its lower reaches it is a river of great breadth even in the dry season.

The Buri Ganga.

The deterioration of the Dhaleswari is especially unfortunate as the city of Dacca is dependent for its water communications on one of its offshoots, the Buri Ganga. This is a river about twenty-six miles in length which takes off from the parent stream a little below Sābhār and rejoins it at Baktatali a little above Tāltala. Of recent years this river like the Dhaleswari has been silting up at the source and considerable dredging operations have been undertaken with the object of deepening the intake. It is encouraging to learn from a letter from Mr. John Taylor in 1800 A.D. that in 1645 A.D. the Buri Ganga was so much smaller than it was in his day that it was bridged opposite Dacca. In the rains the Buri Ganga is open throughout its length to boats of considerable size, but in the dry weather even small steam launches cannot come up as far as Dacca.

The Ichhâmati.

Between the Dhaleswari and the Padmā are the remains of the Ichhāmati which is one of the oldest rivers in the district. It was probably originally connected with the Kosi river and entered the district near Jafarganj. It flows a tortuous course past Katrasin (whence there is a channel connecting it with Ghior), Balla, Jhiktea, Harirāmpur and Nawābganj. It originally fell into the Brahmaputra near Rāmpāl, but like the eastern channel of that river it has almost disappeared, and it now makes its way into the Dhaleswari by several winding routes. Near Shaikernagar another channel turns southwards past Srinagar and Haldia and falls into the Padmā. The antiquity of the Ichhāmati is shown by the fact that there are no less than five sacred bathing ghats on its banks at Tirthagata, Agla, Solpur, Barunighat and Jaginighat, but at the present day it has sunk to the level of a channel that contains hardly any water till the rivers rise in the rains. At that season of the year it forms a valuable means of communication with the interior of the great island formed by the Padmā and the Dhaleswari.

The Ghazikhali and Bansi.

On the north bank the Dhaleswari receives the Ghazikhali, and the Bansi which enters the district from Mymensingh and after flowing past Dhāmrā falls into the Dhaleswari near Sābhār. Neither of these streams are available for traffic during the dry season except by boats of the smallest class.

The Turāg.

In the upper part of its course the Bansi is connected with the Turāg near Kāliākoer, but unfortunately a bar has formed which can only be passed at the height of the flood. The Turāg flows past Mirzāpur and Kāsimpur and falls into the Buri Ganga a little below Mirpur. Above Mirzāpur the Turāg receives three minor streams which rise in the Madhupur jungle, *i.e.*, th Saldaha, the Lavandaha, and the Goalear creek. About seven miles above Mirpur the Tangi stream connects the Turāg with the river Balu which rises in the Madhupur jungle a little to the east of Sripur and falls into the Lakshya at Demra. None of these streams are of much use for traffic during the dry season and the navigation of the Tangi stream is rendered difficult during the rains by the railway bridge near Tangi station.

The Lakshiya. The Lakshya, though not the largest, is by far the prettiest river in the district. In 1780, at the time of Rennell's survey the Layshya was formed from three streams that took off from the old Brahmaputra. One was the Banar which left the parent stream about 45 miles north of Toke, the second took off near Toke, while the third, which was at that time the principal channel, issued from the Brahmaputra at Aralea and united with the second stream at Ekdāla near Lākpur Chur but soon left it again to flow eastwards into the Meghnā at Narsingdi. At the present day the Banar has been almost swallowed up by the changes in the course of the Brahmaputra and the Aralea channel has silted up and no longer communicates with the Lakshya during the dry season, so that the river depends for its stream upon the waters that reach it through the Toke channel. While most of the other rivers in the district flow through low country which is heavily flooded in the rains and is therefore unsuited for anything but marsh crops, the banks of the Lakshya are high and are fringed for the most part with villages buried in groves of the graceful areca palm. The banks themselves are often of red earth instead of the grey and ugly wastes of sand and mud which are usually associated with the rivers of Dacca, and in a country such as this, where there is so very little attractive in the river scenery the Lakshya has naturally earned a high reputation for beauty. During its course of 61 miles it passes several marts of note, such as Barmi, Kāpāsia, Lākpur, Jamālpur, Kāliganj, Rūpganj, Murāparā, Demra, Sidhiganj, and Nārāyanganj and at Madanganj it falls into the Dhaleswari. During the rains steam launches can go up the Lakshya into Mymensingh but in the dry season a boat drawing five feet of water cannot proceed above Lākpur Chur.

The Meghnā. The Meghnā is the name applied to the lower reaches of the river which rises on the southern slopes of the mountain range which forms the northern boundary of Manipur and which carries down the drainage of the Surma Valley to join the mighty Padmā near Rājābāri. It enters the district at Bhairab Bāzār in 24° 2' north and 90° 59' east and flows a tortuous course between the districts of Dacca and Tippera till it joins the Dhaleswari a little below Munshīganj. Its banks are low and ugly and the river is continually cutting new channels for itself and throwing up and washing away again extensive *churs*. The whole of the course of the river within the Dacca district is open to steamer traffic hroughout the year. The principal places of importance on its banks are Rāipura, Narsingdi, Bārodi and Baidya Bāzār. The only tributary of importance which it receives on its left bank below Bhairab Bāzār is the Arial Khān which leaves the old Brahmaputra at Belābo and joins the Meghnā a little above Narsingdi. Even this channel is largely silted up and is only navigable by steam launches during times of high flood.

Islands. There are no islands of importance in the district, though the Munshiganj subdivision and the greater part of the Manikganj subdivision technically form an island as they are surrounded by the waters of the Padmā and the Dhaleswari. The same may be said of the tract of land immediately to the south of Dacca, known as Paschimdi or Parjoa, which is enclosed by the Buri Ganga and the Dhaleswari. Numerous *churs* are thrown up in the beds of the different rivers, but they vary in size from year to year and have no permanent existence.

GEOLOGY. Geologically the district falls into two distinct tracts, the high land of the Madhupur jungle and the alluvial flats surrounding it. The upper soil of the Madhupur jungle is a stiff ferruginous red clay, covered in many places by a thin layer of vegetable mould. Beneath this is a deposit of coarse red sand. Mr. Blanford has suggested three explanations of the origin of this formation: (*a*) that the high land may have been raised; (*b*) that the surrounding land may have been depressed; (*c*) that these deposits may have been laid down by some river other than the Brahmaputra. It is said that in the time of Muhammadan rule iron was extracted in the Bhowal pargana, and near Jaydebpur heaps of a black nodular substance are to be found which appear to be the remains of the ore after the iron had been smelted. The rest of the district consists of deposits of sand and clay mixed in varying proportions. In the north-eastern portion there is more silicious sand in the clay than in the south and west. The soil of the marshes and depressions is generally a deep black clay. Taylor reports that the black vegetable mould occasionally approaches to lignite in appearance and that "in the beds of the deep morasses of the southern subdivision there are found small nodular masses of earth which appear to be composed of decayed vegetable matter: they are hard compact bodies of a jet black colour and of so fine a substance that when pulverised they are occasionally used by the natives to make ink." * No stone is found in the district and there are no mineral deposits which could be profitably worked.

FAUNA. A hundred years ago the Madhupur jungle was full of game of every kind, and was so infested with wild elephants that the villagers found it almost impossible to cultivate the land. In 1790 the Collector wrote of Bhowal, "One half of it is an entire jungle swarming with elephants and every other wild beast." In the same year the zamindārs of Kāsimpur declined to accept

* Taylor's Topography of Dacca, p. 8.

settlement at the rates of the preceding year alleging that their lands were ruined by the depredations of the wild elephants which resorted there in large droves and effectually destroyed the crops of the raiyats.* Tigers also were numerous and in 1804 270 tiger skins were brought to the city for the Government reward.† Elephants have now completely disappeared, though as late as 1868 a herd was said to have taken up its quarters in the jungles near Kapasia,‡ and deer and pig are the only animals found in any considerable numbers. There are a few wild buffalo in the country to the north-west of Srīpur, a few tiger and perhaps a larger number of leopards, but how small is the number can be judged from the fact that during the four years ending with 1910 rewards were only paid for the destruction of 13 tigers and 26 leopards. Deer are of four species, the gaus deer (*Cervus hippelaphus*), the sambar (*Aristotilis rusa*) which is rare, the hog deer (*Cervus porcinus*) and the barking deer (*Cervus muntjak*). The smaller animals include monkeys which in some places are very mischievous, porcupines, jackals, foxes, otters and hares. In 1868 Mr. Clay, the Magistrate-Collector, reported that the so-called black rabbit was found in the jungles to the north of the town. It was said to be a connecting link between the hare and the rabbit and to breed in burrows like the latter animal. It was only found in the jungle and did not enter cultivated land. Four kinds of bats are recognised—the flying fox, the small striped or orange bat, the long-eared bat and the common house bat. Smaller animals include squirrels, rats, both of the ordinary and bandicoot variety, mice and moles. A list of the animals, birds and fishes, which according to Taylor are found in the district, is appended to this chapter.

The following account of the birds of the district is taken from the statistical account by Sir William Hunter, pp. 29 and 30:—"Vultures, crows, several varieties of eagles, fish eagles, kites, and falcons are common. Several species of owls are found, and are regarded by the natives with superstitious dread.§ Swallows and kingfishers are numerous. The blue and red kingfisher with a white breast is the most handsome variety and is caught during the cold season and killed for the sake of its feathers which are exported to China where they are in great request. In former days the Maghs and Burmese travelled all over India in search of these birds, which they caught with birdlime. Akyab was said to be the port of exportation, whence they were taken to China in junks. Professional bird-catchers are still met with in Birds.

* *Vide* correspondence of 1790 in the Dacca Collectorate.

† Taylor's Topography of Dacca, p. 21.

‡ Principal heads of the History and Statistics of the Dacca Division, p. 68.

§ The variety known as *kalpecha* alone is feared, but of this the people have a very lively horror.

Dacca, and they informed Mr. Clay, a late Magistrate of the District, that they were employed by people in Calcutta. The bee-eater, like the kingfisher, inhabits crevices in the banks of rivers and may be met with throughout the whole district. Two varieties of the 'tailor' bird are found, so-called from the ingenious construction of their nest. Sunbirds, or honey-suckers, are also common and are remarkable for the brilliant metallic lustre of their plumage. They flutter about the flowers, from which they extract the juice while on the wing. The weaver-bird, which derives its name from the hanging nests which it builds, and which are usually found attached in clusters to the date tree, is very destructive to the rice crops. Of the several kinds of woodpeckers, the Indian robin may be mentioned; it is trained to fight by the natives. The shāmā bird is much prized for its power of song, a good one being worth from £1 to £2. Two varieties of the green parakeet are common. The wader birds are largely represented, and inhabit the numerous marshes throughout the district. The spoon-bill, sāras and mānikjor, or beefsteak bird, make their appearance about the middle of October and return to the hills at the commencement of the rains. Five species of herons are met with in the district. The pelican ibis is found in the neighbouring district of Faridpur and doubtless also in Dacca. It frequents rivers, tanks and marshes, generally in parties, but occasionally alone. The shell ibis is common, and is called by the natives sāmuk, from the name of a large kind of snail on which it feeds. The adjutant bird is not uncommon, though seldom seen in the vicinity of the town. The bulbul, or Indian nightingale, is found in abundance, and it is taught to fight by the natives who are very fond of the sport. The crested coot, the spur-winged plover, snipe, jack-snipe and plover are common. Among the gallinaceous birds are the florican, which is rare, except in the Sābhār Fiscal Division, and the chakor, or keā partridge, which is met with in many parts of the district, though not in great numbers; jungle-fowl and peacocks are tolerably plentiful, as also several kinds of quail. The common blue or jungle pigeon, two or three varieties of the green pigeon and doves are common. The rāj-ghughu, or imperial dove, is also sometimes found. It is a very handsome bird, the back and wings being dark emerald-green, and the neck, breast, and lower parts red-brown. Wild geese and ducks are plentiful on the river *chars* to the south, with many varieties of teal. Several species of gulls are found on all the large rivers, of which the scissor-bill, or Indian skimmer, is the most remarkable. This bird especially frequents the Meghnā and Ganges rivers and may be seen skimming over the water with its beak close to the surface in search of food. The small cormorant, called pānikaurī by the natives, is common in all the marshes and swamps and the diver-bird is frequently seen perched on trees overhanging the water on the watch for its prey. These birds swim and dive with great rapidity and float so low in the water that nothing but their long necks remains visible."

Since these lines were written the district has sadly deteriorated from the sportsman's point of view. The florican is never seen and jungle fowl, if they exist at all, are very rare. Wild geese are seldom shot and though duck are to be found on the Padmā and the Meghnā and some inland *jhils* they are extremely wary. Snipe are to be had but the shooting can only be described as poor and large bags are seldom made.

The fish-eating alligator or *gharial* and the snub-nosed crocodile occasionally carry off the unwary bather. Snakes also cause considerable mortality, as in the submerged parts they are driven to the village sites when the waters rise. The average annual number of deaths due to this cause during the four years ending in 1910 was 169. The following is a list of the principal snakes known to the natives: poisonous—Cobra, Machhanad, Panas, Goma, Darach, Dubraj; harmless—Ulubora, Jinglabora, Landog, Ghauni, Matishap, Dhora Airalbeka, Shalikbora, Sankhini, Dhauma, and Domukha The latter snake, the Typhlos *lumbricalis*, derives its name from the fact that the tail is almost as thick as the head, while the eyes are very small. It is accordingly supposed by the villagers to possess two heads.

Batrachians are of three varieties, the common frog and toad and the tree frog.

Fisheries. Fish are caught in the rivers and in creeks and *jhils*. The most important *jhils* are the Belai, the Saldaha, the Lavandala, the Bhorontala, the Bhinadai, the Silmandi, the Airal, the Nara, the Raghunathpur, the Dal Samudra, the Doya, the low land round Jainsha, and the low land of Dhāmrāi.

Porpoises are very common in the larger rivers and sharks, ray fish and saw fish are occasionally to be met with. The best eating fish are the *hilsa*, the mango fish, the *rui*, the mullet, the *paftar* (*Callichrous pabda*), the *chital*, the *mirga*, (*Cirrhina mrigala*) and the *catla* Crabs, crayfish and prawns are also plentiful. The fishing castes are the Kaibarttas, Teors, Jhalos, Charals and Mal Bādiyas, the first four being Hindus and the last Muhammadans. The principal difference between the Kaibarttas and the Teors is that the former never allow their women to sell fish at the market while the latter labour under no such disability. The Charals never use the net but catch fish in bamboo traps, while the Bādiyas, a floating tribe who live in their boats, restrict themselves to rod and line. The fishing castes are all poor and the supply of fish is said to have decreased during the last quarter of a century. This is true, for it is an assertion that does not very readily admit of proof, is probably principally due to the silting up of *jhils* and rivers and the consequent contraction of the spawning grounds. The fishermen show no consideration for the future and catch small fry and spawning fish. In this way they contribute to their own growing poverty, but this no doubt is a process which has been going on for long and would hardly in itself account for a sudden shortage of the supply. Some harm may perhaps have been done by the widely extended cultivation of jute as the rotting plant produces a noxious effect upon the water and the fishermen allege that the river steamers cause an undercurrent which drives away the fish.

During the rains the fish are dispersed over so large an area that they cannot easily be caught and some of the fishing classes betake themselves to other occupations. In the winter fish is exported to Mymensingh, Calcutta and Chittagong. Fish are caught with nets, bamboo baskets and spears. The following are the nets most commonly employed :—*berjal* or *jagatber*, a very large net with meshes from three to six inches wide which requires a party of twenty men to use it; cost about Rs. 300; *chotober* a smaller variety of the same net, meshes from one to two inches; cost Rs. 50 to Rs. 70; *athar jal*, a large cast net; *jhaki*, a smaller cast net. The *dharmajal* is a species of bag attached to a bamboo handle and lowered into the water. The *kachki* and *khora jals* are V-shaped nets, the wide end of which is lowered into the water. The *kachki* is used from a boat, the *khora* is attached to bamboo posts erected in the river-bed. The *chai* and *paran* are bamboo traps, the *polo* a basket which is thrust down into the mud in shallow water. The *koch* is a bundle of slender but stout bamboos shod with iron, which is a formidable weapon used not only against the finny tribe but also in agrarian and other riots. Fishing boats are usually built of teak or *sāl* (*Shorea robusta*) planks. *Sāl* is the more durable but its specific gravity is heavier than that of water, so to prevent the boats sinking when overturned, *jarul* (*Lagerstrœmia flos reginæ*) is used with the *sāl*.

CLIMATE.

The climate of Dacca is fairly equable, the difference between the mean temperature of the coldest and hottest months in the year being only 17·6 degrees. The summers are not as hot as in Upper India, but against this must be set the fact that the winters are not nearly as invigorating. The cold weather begins in November and for four months the climate is fairly pleasant. In March, however, the days grow hot and the average maximum temperature of that month is 90°. April is even hotter with an average maximum of 93·2, but the rains of May send the temperature down a couple of degrees. From June to October the average maximum ranges from 88° to 89° but the nights are then warmer than they are earlier in the year and the mean temperature is about 83° which is higher than it is in April. October and the latter half of September are in fact the most trying season of the year. The south-easterly breezes which do so much to mitigate the discomforts of the rains begin to fail, the waters begin to recede into their accustomed channels and the damp fields lie reeking beneath the scorching sun. The nights are still too warm to give much relief and it is not till November comes that there is any pleasant coolness. January is the coldest month in the year, but the cold is but comparative for even at Nārāyanganj, which is cooler than Dacca city, the mean minimum temperature for the month is only 55·2. In the north of the district it is certainly fresher and to an officer, camping in the fields, away from the heat absorbing bricks of cities, the night will occasionally seem quite frosty. Appended to this chapter will be found the average maximum, minimum and mean temperatures recorded at Nārāyanganj which, as a rule, are a little lower than those experienced in Dacca city.

Prevailing winds. From November to March the prevailing winds are from the west, north and north-west. In March sudden storms from the north-west are by no means uncommon and are a source of considerable danger to light craft cruising on the rivers. From April to October the wind is generally from the east and south-east. It is heavily laden with moisture but it does much to mitigate the rigours of the climate and often renders a punkah quite unnecessary. The steady persistence of this wind especially in the afternoons and evenings during the rainy seasons is, in fact, one of the most attractive features of the Dacca climate.

The district is occasionally visited by violent cyclones and it suffered severely from the great earthquake of 1897. A more detailed account of these visitations will be found in Chapter VII.

Rainfall. The mean rainfall at Dacca is 72·03 inches, but the variation from year to year is not infrequently considerable, the rainfall of 1900-01, for instance, being 50·7 inches while in the next year it was 82·3. November to March is the dry season, the total average fall for those five months being about 5½ inches. April and October which usher in and witness the cessation of the monsoon have each about 4½ inches, while May and September have from 9 to 10. Each of the three remaining months receives as a rule from 12 to 13 inches of rain, though here, too, there is great variation from the mean. The statement in the margin shows the average rainfall recorded at the five stations which have been opened for some length of time. Rain-gauges have been recently erected at Kāpāsia and at Nawābganj, but there are not sufficient data yet available to allow of the calculation of a mean. It will be seen that the rainfall for the year is fairly uniform throughout the district but there are often marked differences in the amount precipitated on any given day even at stations lying so close to one another as do Dacca and Nārāyanganj. These two places are only separated by a distance of nine miles yet the daily rainfall is sometimes four or five inches greater in one place than the other.

	Mean annual rainfall.
Dacca ...	... 72·03
Nārāyanganj	... 71·51
Munshiganj	... 78·30
Jaydebpur	... 70·94
Manikganj	... 62·67

APPENDIX I.

Average temperature recorded at Nārāyānganj :—

Months.	Average maximum temperature.	Average minimum temperature.	Average mean temperature corrected to true diurnal mean.
January	77·9	55·2	65·8
February	82·2	58·6	69·9
March	90·0	68·2	78·2
April	93·2	74·3	82·6
May	91·3	75·8	83·3
June	89·0	78·3	83·2
July	88·3	79·2	83·4
August	87·5	79·0	82·9
September	88·5	78·9	83·2
October	87·9	75·3	81·0
November	83·5	66·0	74·6
December	78·0	57·3	67·6

APPENDIX II.

List of animals, birds, fishes, trees and plants which according to Taylor are found in the Dacca district :—

ANIMALS.

Tigers.
Leopards.
Buffalo.
Cervus hippelaphus.
„ *aristotilis.*
„ *axis.*
„ *muntjac.*
Pig.
Jackal.
Fox.
Hare.
Black rabbit (*Lepus hispidus*).
Bandicoot rat.
Mongoose.
Muskrat (*Sorex indicus*).
Civet (*Viverra bengalensis*).
Porcupine.
Otter.
Dysopes murinus.
Pteropus.
Megaderma.
Vespertilio pictus.

Elephant and bear which are mentioned by Taylor are no longer found wild in the district.

BIRDS.

Vulture.
Crow.
Kite.
Fish eagle.
Owl.
Strix candidus.
Strix noctua indica.
Kingfishers.
Bee-eaters (*Merops viridis*).
Notched bill.
Creeper (*Certhiadæ*).
Sunbird (*Cinnyridæ*).
Weaver bird (*Ploceus*).
Woodpeckers.
Picus viridis.
„ *tiga.*
„ *amantius.*
„ *macei.*
„ *bengalensis*
„ *rufus.*

BIRDS.—(*contd.*)

Motacilla picata.
Sylvia sutoria.
Cuculus orientlais.
Coracia bengalensis.
Corvus corax.
Gracula religiosa.
Green parrot.
Wader (various species).
Spoonbill (*platatœa*).
Siris (*Ardea antigone*).
Manickjhor (*Ciconia leucocephelia*).
Manickjhor (*Ciconia mycteria australis*).
Heron.
Ardea orientalis.
„ *modesta.*
„ *negriotostris.*
„ *flavia collis.*
Adjutant (*Ciconia argala*).
Parra sinensis.
Conirostral family.
Cuculus lathami.
Gallenille (*Porphyrio sultana*).
Crested coot (*Fulica crestata.*)
Spurwinged plover (*Caradrus ventralis*).
Snipe (*Scolopax gallingo*).
Peacock.
Partridge.
Quail.
Jungle pigeon.
Scissor bill (*Ryncops nigra*).
Pelican.
Darter (*Plotus valenti*)
Duck.
Anas indica.
„ *clypeata.*
„ *crecca.*
„ *pœcilorhyncha.*
„ *girra.*
Goose.

FISH.

Ray (*Raia fluviatilis*).
Shark (*Squalus carcharias*).
Saw fish (*Squalus pristis*).
Tetrodon potka.
„ *cutcutia.*
„ *tepa.*
Marœna.
Macrognathus.
Ophisurus.
Unibranchapertura.
Cuchia.
Gobius.
Ophiocephalus.
Coius.
Trichopodus.
Labrus bola.
Chanda.
Ophiocephalus lata.
Coius cobojius.
Trichopodus colisa.
Bola pama.
Macronopterus magur.
Silurus singio.
Silurus pabda.
„ *garua.*
Boalee.
Pimelodus aor.
„ *pangas.*
„ *tengra.*
„ *batassia.*
„ *rita.*
„ *bagharia.*
„ *jagore.*
„ *silondia.*
Esox cancilla.
Mullet (*Mugil corsula*).
Mango fish (*Polynemus risua*).
Clupea phasa.
Hilsa (*Clupanadon ilisha*).
Mystus chitala.
„ *ramcarati.*
Cysrinus rohita.
„ *cutla.*
„ *culbasia.*
„ *putitoria.*
„ *puntius.*

FLORA.

Nymphæa lotus.
Panee-kela.
Singhara (*Trapa biscinosa* and *quadrispinosa*).
Rukta komol (*Nelumbium*).
Pokol (*Anneslia spinosa*).
Ghetchoo (*Aponogeton monostachion*).
Culmee-shag (*Convolvulus repens*).
Ksherni (*Mimusops kanki*).
Lutkha (*Pierardia sapida*).
Kamaranga (*Averrhoa carambola*).
Julpai (*Elœocarpus serrata*).
Dephul (*Artocarpus lakoocha*).
Chalta (*Dillenia speciosa*).
Imlee (*Tamarindus indica*).
Kuthbel (*feronia elephantum*).
Ficus glomeruta.
,, *carica.*
,, *vagans.*
Amoora.
Mango.
Jungli khajoor (*Phœnix farinefera*).
Cane (*Calamus rotang*).
Jungli huldee (*Curcuma zedoaria*).
Jaman.
Sutumoollee (*Asparagus racemosus*).
Juyuntee (*Æschynomene sesban*).
Sonali (*Cassia fistula*).
Sona (*Bauhinia purpurea*).
Kat kaleja (*Cœsalpinia bonducella*).
Apurajita (*Clitoria ternata*).
Rukhta chandana (*Adenanthera pavonia*).
Khadira (*Acacia catechu*).
Mashanee (*Glycine labialis*).
Kala kalkashanda (*Cassia purpurea*).
Gooluncha (*Menispermum glabrum*).
Chitra (*Plumbago zeylanica*).
Bichittee (*Trajia involucrata*).
Basoka (*Justicia adhotoda*).
Mootha (*Cyperus rotundus*).
Shyamaluta (*Echites frutescens*).
Bhoii koomra (*Trichosanthes tuberosa*).
Shanci (*Achyranthes triandra*).
Bala (*Pavonia odorata*).
Nag keshur (*Mesua ferrea*).
Poonurnuva (*Bœrhavia procumbens*).
Nisinda (*Vitex nigundo*).
Taruka (*Althœa alhugas*).
Harjorah (*Cissus quadrangularis*).
Bangra (*Verbesina prostrata*).
Jirjul (*Odina wodier*).
Toolsi (*Ocymum villosum*).
Shimool (*Bombax heptaphylla*).
Champa (*Michelia champuka*).
Nagphunee (*Cactus indicus*).
Shephalika (*Nyctanthes arbortristis*).
Juba (*Hibiscus rosa-sinensis*).
Palita mandar (*Erythrina indica*).
Akund (*Asclepias gigantea*).
Seej (*Euphorbia nercifolia*).
Isharmool (*Aristolochia indica*),
Kadumba (*Nauclea cadumba*).
Matura (*Callicarpa incana*).
Bhika purni (*Hydrocotyle asiatica*).
Jyostee madhoor (*Glycirrhiza glabra*).
Bukool (*Mimusops elengii*).
Jamp tokuri (*Sida asiatica*).
Sujna (*Hyperanthera moringa*).
Koondooree (*Bryonia grandis*).
Patur choor (*Plectranthus aromaticus*).
Rukta kumbula (*Nymphœa rubra*).
Jumulgota (*Croton tiglium*).

FLORA—(*contd*).

Koochila (*Strychnos nux vomica*.
Neem (*Melia azadiracta*).
Dhatura (*D. metel*).
Bhorenda (*Ricinus communis*).
Bena (*Andropogon muricatus*).
Oolloa (*Saccharum cylindricum*).
Kagura (*Saccharum spontaneum*).
Null (*Arundo karkha*).
Baksha (*Rotbœllia glabra*).
Koosha (*Poa cynosuroides*).
Doobla (*Panicum dactylon*).
Hoogla (*Typha elephantina*).
Jow (*Tamarix indica*).

CHAPTER II.

HISTORY.*

EARLY HISTORY. Buddhist traditions.

There can be little doubt that a portion, at any rate, of the district of Dacca was included in the ancient kingdom of Pragjyotisha or Kamrup—a passage in the Yogini Tantra distinctly stating that the southern boundary of that kingdom was the junction of the Brahmaputra and Lakshya, which is situated near the modern town of Nārāyanganj. The early traditions that have come down to us indicate that Dacca and several of the neighbouring districts were originally under the sway of Buddhist kings. According to the Tibetan legends a Buddhist king named Vimala was master of Bangala and Kamrup, and therefore of Dacca. Hiuen Tsiang who visited Kamrup in the second half of the seventh century states that Samtata, which probably included the pargana of Bikrampur, was a Buddhist kingdom although the king was a Brahman by caste. In the Raipura thana brass images of Buddhist origin have been discovered and two copper-plates with inscriptions of Buddhist kings. These have been assigned by experts to the end of the eighth and beginning of the ninth century, and a copper-plate found in the Faridpur district, which is ascribed to the same period, proves that the Bikrampur pargana was also under Buddhist rule.

The names of a few local Rājās have come down to us, but we know little more about them than their names. One of the best known is Haris Chandra, the ruins of whose capital close to Sābhār can be seen even at the present day. The capital of another local princeling called Josh Pal was at Dakurai, 18 miles north of Sābhār where there are several tanks and an old road called the Rathkhola Sarak, leading to a place called Jatrabari, names which tend to suggest that Josh Pal was not a Buddhist. The remains of another town which is said to have been the headquarters of a chief called Sisupal are to be found at Singher Dighi, near Māhona, in the north-west of the district. About eight miles away, at Pīrōjāli, are the ruins of a fort ascribed to one Indra Rājā; and there are traces of old buildings and a moat close to Rājābāri five miles west of old Kāpāsia at a place which is said to have been the capital of the Chandal Rājās.

Overthrow of Buddhism.

In the ninth century A.D., one Adisura, a Kshatriya by caste, came from the Deccan and after overthrowing the Buddhist king of Bikrampur established himself at Rāmpāl near Munshiganj.

* This chapter was originally written in a longer form by Mr. J. T. Rankin, I.C.S., but owing to exigencies of space it has been condensed.

He sent to Kanauj for Brahmans to teach the people the religion which even the priestly class in the district had forgotten and five Brahmans, accompanied by five Kayasthas, in due time arrived. Tradition says that their reception by the king's underlings, when they reached Rāmpāl, was so rude that they were about to take their departure again in anger and had even bestowed the blessing intended for the king on the stump of a Gajari or Sāl tree to which the court elephants used to be tied. The old stump took life again and is still to be seen at Rāmpāl, the only Gajari tree in Bikrampur, where it is an object of veneration and worship to all Hindus. The king fortunately got word of the arrival of the Brahmans and was able to make his peace with them.

The Sen kings. From copper-plates and other inscriptions discovered in recent years we learn the names of several kings of the Sen dynasty, who appear next upon the scene. This source of information is more reliable than the Ain-i-Akbari and the names given in the latter need not be discussed here. The kings referred to ruled in Eastern Bengal in the following order: Vira Sen, Samanta Sen, Hemanta Sen, Vijaya Sen, Ballāl Sen and Lakhshman Sen. It has been conjectured that Vira Sen is identical with Adisura and this is not altogether improbable if, as the inscriptions give us to understand, a considerable interval elapsed between him and the next king. Of the next two kings, Samanta and Hemanta, nothing of note is recorded. Vijaya Sen, however, we are told, was a great warrior who conquered the king of Gaur, probably, the Pāl Rājā of the time reigning in Northern Bengal, and it is more than likely that this was the death blow to Buddhism in this part of India.

Ballāl Sen. The greatest of the Sen kings was Ballāl Sen, famous alike in literature and in tradition, whose residence is still pointed out at Ballāl Bāri, at Rāmpāl. It is a raised piece of ground rectangular in shape, surrounded on all sides by a moat two hundred feet wide. This is all that is now visible, but in the surrounding country bricks are constantly being turned up and treasure is not infrequently found. Close by are the Tantipārā and the Shankhari Pārā which bear witness to colonies of weavers and shell-cutters who at one time lived there in attendance on the court.

There are two bridges in the neighbourhood which tradition ascribes to Ballāl Sen. One is over the Mirkadim Khal and is called the Ballāli Bridge; it has three arches and the piers are six feet thick. The other is a little further to the west and spans the Tāltala Khal; this also has three arches but was blown up in the early days of British rule to enable large boats with troops to pass to and from Dacca.

Ballāl's was a long reign. The last trace of Buddhism had been destroyed by his father and he was free to devote himself to the internal administration of the kingdom. We know that he reorganised the caste system and founded Kulinism, a kind of Hindu aristocracy, and that he was the originator of several social reforms. We know also that he wrote two Sanskrit works, the Dānā Sagāra and the Adbut Sagāra. He abdicated in favour of his son in 1170 A.D. and died two years later. His name is still a household word in every Hindu home in the district and his fame is such as only a great and wise king could have inspired.

Fall of the Sen Kings.

Ballāl was succeeded by his son, Lakhshman Sen, who gave his name to Lakhnauti (Lakhshmānā Bāti) and lived latterly in Nadia. We are told that after the capture of Nadia by Bakhtyār Khilji he fled to Bikrampur where he and his sons exercised a precarious sovereignty for the next hundred years. He had three sons--Madhab, Keshab and Viswa Rup—the last of whom succeeded him in Bikrampur and evidently had some fighting with the Muhammadans. Eventually the Sens were driven out and we find that the Rājā of Mandi claims descent from them and alleges that one of his ancestors, Rup Sen, fled to the Punjab where he founded the present city of Ruper. Beyond these legends all trace of this once powerful dynasty has completely disappeared.

Early Muhammadan period.

Little is known of the movements of the Muhammadans in Dacca in the earlier part of the thirteenth century. In 1223 A.D., the Governor of Bengal, Ghiyās-ud-dīn, marched towards Kamrup and Eastern Bengal, but was recalled by an attack on his capital. Another governor invaded Eastern Bengal in 1260 A.D., and according to Marco Polo the country was subdued by the Khāns of Tartary in 1272 A.D. He gives the following account of these parts :—

"The province Bengala bordereth upon India toward the south, which Great Can subdued, when Marco Polo lived in his court. The country hath a proper king and peculiar language. The inhabitants thereof are all idolaters : they have masters which keep schools and teach idolatries and inchantments : a thing common to all the great men of that country. They eat flesh, rice and milk: they have cotton in great plenty, and by reason thereof, much and great trading is exercised there: they abound also with spike, galangal, ginger, sugar and divers other spices. Huge oxen are also there, comparable with elephants in height but not in thickness. Many eunuchs are made in this province, which are afterwards sold unto merchants."

In 1279 A.D., the district was visited by the Emperor himself who advanced beyond Sonārgaon in pursuit of Toghril, the governor of Lakhnauti, who had thrown off his allegiance and proclaimed himself an independent sovereign.

Bahādur Khān.

Subsequently the Emperor Alā-ud-dīn, finding that the viceroy of Bengal had become too powerful, effected a partition of the province and appointed Bahādur Khān to be governor of Eastern Bengal with his head-quarters at Sonārgāon. A Bengali historian of Sonārgāon tells us that after capturing the main forts and subduing the Rājā of the locality, Bahādur governed in his name and introduced but few changes in the form of the administration. Certainly, so long as Alā-ud-dīn lived, Bahādur ruled circumspectly, but on his death he declared himself independent with the title of Bahādur Shah. This so enraged the new Emperor (Ghiyās-ud-dīn Tughlak Shah) that he marched into Bengal (1324 A.D.) and, defeating Bahādur, took him to Delhi with a rope round his neck, appointing Tatar Khān, his adopted son, to be governor of Sonārgāon in his place.

Tatar Khān was succeeded in 1338 A.D. by his armour-bearer Fakhr-ud-dīn who declared himself to be independent. He was, however, defeated by Qadir Khān who occupied Sonārgāon where he amassed great treasure. This treasure proved his destruction for his soldiers went over to Fakhr-ud-din who offered them this immense reward as the price of their treachery. Coins minted by this chief prove that he reigned ten years, when he met his death, probably at the hands of Alī Mubārak, governor of Lakhnauti. The following account of the country in the time of Fakhr-ud-din is given by Ibn Batūta. Writing of the Brahmaputra he says, "it descends from the mountains of Kamrup and is called the Blue River, by which people travel towards Bengal and Lakhnautī. Along this river are hydraulic wheels, gardens, and villages, on the right and on the left, just as they are to be seen along the Nile in Egypt. The inhabitants of these villages are non-Muhammadans who pay a protection tax. From them is exacted half of the produce of their lands besides tribute. We remained on this river for fifteen days sailing between villages and gardens just as if we had been passing through a market. On this river there are innumerable ships in every one of which there is a drum. Whenever two ships meet the crew of both of them strike their drums and salute each other. Fakhr-ud-dīn, the Sultan, of whom we have spoken, has ordered that no duty should be levied from fakirs on that river and that provisions should be given to such of them as had not got them so that whenever a fakir arrives in a village he is given half a *dinar*." **Fakhr-ud-din.**

At Sonārgāon the travellers found a jonk which was bound for the country of Java and embarked on it.

In 1352 A.D. Hāji Ilyās conquered Eastern Bengal and founded a dynasty which continued with a brief interval to reign over that province for nearly a century and a half. In 1354, he was attacked by the Emperor Feroz Shāh and fled to the fort of Ekdala. It is said that during the siege of the fort the saint Shaikh Rājā Biyabāni died, and Ilyās, coming out of the fort disguised as a mendicant, joined the Shaikh's funeral procession and afterwards went to see the Emperor without himself being recognised. **Dynasty Hāji Ilyās.**

Ilyās died in 1359 A.D. and was succeeded by his son Sikandar Shāh in whose reign the emperor Feroz again invaded Bengal. Hearing of the Imperial advance Sikandar, like his father, fled "into the islands of Ekdala." Another siege ensued during which one of the chief towers of the fort fell owing to the pressure of the people upon it, but the fort being built of mud **Sikandar Shāh.**

was speedily repaired. Negotiations for peace were opened and presents were exchanged. It is related that the Sultan sent into the fort of Ekdala by the hands of Malik Kabul a crown worth 80,000 Tanka and 500 valuable Arab and Turki horses with the expression of his wish that henceforth they might never again draw the sword. Sikandar seems to have paid great attention to internal administration and it is said that he made a regular survey of the province, his name surviving to the present day in the term Sikandari *gaj*. His end was however an unhappy one as he was defeated and killed by his son Ghiyās-ud-dīn at Garpārā in the Manikganj subdivision in 1368 A.D.

Ghiyās-ud-dīn.

Ghiyās-ud-dīn held his court at Sonārgāon. He was a man of some literary attainments and invited the celebrated poet Hafiz to visit him. At the same time he was an able and enlightened ruler. We learn from Chinese sources that he despatched embassies to China and received presents in return. He died in 1373 A.D. and the remains of his tomb are still to be seen in Mahalla Baghalpur at Sonārgāon. At the present day it is in a very dilapidated condition but it was described by Dr. Wise in 1874 in the following terms:—"This mausoleum formerly consisted of a ponderous stone which occupied the centre, surrounded by pillars about five feet high. These stones are all beautifully carved and the corners of the slabs and the arabesque tracery are as perfect as the day they left the workman's hands. The stones are formed of hard, almost black, basalt. At the head is a prostrate sandstone pillar, half buried in earth. It was evidently used when erect as a Chiraghdan, or stand for a light."

Ghiyās-ud-dīn's coins were struck at Muazzamabād, where a mint had been established by his father. This place appears to have been close to Sonārgāon, and may have been the same as Muazzampur, a village lying a few miles to the north of Sonārgāon, which we know as the seat of a saint in the reign of Jalāl-ud-dīn a few years later.

Rājā Kāns and his descendants.

In 1405 there was a brief recrudescence of Hindu sovereignty, the throne of Bengal being seized by Rājā Kāns who reigned till 1414 A.D. His son and successor Jalāl-ud-dīn was, as his name implies, a convert to the Muhammadan religion. He was followed by his son Ahmad Shāh to whose reign belongs the oldest inscription yet found in the district. It is to be seen in the mosque of the saint Shāh Langar at Muazzampur.

Nāsir Shāh.

In 1432 A.D., the dynasty of Ilyās Shāh was restored in the person of Sultan Nāsir-ud-din Abul Muzaffar Mahmud Shāh who reigned till 1460 A.D. He restored to his throne Meng Soamwun, the king of Arakan, who had been expelled by the Burmese in 1406, but only on condition that he should remain a vassal of Bengal. The mosque of Binat Bibi at Naraindia in the city of Daccā was erected during his reign, but otherwise there is little known about this prince.

The records of his immediate successors are equally meagre but in 1494, Shāh Alā-ud-dīn Husain Sharif Maki, known as Husain Shāh the Good, came to the throne. He made his capital at Ekdala and captured Kamātapur in 1498 leaving his son Danyal as governor there. The young prince and his followers were however killed and a subsequent expedition sent into Assam was completely routed by the Ahoms. Husain Shāh also sent two expeditions into Tippera. The first under Gaur Malik was driven back, the Tipperas damming the river Gumti and then letting loose the waters upon the invaders. The second, under Hyten Khān, was at first successful but was subsequently routed by the same expedient as had proved so successful against the former expedition. Some time after this (the date is uncertain and it may have been after Husain Shāh's death) Bijaya, the Rājā of Tippera, in retaliation, invaded Bengal with an army of 26,000 infantry and 5,000 cavalry, besides artillery. He travelled with 5,000 boats along the rivers Brahmaputra and Lakshya to the Padmā, spent some days at Sonārgāon in debauchery and then crossed to Sylhet. Husain Shāh

After Husain Shāh there were three other independent kings, *viz.*, (i) Nasrat Shāh, his son, (ii) Fīroz Shāh, his grandson, and (iii) Mahmud Shāh, his son. The last named was defeated by Sher Shāh and with him ended the line of independent kings.

Before proceeding to describe Dacca under the Mughals it will be convenient to record here a few of the facts relating to the period intervening between the defeat of Mahmud Shāh and the final annexation of Bengal by Akbar in 1576. Administration of Sher Shāh.

Sher Shāh appointed one Khizr Khān Bairak to be governor of Bengal but he married a daughter of Mahmud Shāh and declared himself independent. For this he was imprisoned by Sher Shāh who took the opportunity of dividing Bengal into provinces, making Kazi Fazilat the Amir or Superintendent. Sonārgāon was probably one of those provinces and the governor in the year 1542 seems to have been Saiyid Ahmad Rumi. Sher Shāh's short but able administration extended as far as the Dacca district. The trunk road made by him from Sonārgāon to Upper India is famous. Rest-houses were maintained at every stage and every few miles there was a well.

Islām Shāh, son of Sher Shāh, garrisoned the whole country with troops from the borders of Sonārgāon, but he reversed his father's policy and once more appointed one governor for Bengal. Muhammad Khān Sur was selected for the post, and he on Islām Shāh's death declared himself independent, as did his two sons after him. Neither these kings nor any of the rulers who followed ever apparently held the whole of Bengal, nor was their right recognised by contemporaries, and consequently, as Stewart says, they cannot be considered absolute sovereigns.

After the final extinction of the Sur dynasty the Afghāns in Bengal were dispersed, some, it is said, became faqirs and some attached themselves to Sulaimān Karānī who had meanwhile been amassing much influence and power. He brought nearly the whole of Bengal under his sway, including the district of Dacca, as appears from the inscription on a mosque in Rikabi Bāzār (about three miles from Munshiganj) which was built by one Malik Abdulla Miyan during the reign of Hazrat Ala (His Majesty) Miyan Sulaimān, in the year 1575 A.D.

Sulaimān was succeeded first by his son Bāyazīd and then by his second son, Daud. The wars between these rulers and the generals of Akbar have no concern with the district. But there was fighting in Ghorāghāt, in which Kālā Pāhār and other Afghāns were concerned, and this may have had an effect in and around Dacca. Daud was finally killed in 1576, when Bengal was annexed to the Mughal Empire.

The twelve Bhuiyas.

It was some years, however, before the whole of Bengal was actually reduced to subjection. Several tracts continued to be under the rule of petty chiefs who refused to own allegiance to the Emperor and gave shelter and a hearty welcome to the numerous Afghāns whom Daud's death had thrown out of employment. Foremost among those chiefs were the twelve Bhuiyas of Bengal. In this place it is only necessary to refer to those who ruled over portions of the Dacca district. These were (i) Fazl Ghāzī of Bhawāl, (ii) Chānd Rai and Kedar Rai of Bikrampur and (iii) Isa Khān, Masnad-i-Alī, of Khizrpur. The first named traced his descent from one Pahnun Shāh who lived about six hundred years ago. His son, Karfarma Sāhib, went to Delhi, and there received from the Emperor the grant of pargana Bhawāl in return for uniting the two roofs of a building, which all the court architects had hitherto failed to accomplish. According to tradition the area ruled over by this family comprised the parganas of Chānd Ghāzī (now Chānd Pratāp), Tala Ghāzī (now Talipabād) and Bara Ghāzī (now Bhawāl). They had not, however, the faculty of keeping what they had gained and some time in the eighteenth century these estates passed into the hands of their Bengali servants. The family still resides at Chaura near Kāliganj in a state of pitiable poverty. Chānd Rai and Kedar Rai who built the Rājābāri *math* are the only two Bhuiyas of Bikrampur whose names have come down to us. Their capital at Srīpur, not far from Rājābāri, has long ago been washed away by the Padmā river but it was of sufficient importance to be mentioned by more than one European traveller.

Isa Khān.

The greatest of all the Bhuiyas was Isa Khān, son of a Bhis Rājput of Oudh who had accepted the Muhammadan faith. His principal strongholds were at Khizrpur, about a mile north of Nārāyanganj, and at Diwān Bāgh, and he formed a rallying point for the Afghāns of Eastern Bengal who offered a stern resistance to the Mughal arms. In 1584 the Viceroy Shāh Baz entered Dacca in pursuit of the rebel Masum and captured Khizrpur and Baktarapur, another of Isa Khan's strongholds. That chief endeavoured to create a diversion by laying siege to the fort of the

Koch Rājā at Jangalbari (Mymensingh) and then attacked the imperial forces on the Brahmaputra. But he was defeated and in the following year (1585) submitted to the Emperor. He was, however, but a turbulent vassal and in 1594 Rājā Mān Singh, the viceroy of that time, made Dacca his head-quarters in a campaign against him, the troops encamping at Urdu near the site of the present central jail. Isa was driven from Khizrpur to Egara Sindu where he challenged Mān Singh to single combat. His conduct was so chivalrous that the two warriors became firm friends and went together to the court at Delhi where Isa Khān received a grant of twenty-two parganas. Even at the present day several of the parganas in the district are described as being situated in *tappa* Isa Khān. Munawār Khān's bāzār close to the Nawābpur road in Dacca takes its name from the great-grandson of this sturdy soldier.

Further opposition to Mughals.

Resistance to the imperial arms did not, however, terminate with the submission of Isa Khān. The Afghāns under Osmān Lohani held out obstinately at Dhāmrāi and defeated the 'thānadār' while the king of Arakan laid siege to a fort near Sonārgāon. The zamindār of Bikrampur assisted him by making a diversion in the south of the district and attacking Srīnagar but Mān Singh put both of them to flight with heavy loss.

The Portuguese.

The earliest records of the Portuguese in the district date from this period. In 1586 Ralph Fitch sailed from Sripur for Pegu in a ship belonging to one Albert Caravallos. In 1599 we know that Francis Fernandez, the first Missionary to Bengal, was at Srīpur and again, in 1602, we find that one Carvalho (Carvallos ?) was in the service of Kedar Rai of Srīpur. Dr. Wise tells us of a tradition to the effect that in 1599 Fre Luis des Chagos was stopped on his way to Sylhet by Christians who besought him to relieve them from their landlord's tyranny. On his return he bought the villages of Nagari and Bhagari in Bhawāl and a piece of land was also purchased at Nārāyandia. It is doubtful if the church at Nagari was founded at this time but we know that an Augustine church did exist at Nārayāndia early in the seventeenth century. The parochial church of Dacca was at Tezgāon about a mile north of the new civil station. This was founded soon after the one at Bandel (Hughli), but the exact date is not known. The following extract relating to the visit of Fernandez to Srīpur is taken from Purchas:—

"At Srīpur in December, they arrived and were received as angels from heaven, by reason of the Bishop of Cocin had excommunicated the new Captayne with his followers from which sentence they hoped the Jesuites would exempt them and although we were loth to intermeddle, yet we could not but give answer to them. At Sripur the Governor gave us leave to preach and assigned six hundred pieces of gold for revenue, and roome to build a church, with promise of all necessaries." The Captain referred to was evidently a leader of Portuguese who were settled there already. The church does not seem to have been ever built.

Ralph Fitch's account of Dacca.

The following description of the district by Ralph Fitch, who visited it in 1586, is interesting:—

"From Bacola I went to Serrepore (Sripur) which standeth upon the river of Ganges: the king is called Choudery (*i.e.*, Chaudhuri). They be all hereabouts rebels against their king Zebaldim Echebar (*i.e.*, Jalāluddīn Akbar): for here are so many rivers and islands that they flee from one to another, whereby his horsemen cannot prevail against them. Great store of cotton cloth is made here. Sinnergan (*i.e.*, Sonārgāon) is a town six leagues from Serrepore, where there is the best and finest cloth made of cotton in all India. The houses here, as they be in the most part of India, very little and covered with straw and have a few mats round about the walls and the door to keep out the tigers and the foxes. Many of the people are very rich. Here they will eat no flesh nor kill no beast: they live on rice, milk and fruits. They go with a little cloth before them and all the rest of their bodies is naked. Great store of cotton cloth goeth from hence and much rice, wherewith they serve all India, Ceylon, Pegu, Malacca, Sumatra and many other places."

THE NAWĀBS OF DACCA.

At the beginning of the seventeenth century the district and city sprang into prominence as the head-quarters of the Nawābs of Dacca.

Islām Khān.

In 1607 Islām Khān was appointed viceroy of Bengal and in 1608 he transferred the seat of government from Rājmahāl to Dacca which was for several reasons a more convenient capital. It afforded a good centre for operations against Usman, the Afghān chief, who was still unsubdued, against the Portuguese, who after their alliance with Arakan had become a serious menace to the waterways of Eastern Bengal, and against the Ahoms in Assam. But the chief reason, perhaps, for making the removal permanent was that a change in the course of the river at Rājmahāl had resulted in a great decline in the trade of that place. It is said that before fixing the site of the new capital at Dacca, Islām Khān had serious thoughts of establishing it at Dhāmrāi where he halted some time and where a portion of the village is still known as Islāmpur. It must not, however, be supposed that Dacca first came into existence in the time of Islām Khān. Two mosques in different quarters of the town had been built many years before this date, Rājā Mān Singh had lived for a time at Dacca and the town was the seat of an imperial thānadār. Further, the Basaks of Dacca have records to show that their ancestors first settled here some years before Islām Khān's time, and only a trading centre of some importance would have attracted such a community as theirs.

Islām Khān, the first Nawāb of Dacca, was foster brother of the Emperor Jahāngīr. He was a strict Musalman, simple in his personal habits and dress, but as Nawāb he lived in regal style. He had 20,000 horse and footmen in his service; he had his *jharoka* and *ghuslkhāna* and he spent Rs. 80,000 a month on dancing-girls. Testimony of his piety is to be found in a mosque in Islāmpur in the town—a small unpretentious building said to have been erected by him—and the quarters Islāmpur and Nawābpur of the city owe their names to him. He died in 1613 at Dacca and his body was taken to Fatehpur Sīkri, his birthplace, and buried there.

From the first, probably, Usmān must have been a source of anxiety to Islām Khān. But in 1612 A.D., when he was threating Dacca itself, he sent Shujāat Khān with an army against him. A battle was fought "near Usman's fortress and country" on the banks of a stream, in which Usmān was killed and the imperial forces gained a victory which sheltered once for all the power of the Afghāns in Bengal.

About that time Lakshmī Nārāyan, king of Koch Bihar, came in person to Dacca and appealed to Islām Khān for help against his cousin, the king of Koch Hajo, and simultaneously the Rājā of Susang begged asistance against the latter's tyranny. Islām, glad of the opportunity to humble a Rājā who had always prided himself on his independence, and keen, no doubt, to add fresh territory to the empire, sent an expedition to Koch Hajo under Mukarram Khān. The Rājā was defeated, taken prisoner to Dacca and thence sent to Delhi, while a garrison was left in Hajo.

Next year Islām Khān set himself to subdue the country east of the Meghnā which had submitted to the king of Arakan. Gonsales of Sandip made an alliance with the latter to repel their common foe. The Arakanese (Mugh) army marched as far as the Noakhali district, but Islām Khān succeeded in defeating it and sent to the Emperor, in charge of his son Hashang Khān, a number of the Mughs who were captured.

Kāsim Khān.

On Islām Khān's death, the Emperor appointed his brother Kāsim Khān to be viceroy in his place. During his time the king of Arakan took Sandip and a portion of the Bakarganj district and, according to Arakanese records, occupied Dacca also, but this, if true, must have been later, when the Mughal troops were elsewhere engaged during Shāh Jahān's rebellion. For his failure to repel the Mughs and for allowing the Assamese to make an incursion into Koch Hajo Kāsim was recalled in 1618 and Ibrāhīm Khān appointed to Bengal. The out-going and in-coming viceroys met and quarrelled over the return of Islām Khān's elephants but Kāsim's party was worsted and he left Ibrāhīm in possession of all his treasures.

Ibrāhim Khān.

Ibrāhīm Khān Fath Jang was the brother of the Empress Nūr Mahal. A strong and capable governor, he held the Afghāns in check, repelled the Assamese and kept a strict watch on the Arakanese by means of a fleet of war boats. For five years agriculture, manufactures and commerce all flourished, and the province enjoyed great prosperity. But these peaceful times were not to last. Prince Shāh Jahān rebelled and invaded Bengal and the viceroy, recovering from his first panic, marched from Dacca with what troops he could collect. He was handicapped by part of his army being employed in Chittagong and portions of it being scattered over the country for the purpose of enforcing the revenue collections, but he was loyal to the Emperor, and attempts to gain him over were made in vain. A battle was fought near Rājmahāl, resulting in the death of Ibrāhīm and the dispersal of his forces. Shāh Jahān thereupon proceeded to Dacca, where Ahmad Beg, nephew of Ibrāhīm, was compelled to make over to him all the elephants, horses and other property of his uncle, together with forty lakhs of rupees belonging to Government. He stayed in Dacca for a short time giving audience to public and private gentlemen and otherwise conducting himself as ruler. On leaving he appointed Darab Khān to be governor but on his retreat from Bengal another viceroy was appointed.

From Arakanese sources we learn that in 1622 the Rājā of Arakan enforced payment of tribute from Dacca. This he would be able to do in the absence of Ibrāhīm and his army.

In the Rājmālā we read that the Muhammadans invaded Tippera to capture horses and elephants. Headed by Nāwab Fatteh Jang they were victorious, the capital was taken and the Rājā sent a prisoner to Delhi. The Muhammadans remained in that country two and a half years, committing great atrocities, plundering the temples and robbing the inhabitants. They were at last forced to leave owing to the outbreak of a dreadful plague. Again, soon after 1625, the Rājā of Tippera refusing to pay tribute, the Nawāb led or sent an expedition against him which was defeated. On this occasion we are told that his troops had with them a famous cannon made of leather.

Mahābat Khān.

After Shāh Jahān quitted Bengal, the province was made over to Mahābat Khān and his son Khānahzād Khān. The former had distinguished himself in the war in the Deccan and so risen to favour. He incurred the Emperor's displeasure for failing to send him the elephants he captured, as well as for failing to submit accounts. Leaving his son in charge he set off to interview the Emperor. Peace was made but the viceroyalty was conferred in 1626 on Mukarram Khān.

Mukarram Khān.

The new Nawāb was son-in-law of Islām Khān and he it was who led the expedition into Koch Hajo. While at Dacca he took great pleasure in boating and kept up a large establishment of boats of every description for war as well as for pleasure. Going out one day in state to meet the Emperor's envoy his boat upset and he was drowned.

Mirza Hidāyatullah. Kāsim Khān.

Mirza Hidāyatullah known as Fidai Khān was appointed in 1627. Nothing is known of his viceroyalty. On Jahāngir's death he was replaced by the new Emperor's own nominee, Kāsim Khān, who had been Khazanchi or Treasurer of Bengal under Islām Khān. He rose to favour owing to his skill in archery which he taught to the new Emperor and by marrying a sister of Nūr

Jahān he secured himself in the royal favour. The chief event of his rule was the war against the Portuguese at Hughli, in which the fleet from Dacca which mobilised at Sripur took part.

He died in 1631 A.D. and was succeeded by Mir Muhammad Baqir, whose titles were Irādat Khān and afterwards Azīm Khān. At a later period he became Shāh Shujā's father-in-law. During his time the Assamese destroyed the garrison in Assam, carried off the governor Abdus Salām and invaded Bengal, penetrating almost as far as Dacca. Azim Khān.

For this reason Azīm Khān was superseded by Islām Khān Mashadi, whose real name was Mir Abdus Salām. Soon after his accession in 1638 A.D. he received a visit from Makat or Manik Rai, the governor of Chittagong under the Rājā of Arakan, who had incurred that king's displeasure and now hastened to declare himself a vassal of the Mughal Empire. He made over his province to Islām Khān who took possession and renamed the town of Chittagong Islāmābād. The Nawāb then despatched an expedition into Assam and terms were negotiated with the Assamese fixing a boundary between Muhammadan and Assamese territory, which was maintained for the next twenty-five years. It is possible that the results of this expedition might have been less favourable to the Assamese had not the viceroy been recalled by the Emperor to the post of Vazir at Delhi, thus making room for Prince Muhammad Shujā, commonly known as Shāh Shujā. Islām Khān Mashadi.

The fort at Dacca, which stood on the site now occupied by the Lunatic Asylum and Central Jail, was built by Islām Khān Mashadi. The courts of justice and the mint were within its walls. The building opposite the main gate of the jail is said to have been the residence of the *kotwal*. Islām Khān also increased the *nawara* (or fleet) and the artillery, and in his time the arsenal must have been in a state of considerable efficiency for there exists now in Murshidābād a gun made at Dacca during his viceroyalty. It is seventeen and a half feet long and its muzzle is six inches in diameter; the weight is said to be about seven and three-quarter tons.

Shāh Shujā came to Bengal as viceroy in 1639. The Emperor sent with him as an adviser his father-in-law, Azīm Khān, who had himself filled the post, and, further to curtail his power, put Shāista Khān in charge of Behar. After a short residence in Dacca, Shāh Shujā for some reason transferred his capital to Rājmahāl, leaving his father-in-law as his deputy in Dacca. The latter disliked this subordinate position and soon resigned. For nearly twenty years, with a short break, Shāh Shujā ruled over Bengal. In spite of the absence of the viceregal court, this was apparently a period of prosperity for the city of Dacca and several of its important buildings date from this time. Shāh Shujā.

Shāh Shujā proved an able administrator and one of his achievements was the preparation of a new rent-roll of the province. But his ambition proved his ruin. Hearing of his father's illness, he started at the head of an army with the intention of seizing the Empire. Details of this exploit belong more properly to a history of India or of Bengal. Suffice it to say here that he was defeated by Aurangzeb's general, Mīr Jumla, and fled to Dacca, whither he was pursued by Mīr Jumla. He sent his son, Zainuddīn, to arrange for an asylum with the king of Arakan. Zainuddīn was well received by the latter and came back to Dacca with a fleet of boats manned by Portuguese and Arakanese, on which poor Shujā embarked with all his family and treasure and escaped to Arakan where he died.

Mir Jumla.

On the defeat and flight of Shāh Shujā, the Emperor appointed Mīr Jumla to be viceroy. He was above all things a soldier and a soldier with great ambitions. It has been suggested that Aurangzeb gave him this appointment not merely as a reward for his services (especially against Shāh Shujā) but also as an expedient for keeping a dangerous man at a distance, fully occupied with congenial employment. The relics in Dacca attributed to him are all the works of a military governor. At the confluence of the Lakshya, Dhaleswari and Meghnā rivers he built the Idrakpur fort, where the town of Munshīganj now stands. Much of this fort still remains and within its walls the Subdivisional Officer has his residence and the jail is located. The forts at Khizrpur and Sona Kanda are attributed to him, but both probably existed before his time and in all likelihood he only strengthened them. There were at one time two forts on the Buri Ganga below Dacca, one at Fatulla and the other opposite. These were probably built by him. The bridge at Pagla, Tavernier tells us, was his work, and it is more than probable that he also constructed the road from Dacca to Khizrpur, *viâ* Fatulla, which passes over this bridge. Finally, the road to Mymensingh and the bridge on it at Tongi were both made by him.

Before Mir Jumla took up the government of Bengal the Assamese had been giving much trouble, and as soon as he had leisure he turned his attention to them. He sent out two small expeditions, one under Rashīd Khān and another under Rājā Sujan Singh, which had little or no result. Then, in 1661, he started himself, leaving Ihtishan Khān at Khizrpur to guard Dacca and its environs. While away he contracted a serious illness which neither his Dutch nor his French doctor, nor his Hakīm from Delhi could cure and he died not far from Khizrpur in 1663.

Shāista Khān.

On the death of Mir Jumla, Shāista Khān, brother of the Empress Momtaz Mahal and nephew of the Empress Nur Mahal, was appointed to the vacant viceroyalty. He ruled Bengal from 1664 to 1677 and again from 1679 to 1689, and during this period Dacca attained to the zenith of its prosperity and grandeur.

One of the first of Shāista Khān's acts was to clear the rivers of the pirates that infested them and to sack the stronghold of the Mughs at Chittagong. He won over many of the Portuguese from their allegiance to the king of Arakan and planted a colony of them at Feringhi Bāzār near Munshīganj. He next turned his attention to Tippera and captured and sent to Delhi the heir-apparent of the kingdom who had been guilty of great cruelty, but like many viceroys the remoteness of Delhi encouraged him in an undue sense of his own importance and he gave grave offence by refusing to send the surplus treasure to the capital. He was recalled in 1677 and during his absence the province was administered by Azīm Khān and, on the death of that prince, by Muhammad Azam, who commenced the construction of the Lal Bagh which contains the beautiful tomb of his wife Peri Bibi.

In 1679 Shāista Khān returned to Dacca. Three years later William Hedges came to his court to seek concessions for the Company and has left the following account of his visit:—

"At 9 in ye morning I went to wait on ye Nawab, who after ½ hour's attendance sent officers to bring me into his presence, being sat under a large canopy of state made of crimson velvet richly embroidered with gold and silver, and deep gold and silver fringes, supported by 4 bamboos plated over with gold. I was directed by ye Emir Tusuk, or Master of the Ceremonies, to sit over against ye Nawab, nearer ye canopy than his Duan or any other person. At my first entrance ye Nawab was very busy in despatching and vesting divers principal officers sent with all possible diligence with recruits for their army lately overthrown in Asham and Sillet, two large plentiful countries 8 days' journey from this city, which are all lost except one little place held out and kept by 40 or 50 persons only: ye rest of ye souldiers being all fled out of ye country. Amongst ye rest I saw a Portuguese who was to be Commander of 5 or 600 of his countrymen."

Further on, we read:—

"*November 13th.*—News being brought me last night that ye Nabob (in ye 82nd year of his age) had a son born this day, and 'twas expected I should make him a visit and give him a present, I went this morning to ye Durbar and gave him 13 gold mohurs and 21 rupees, which he accepted so kindly that I took ye opportunity to request his perwanna."

Later on he tells us of a very severe flood that occurred in Dacca on the 4th September 1684.

Shāista Khān governed Bengal with signal success until 1689, when, verging on ninety years of ago, he obtained permission to resign. When leaving the city he ordered the western gate to be built up in commemoration of the price of rice falling in his time to the rate of 640 lbs. per rupee, and an inscription was placed on it forbidding any future governor to open it until that rate was again attained.* He died shortly afterwards at Agra. The parganas of Talipabād and Shāistanagar still exist to perpetuate his name in the district.

Murshid Kuli Jafār Khān.

The administration of Shāista Khān's two immediate succesors Bahādur Khān and Ibrāhim Khān was uneventful, and the latter is best known as the builder of the palace at Jinjira opposite the city of Dacca which was connected with the Bara Katra by a wooden bridge. The next viceroy Azīm-ush-shan was so oppressive in his treatment of the trading classes that the son of a poor Brahman, Murshid Kulī Jafār Khan, was sent to him as finance minister with plenary powers. As soon as this man arrived in Dacca he reorganised the collection staff, assessed accurately the imperial and *saiyar* taxes, and prepared a complete revenue roll of the province. He also resumed many of the Bengal *jaghirs* giving less valuable lands in Orissa in exchange. These reforms enabled him to remit a crore of rupees to the Emperor but did not endear him to the viceroy, who endeavoured to procure his assassination. Jafār Khān withdrew to a town, that he called after himself Murshidābād, and the Emperor recalled Azīm-ush-shan to Behar. From this date Dacca became the head-quarters of a Deputy or Naib-Nazim only.

Dacca under Deputies.

But many even of these officers resided outside the district and only sent deputies to Dacca. Of these Mīr Habīb was an oppressive, and his successor in the *diwānship* Jaswant Rai a good administrator. So prosperous indeed was Dacca in his time that the price of rice once more fell to 640 lbs. per rupee and the gate closed by Shāista Khān was thrown open. After him the district seems to have fallen upon troublous times, one deputy succeeding another in quick succession and the Marāthās being a constant source of terror. It was at this period that Rājā Rāj Ballabh acquired wealth and power. His father had been a clerk in the *nawarra* (naval department), but the son starting from equally humble beginnings rose to be the richest and most powerful man in Eastern Bengal. He acquired great estates including the pargana of Rājnagar and erected numerous temples all of which have since been washed away by the river Padmā. After the battle of Plassey, Mīr Jafār became Nawāb Nazim but he fell into disgrace for authorising or conniving at the murder of the widow mother and daughter of Sirājuddaula and the widow and adopted son of Alī Vardi Khān who had been confined at Dacca, and was for a time deposed. He was reinstated in 1763 and in that year Dacca seems to have been the prey of three separate armies, being captured by the followers of Mir Kāsim, retaken by Muhammad Feza Khān, and pillaged by the Sannyāsis.

*It is difficult to understand how it can have paid to reap, thresh and husk rice and bring it to market if the price was only 2 annas a maund. At the end of the eighteenth century when rice was selling for four annas a maund at Sylhet it was reported that this price barely paid the cooly hire to market.

Jasarat Khān was then appointed Naib Nazim and it was from him that Lieutenant Swinton took over charge after the Company had decided to assume the Dīwāni of Bengal.

The last Nawābs.

On Jaṣarat Khān's death in 1799 he was succeeded by his eldest grandson, Hashmat Jang. He in his turn gave place six years later to the elder of his two brothers, Nasrat Jang, who held office for thirty-seven years and on that account is the best known of the last Nawābs of Dacca. When he died in 1822 it was decided that it was unnecessary to retain any longer the office of Naib Nazim, and Shamsuddaula, the youngest of three grandsons of Jasarat Khān, was recognised only as the head of his family. This man had been arrested in 1799 on a charge of high treason and was not released till 1805. Even then the Court of Directors were doubtful as to the expendiency of showing him clemency as will be seen from the following extract from their proceedings :—

"But when we consider the serious magnitude of the crimes of which Shumsooddowleh was convicted and the number and variety of the projects in which he was engaged for the subversion of our empire, extending from Behar to the court of Zemam Shāh and even to Persia, including also a plan concerted with persons at Muscat for the introduction of body of Arabs into our provinces, in consequence of which Arab ships actually arrived in 1796 and 1797 at the fort of Calcutta, having on board armed men and military stores, the commanders of which ships had orders to obey such directions as they might receive from Shumsoodowleh, we cannot but feel some doubt concerning the wisdom and prudence of setting free a person of so dangerous a character." Their reasons for abolishing the office of Naib Nazim are set forth by the Honourable Court in the following passage :—

"It is quite obvious that the office of Naib Nazim in the Dacca division of Bengal was purely ministerial like the corresponding situations in the Murshidābād division and Behar, and can in no way be considered hereditary, or as having any of the attributes of property or sovereignty attaching to it (like the dignity of Nazim). Its duties are defined in the Sunnud granted to Nawab Nusrut Jung (conformably to old forms) to be as follows :—

"To conduct generally the administration of the affairs of the districts placed under his jurisdiction, to chastise the turbulent and rebellious, to protect the weak and the malgoozars, to administer justice to complainants according to the Mahommedan law, to prevent iron-smiths from making match-locks, to be cautious that no one should sell to ill-disposed persons lead, powder or any implements of war, to exert himself in collecting the revenues of the mehals under his charge and to pay regularly the public revenue into the Treasury according to the instalments, to disburse no part of the public money without a sufficient warrant, to maintain the establishments of war and state boats, etc. (nowareh) on an efficient footing etc., etc.'

"Most, if not all, of the above functions must have been nominal and quite inapplicable to the state of things existing even in 1785: but in the present day it would be farcical to talk of an office having such duties annexed. The Nawab Shumsooddowleh does not himself now apply for a Sunnud as his brother did in 1785, but merely asks generally that the honour and consequence of his family may be maintained. As there are no engagements in existence which bind Government to keep up the office of Naib Nazim at Dacca, as the corresponding offices in Behar and on this side of Bengal have long since been abolished, and as there is nothing in the circumstances of Shumsooddowleh to give him any peculiar claim to indulgence, it will probably be thought expedient to pass over and omit altogether the appointment of Naib Nazim in announcing the provision authorised for the family."

Extinction of family of Naib Nazim. In 1831 Shamsuddaula died and was succeeded by his son Jalāluddīn Muhammad Kamiruddaula who on his death in 1834 was in his turn succeeded by his son Ghāziuddīn Haidar, known as the Pagla Nawāb. He incurred debts and behaved in such a manner that Government had to make over the management of his property to an agent. He died heirless in 1843 and the title as well as the office of Naīb Nazīm became extinct. His property was sold by auction and one of the state howdahs passed into the hands of the Basaks of Nawābpur by whom it is paraded on the occasion of the Janmastami festival. Troops were present at Nawāb Ghāziuddīn's funeral, which was conducted with military honours "as customary."

The English Factory at Dacca. We must now turn back to trace the origin of the English factory at Dacca. It is not known when or by whom this factory was first established. Thomas Platt, or Pratt, who was Mīr Jumla's ship-builder, would seem to have represented the East India Company at the Durbar and he appears to have been the Company's Agent when Tavernier visited Dacca, for he mentions Mr. Pratt as being the English chief or President. Before his time there was another Englishman in Dacca, for we read that a few years later a deed purporting to be signed by James Hart and dated 1658 was produced in support of a claim for the land on which the English factory stood and which was formerly owned by this James Hart. The deed was treated as a forgery, but the fact that Hart was in Dacca in 1658 and owned the land was not disputed. Nothing further is known about this man, and he may have had nothing to do with the Company.

In 1672-73 the Company was represented by Messrs. John Smith and Samuel Harvey, but the two seem to have fallen out, for we find that in 1677 the former alleged "that Mr. Harvey said to me that there was no such thing as god or divell that religion was broached to keep ye world in awe, that it was done by ye cunning of Moses and afterward Christ, or words to ye same effect." The court charged Harvey with "atheistical notions," and he was put on his trial but acquitted. In 1676 Mr. Fytch Nedham was the Agent at Dacca, but in that year Mr. Harvey was sent back there as chief with Nedham as his second. One of the first things he did was to procure sanction for the erection of brick buildings for the Company's factory. Ten years before, Tavernier tells us, the English house was "fairly good" but it was probably not of brick.

Even at this early time the English appear to have had some prestige and influence at the Durbar, for one "Emin Cooly" the former "faujdār" of Hughli, got a letter of introduction to the English officers at Dacca to help him in some business he had with the Nawāb.

Much of the chief's time was occupied then, as for many years later, in endeavouring to procure the Nawāb's parwana on advantageous terms for the English trade. For this purpose visits were paid to the chief Durbar officials as well as to the Nawāb. Presents also were an important factor in the case.

In May 1678, we read of the gentlemen at Dacca presenting the Nawāb with an Arabian horse; in July of the same year they lamented their inability to make a present to the new daroga "because we had presented two great men twice this year, first ye Nawab Azum Cawn, and now ye Prince."

In July 1678 Mr. Matthias Vincent, the chief at Hughli, visited Dacca to see if he could personally induce the Nawāb to grant the necessary parwanas for the trade. It is interesting to observe how he first visited "the Prince's Duan," then "the King's Duan," then "the Prince's Nazarr or Controller of ye house," and so on. A few days later he was granted an audience of the Prince, to whom he presented 27 gold mohurs and a hundred rupees in silver (the actual present including two horses was sent later). After two months spent in constant visits first to one official and then to another, Mr. Vincent obtained the Prince's order for free trade and left Dacca.

In the same year a third officer was sent to Dacca, *viz.*, Mr. Powncett, while Mr. Fytch Nedham was replaced by Mr. Trenchfield. In 1681 the Dacca diary was signed, during Mr. Harvey's illness, by Messrs. John Powncett and Charles Eyre (the latter was warehouse-keeper).

The amount expended on presents at this time must have been considerable as the following extracts of the year 1681 will show :—

"*9th June.*—James Price acquainted us that the Duan's Phurwana would speedily be perfected upon our gratifying the mutsuddies: we thought convenient (tho' a greater matter was urged by ye said James

Price) to send 15 rupees to the Munshy, 3 yards of scarlet to the peshdust and 4 yards of ordinary to ye cullumburdar."

"*11th June.*—Hodge Sophe Chaan, the king's duan, seeing our Vaqueele this day at ye Nabob's durbar and signifying to him his desire of such wax figures, etc., we had formerly given the Nabob Shasteh Chaan, on notice hereof we concluded it most necessary (considering how much and how constantly we were obliged to him) to present him 2 wax figures, together with those curiosities in the flint ware we received lately from Hugly."

"*9th July.*—Coda Bux Chaan, the king's Buxie and third officer in the kingdom of Bengal, this day doing us the honour of coming to our factory, we thought necessary, acccording to all decency and custom * * * * to present him with etc."

"*26th December.*—Having understood from Mirza Muduffer* that part of the flint ware he lately bought was for Buzurgh Omeed Cawn ye Nabob's eldest son, and being instructed by him also that it would be convenient for us to give him a visit with some small nuzzar or present, as is ye custom of ye country (noe visit of this nature being made empty handed) we concluded to see him this day and present him, a large burning glass, a penknife, a large prospective glass, a Meridian sun dial."

The Dutch † would seem to have been equally lavish and were granted leave to export rice on promising elephants, horses, etc.

In 1682 William Hedges arrived in India to be Governor and Superintendent of the factories in the Bay of Bengal, with the title of Agent of the Bay. "The several affronts, insolencies and abuses dayly put upon us by Bool Chund,‡ our chief customer (causing general stop of our trade), being growne insufferable, ye Agent and Councell for ye Hon'ble E. Indian Comp's affaires at Hughly resolved upon and made use of divers expedients for redress, and concluded in consultation that the only expedient now left was for the Agent to go himself in person to the

---

* Son-in-law of Nawāb Shāista Khān's eldest son Buzurg Umed Khān.

† The Dutch were established in Dacca before the English.

‡ He was Daroga of Hughli; on his appointment in March 1682 he presented the Nawāb with Rs. 2,00,000 and received from him "four large pearls, with two rubies for his ears, a golden standish, a golden lutted sword" and other articles and from the Diwān a Persian horse.

Nabob and Duan at Dacca, as well to make some settled adjustment concerning ye customs as to endeavour the preventing Interlopers trading in these parts for ye future: in order to which preparations were caused to be made. Mr. Richard Frenchfield and Mr. William Johnson were appointed to go along with ye Agent to Dacca." The Agent arrived in Dacca on 25th October 1682 and succeeded in obtaining parwanas fixing the duty on bullion at the mints, allowing trade free of customs duties (on security) for seven months pending an order from the Emperor and for several other smaller matters. Like Mr. Vincent, the Agent only secured these concessions by constant visits to the various Durbar officials.

Seizure of factory in 1688.

In 1688 Bahādur Khān seized the factory and imprisoned the merchants and their followers. At first they were not harshly treated, but on the arrival of "Mr. Henry Hanley and Mr. James Ravenhill with 14 persons more......in company, all in a most miserable and tattered condition, laden with fetters of about 8 lbs.," they were thrown into the prison allotted to the new-comers, fettered and chained together at night two and two. Relief, however, came with the arrival of Ibrāhīm Khān who reinstated them in their possessions and obtained for them from the Emperor in 1691 full authority to trade free of all dues and charges in return for an annual payment of Rs. 3,000.

Presents to the Nawāb continued to be a heavy charge upon the Company. Its local representatives were not however ungrateful and protested at the meanness of the gifts sent for the acceptance of the generous Ibrāhīm Khān. They were informed by their superior officers that the Rt. Hon'ble Company, in their advices, had blamed them for "the abominable large pishcashes at Dacca and the great expense yearly made at that durbar," and had ordered that frugality be used for the future, but, and this was the important point, the present was increased. Even after the removal of the Nawāb Nazim from Dacca the benevolences to his deputy constituted a serious drain and in 1737 arrived one Sciadradgecaun. "This man acts here in the most tyrannical manner not only in his own office but also in those appertaining to the Nabob's government, whipping and killing whosoever refuse to give him any sums of money he demands." He seems to have had no reasonable title to be placated with a gift of money, but he refused with scorn the offer of Rs. 500, and subsequently when he became Naib Nazim's Deputy he boycotted the factory till his demands were satisfied. In those days the judicial officers required propitiation no less than the executive, as will be seen from the following naive account of Kazi's justice:—"The Faqueer that had lived for many years on our wharf and which some months since we got turned away by our Nabob's order, having been at Muxadavad to complain, had obtained a purwana directed to the Cozzee here to enquire into the affair, and if he found the Faqueer had a right to the ground and that a

Mussulman's bones were buried there that then he should restablish him in his right and permit him to build a place of worship on the ground: and the Cozzee having offered, in consideration of 250 Rupees to give a Sunnud setting forth the Faqueer's complaint to be groundless and false and liberty for us occupy the ground and build on it: and we considering the great inconveniency of having a Moore's place of worship in the midst of our ground, especially if our Hon'ble Masters should think proper to have a factory house built there. Agreed we do pay the Cozzee 250 Rupees and receive from him a Sunnud accordingly."

Military establishment of the factory.

It is not clear when a military guard was first entertained at the factory. In 1736 the military stores included "3 Brass Swivel guns, 2 Mortars, 3 long Swivel guns, 4 large Brass Swivel Blunderbusses, 10 small (3 of which are iron), 2 iron Canon, 10 spare Bayonet pieces, 4 Carbines, 5 Pistols, 5 Swords," etc., etc. These would hardly have been kept had there been no persons to use them, but no fixed establishment seems to have been entertained. In the following year the presence of some military officers from Calcutta caused the Dacca Council to consider their requirements. "Taking into consideration what military are necessary to be kept at this Factory, it appears that it is necessary to have sentinals at the doors of the Treasure Godown and other Warehouses of the Factory, as well as at the gates, and that at some of the adjacent petty chowkeys stopping boats that are bringing the Hon'ble Company's goods, a party of soldiers are often necessary to be sent to clear such goods. Agreed therefore that we keep one Ensign, one Sergeant, one Corporal, one Drummer and 17 sentinals, and that we send the remainder of the Military to Calcutta." Such was the beginning of the military guard at Dacca. In 1745 it had increased to one Lieutenant, five Sergeants, six Corporals, 47 European privates, and several others. In the following year some further additions were made on account of the Marāthā scare, the force then standing at one Lieutenant, one Ensign, seven Sergeants, eight Corporals, 71 European "private men," 42 Portuguese (who were shortly after dispensed with) and others. In 1761, this had been replaced by a guard of sepoys, one battalion being distributed between Chittagong, Dacca and Lakhipur. Later, it consisted of a regiment of infantry and a detachment of artillery, and in 1836 (exactly one hundred years after the first entertainment of a permanent guard) the 50th Regiment of Native Infantry were stationed here, with eighteen commissioned officers, besides a Surgeon.

The original cantonments at Dacca were near Tezgāon, in a village called Bāigun Bāri. The place is still called Kālipaltan, and a portion of it still retains the name of Chāndmāri (shooting range). Some time about the beginning of the nineteenth century the cantonments were moved nearer the town to the Purānā Paltan, but the site was thought to be unhealthy and a few years before the Mutiny the troops were transferred to the Lal Bagh.

At first the Company's establishment consisted of two Europeans, but by the year 1736 there were five posts at the factory, *viz.*, the Chief, the Accountant, the Export Warehouse-keeper. the Buxi and the Import Warehouse-keeper. In 1758 the Court directed that the business should be conducted by a Chief, a Second and two Writers. The Chief and his Assistants had small salaries, but to compensate for this they were allowed the privilege of trading on their own account provided this did not interfere with the Company's investments. A common table was maintained at the Factory, at the expense of the Company, and in 1737, the Company allowed Rs. 700 yearly for Factory provisions. This sum was increased considerably in later years and in 1758 Rs. 3,000 were allowed for keeping a table, with instructions "that the Junior servants * * * shall partake thereof: and, in case they shall desire to diet apart, each junior servant above the rank of Writer shall get out of the Chief's allowance 30 current rupees per month, and each Writer 20." The first mention of a Factory Surgeon is an entry dated the 16th December 1737: "Mr. John Coleman, our late Surgeon, having died intestate, etc." He was succeeded by Mr. Holwell and then by Mr. John Canty. A Surgeon seems to have been attached to the Factory regularly thereafter. The salary of the post was forty rupees per mensem.

Establishment at factory.

The extent of the private trade of the Company's servants can hardly be realised in these latter days. Mr. Cooke, who was dismissed for embezzlement, forfeited all his property to the Company to make good the loss: this property included the articles in which he was trading and it took many months to gather in from the various trading centres (aurungs) the articles that had been secured for him. As the Company recognised this trade, certain of the factory charges (*viz.*, Charges General, Servants' Wages and Charges Durbar) were divided proportionately between the Company and its servants according to the amount of trade. The following figures give the trade and the proportion of the charges payable in 1744:—

Private trade.

—	Annual salary.	Amount of trade.			Proportionate share of charges.		
		Rs.	a.	p.	Rs.	a.	p.
The Hon'ble Company... ...	...	5,67,791	3	0	15,749	14	0
Thomas Joshua Moore, Esq., Chief	£40	1,01,515	0	3	2,815	15	9
Mr. John Smith, Junr. Mercht ...	£30	10,015	13	0	277	13	0
Mr. Samuel Ropper, Factor ...	£15	16,157	7	3	448	3	3
Mr. James Blachford, Factor ...	£15	66,116	8	0	1,823	0	9
Mr. Thomas Man, Writer ...	£ 5	13,017	12	3	361	1	9
Total ...	...	7,74,613	11	9	21,476	0	6

One of the best known instances of private trade at the Dacca Factory is that of Mr. Richard Barwell, who, while Chief here, made a fortune in salt transactions in Bakarganj. Six months after he arrived in Dacca he applied for permission to remit a lakh of rupees in bullion to England. When threatened by Clavering with legal proceedings, he wrote:—"He (Clavering) threatens me with the terrors of the law—he brings forward a false charge touching the benefits I derived from salt while at Dacca. I do not deny the profits I made. I avow them. I always avowed them. They were neither secret nor clandestine, but I object to the conclusions drawn, and refute them, etc."

Robert Lindsay, when at Dacca as a very junior servant of the Company a few years later, also speculated largely in salt in his private capacity. His account of his first venture is interesting. He writes: "Among the numerous articles of commerce carried on in the interior of the Dacca district salt is not the least considerable: it is manufactured by the Agents of Government on the sea coast and preserved as a monopoly for the benefit of the Company. At certain periods it is brought up in large boats to Dacca and there exposed to public sale. My commercial education at Cadiz was now beginning to show itself of use to me. In the mode of exposing the lots to sale I could perceive no small intrigue was carrying on: for I saw that the natives had not that free access to the public sale to which they were entitled, and that the lots fell, as they were put up, to the dependents of the Members of Council, who by this means gained to themselves a considerable advantage. A fair opportunity I thought, now occurred of bettering myself without injury to the public: I therefore conversed with a wealthy native on this subject, who fully entered into my views and proposed to advance me a large sum of money upon a mutual concern, provided I would appear as the ostensible person. I in consequence appeared at the next sale and became the purchaser of salt to the extent of £20,000; and the speculation turned out so well as fully to enable me to pay off all the debt I had contracted during my long residence in Calcutta, and to place a few thousand rupees in my pocket." Such a clever young man could not have acquired any popularity among his superiors by this *coup* and he naively adds:—"This, I have reason to think, soon after facilitated my removal from Dacca."

It is not perhaps so well known that Warren Hastings engaged in private trade within the jurisdiction of the Dacca Factory. A complaint was made in 1763 to Calcutta by the Dacca Council of the illegitimate uses to which sipahis were put by Hastings' agents. In reply Hastings recorded the following note:—"Some time ago a large body of Fakeers infesting the country about Backergunge surrounded Mr. Kelly, my Agent, and put him in great danger of his life * * * For this reason I requested the Governor to send a few people to his rescue. The Fakeers have since quitted the country and it was my intention to have recalled the seapoys but by ill health and attention to the other affairs I forgot it ; so far only I am willing to take upon me the blame of the seapoys continuing yet with Mr. Kelly, who were ordered to be employed only in the protection of his own life and effects, and if he has made any ill use of them let the gentlemen of Dacca prove it, and I desire he may be brought down and publicly punished for it. My reason for procuring a guard of 4 seapoys for Captain Rose is that he is employed in collecting a great number of timbers belonging to me and other gentlemen which are now scattered in many different places in the river lying between Dacca and Backergunge and where you, gentlemen, will easily conceive the necessity of having some defence against the robbers which continually infect these parts. If you think them improper they shall be immediately recalled."

Seizure of factory in 1756.

Two other incidents in the history of the Dacca Factory remain to be recorded. The first occurred in 1756. Sirāj-ud-daula, when he marched on Calcutta, sent orders to the Naib at Dacca, Jasarat Khān, to seize the English factory and imprison the Company's servants. The factory was unfortified and the garrison but small, so, when Mr. Becher, the Chief, ascertained from the French that Calcutta had been captured, it was decided not to make any resistance but to secure the best terms possible through the French. It was then arranged with Nawāb Jasarat Khān that all the ladies and gentlemen should go to the French factory and remain there pending Sirāj-ud-daula's orders. The soldiers were to lay down their arms and be the Nawāb's prisoners. After two months' stay at the French Factory, the English obtained their release owing to the exertions of M. Law at Kāsimbāzār and sailed to Calcutta in a sloop provided by M. Courtin. The English factory was not restored to the Company until the following year.

Capture of factory in 1763.

The other incident is the capture of the factory in 1763 by a body of Sannyāsis or Fakirs. Mr. Leycester, the then Chief, justified its abandonment as follows :—

"Regarding the retreat and loss of treasure, he knows not how it could have been avoided nor what precautions could have been taken, that were not, to prevent the misfortune. The gentlemen of that Factory were fully sensible of the importance of saving their treasure and tried every possible method as they did for retreating in a regular manner. In an entire want of cooleys it was resolved to disarm some of our seapoys and employ them in that capacity—first to convey the sick and wounded, then our treasure, and at last retreat with the remainder of our garrison. The sick had mostly been sent to the waterside, in pursuance of this resolution, to be put on board the few boats we had been able to collect at the Gaut, when many of our seapoys left the Factory, and Mr. Leycester assures the Board that while he was in the Factory expecting to hear that boats were come to the Gaut sufficient to secure the treasure and remainder of the garrison, all the seapoys in a body left the Factory without any orders and fled to the few boats that were already come in the utmost irregularity and confusion, rendering their own retreat under such circumstances very precarious and putting it out of the power of the gentlemen to conduct the affair in the manner that had been really proposed. * * * * * He begs leave further to observe that the so sudden recovery of the Dacca Factory was entirely the result of the gentlemen's own resolution on the first account they had ever received of the Meckly detachment's having left that country, Captain Grant not having joined our party till we had left Luckypore, and that such their resolution and application afterwards has been attended with the happy consequence of procuring to his Hon'ble Masters nearly as large, and, he may venture to say, as good an investment as hath been known for some years to come from this Factory." Quite another version of the story, however, is given by Clive in a minute, dated 29th January 1766:—"That gentleman's (*i.e.*, Mr. Leycester) behaviour at Dacca, when he abandoned the Factory which commanded a very considerable proportion of the Company's treasure and merchandise would in all probability have lost him the service if General Carnac had not prevailed upon Mr. Vansittart to let him soften the paragraph written upon that subject in the general letter. For further particulars I refer the world to old Mr. Delaport, who very quietly smoked his pipe in the Factory an hour and a half after Mr. Leycester had forsaken it, and then found leisure to carry off all his own effects, without any molestation from the enemy, who proved to be no other than a rabble of Fakeers. Nor was his zeal for the service greater when Captain Grant with a very small detachment retook the place, without the loss of a man; for Mr. Leycester who had just run away from the Factory, although he would have been a very proper person to have pointed out the road to the Captain, who was a stranger to that part of the country, chose rather to remain on the other side of a navigable river until he was informed that the Factory was again in our possession, when he returned to resume his former employment."

Site of factory.

The original factory building seems to have been situated in Tezgāon. In 1682 Hedges writes: "This afternoon I went to visit Haggai Sophee Chan * * * * * took my leave and returned to ye English factory which is at least 3 miles distant from this, or ye Nabob's durbar, a most inconvenient situation for doing of business, being far from ye Courts of Justice, Custom House and ye waterside." Also in 1775 we read of a factory house at Tezgāon in addition to the principal factory building. The old factory is said to have been a one storied house having a large central hall with sleeping apartments and offices around it. Mr. Harvey had it re-built—but for years it seems to have caused considerable anxiety in times of storm and flood—and repairs were constantly required. Between the years 1724 and 1730 a new building was erected nearer the river on the site occupied till recently by the Dacca College and now by the Collegiate School. It was constructed in the form of a square and enclosed a considerable extent of ground. Low ranges of warehouses surrounded it and in the centre was a house for the factors, besides offices and accommodation for servants and guards and in later years a mint and magazine were added. Tezgāon, however, was not altogether abandoned. Besides a garden house and several bungalows, and probably the old factory, the quarters of the washermen were there. In 1771 on the abolition of the Baghmaras (shikaris) we find the Collector writing: "The consequence of which, I apprehend, will be that the Company will lose many of their washermen and Tezgong will be rendered uninhabitable by these animals (*i.e.*, tigers)." The following extract from a Government letter dated the 23rd January 1775, on the subject of the Dacca houses, is interesting:—"It has been thought proper to make a distribution of the houses belonging to the Company at Dacca between the covenanted servants who are to reside on the part of the Board of Trade and those employed in the Revenue branch—and it is directed that the Commercial Resident be put in possession of such as are allotted for the use of his department. That the Factory, the warehouse, the Factory house at Tezgong and the houses occupied by Messrs. Day and Hatch and either the houses occupied by Mr. Leigh* or that occupied by Mr. Russell, at the choice of the Revenue Chief, be appropriated to the use of the Chief and Assistants of the Commercial Factory. That either of the houses occupied by Mr. Leigh and Mr. Russell, at the option of the Revenue Chief, as above specified, the house occupied by Mr. Kerr and the garden houses at Tezgong occupied by Mr. Law and Mr. Leigh be appropriated to the Revenue department. That the temporary buildings raised by Mr. Shakespear at his own expense within the walls of the Factory be continued to him, and the temporary building (? erected) at private expense in the same place for Messrs. Evelyn and Cator, be continued to them."

The Provincial Council.

In 1774 a Provincial Council consisting of a Chief and four members was appointed to superintend the revenue and commercial affairs and some changes were made in the

* Mr. Leigh's house lay to the south-east of the factory "on the esplanade" and was used for a time as the Collector's Cutcherry. In the accounts it is called the second house and was usually the residence of the Buxi. Mr. Kerr's house was a short distance to the west of the Factory and was pulled down in 1778 by Mr. Broughton, an Assistant in the Revenue Department. At Tezgāon there were in 1780 four houses besides the Company's factory—two of them (a house and a bungalow) belonged to Mr. Law, one to Messrs. Hatch and Day, and one (called Champa Bagh) to the Company. Mr. Law's house and bungalow were disposed of by lottery—the former (in 1800) being in possession of Mr. Ranking and the latter in that of Mr. Pattenson. The third house was transferred to a Mr. Sameeda and the fourth fell down.

conduct of the factory business. Brokers were abolished and in their place agents (*gomastas*) were appointed to the different *aurungs*; *naibs* were also appointed to decide cases in which weavers were concerned. These reforms were not successful; abuses grew up and in 1787 a Commercial Resident was appointed to conduct the affairs of the factory. The dealings with the weavers were then conducted in a more regular and sympathetic manner. The Resident in 1800 writes:—"At this Factory it is an annual instruction to the *Aurung Gomastas* that the Regulation which respects the weavers and the commercial residents be read to the weavers before any engagements for the new year are entered into. Every individual weaver executes a separate written engagement for the provision of the cloths which he voluntarily contracts to deliver and these engagements are in no instance departed from except by a written request on the part of the weavers or their representatives. The weavers' accounts are annually adjusted and each weaver has throughout the year a copy of his running account (called a *haut chitty*) regularly brought up constantly in his possession." These arrangements appear to have been continued down to 1817 when the factory was closed.

The Dutch.

The Dutch settled in Dacca for trading purposes before the English. Nawāb Nasrat Jang writes of them:—"At first *Gomastas* made purchases at the Factory; afterwards, in the time of Hossein-ud-dīn Khān (*i.e.*, between 1742 and 1753) Mr. Ilsam, being appointed Chief of the Factory, came and resided at Dacca." This, however, hardly represents the true facts. In 1666, Tavernier tells us, the Dutch "finding that their goods were not sufficiently safe in the common houses of Dacca have built a very fine house." He attended a banquet given in his honour by the Dutch and, on his departure from Dacca, the Dutch gentlemen accompanied him for two leagues. In 1682 William Hedges received a visit from "ye three Dutch Factors, *viz.*, Jno Bonstoe, Alexander Urwin and Jacob Smith, who supped with me." As in the case of the English a new factory may have been built in the eighteenth century, and to this the reference above quoted may have been made. In 1775 the Dutch Chief, Mr. Daniel Lank Hiet died and was buried in the English cemetery. In 1781 the Dutch factory surrendered to the East India Company and the solitary Dutch subject in Dacca (Mr. Heyning) was released on parole. The property seized included a garden house at Tezgāon This appears to have been the end of the Dutch regime at Dacca. In 1801 the Collector received charge of the Dutch factory from the Magistrate and we read that police officers took away bricks and *surki* from the ruins for repairing the streets of Dacca. In 1810, it was proposed to erect a hospital on the site, but the idea was dropped as it was not known what the relations between England and Holland were at the time. In 1824, a treaty was signed between the English and Dutch Governments by which the latter ceded to the former all their establishments in India and in June of the year following the formal transfer was made by Mr. Vanas, the Dutch Commissioner, to Mr. Dawes, the Magistrate. The Dutch factory stood on a portion of the land now occupied by the Mitford Hospital, the site is known in the old Collectorate papers as *Kuti Ollandaz*.

Of the French settlement in Dacca, Nawāb Nasrat Jang writes:—"During the naibut of the said Moorshid Cooly Khān (*i.e.*, from 1726—38) a gomasta, named Gopaul Sein, came to Dacca on the part of the French, and having purchased cloths sent them to the French merchants at Chandernagore. In this way the French business was at that time carried on at Dacca. But after Nawazish Mahomed Khān, towards the close of the reign of the Emperor Mahomed Shāh (*i.e.*, between 1740 and 1742) became Naib Nazim of Dacca, Messieurs Deveuz and Chamauz, arriving at Dacca, built with the permission of the said Naib a Factory and commenced business there." This account may be misleading as those given in respect of the English and Dutch, but another authority has given 1742 as the date of the building of the French factory and as we have no information of their being settled in Dacca before that time Nawāb Nasrat Jang's account may possibly be correct. It has been narrated above how, in 1756, disaster to the English was averted by the courtesy and kindness of M. Courtin, in which he was nobly seconded by M. Fleurin. In the following year M. Courtin sent a detachment to Kāsimbāzār to reinforce M. Law in his efforts to support Sirāj-ud-daula and he himself followed (having delayed only for the arrival of M. Chevalier from Assam), taking with him "about 35 boats, Mm. Chevalier, Brayer, Gourlade, the Surgeon, and an Augustine Father, Chaplain of the Factory, 8 European soldiers, of whom several were old and past service, 17 topass gunners, 4 or 5 of the Company's servants and 25 or 30 peons." But the battle of Plassey occurred before he could join M. Law. The French property and possessions that came into the hands of the English were made over again in 1785 to M. Champigny and in 1786 a convention was signed affirming the French rights and privileges at their factories. Their factory and lands seem however again to have been taken for in 1801 they passed from the charge of the Magistrate to the Collector and in 1802 to the Commercial Resident while in 1824 the factory was converted into a depôt for the reception of military stores. In 1819 M. Darrac arrived in Dacca to demand to be put in possession of the French factory with its dependencies in accordance with the terms of the Treaty of Paris (1814). But it is not until 1827 that we read of this being complied with. Soon after M. Darrac's arrival in Dacca the Magistrate had occasion to complain of his conduct and Government in reply wrote:—" * * M. Darrac has exceeded his official competence and you very properly remonstrated with him on his unwarrantable procedure in

The French

apprehending and confining Sooroop Chund, in inflicting corporal punishment on the Custom House chaprassy and in assuming the right of licensing a shop for the sale of spirituous liquor contrary to the regulations of the British Government. * * * M. Ravier has at the same time been required peremptorily to instruct M. Darrac to abstain in future from usurpation of powers which do not belong to his station and to confine the exercise of his authority to the mere superintendence of the commercial affairs of the Factory without interfering in any degree whatever in matters beyond the limits of his public duty as a Commercial Agent, * * * M. Darrac is not to be permitted to exercise any authority implying sovereign power or, in strictness, beyond what may be admitted in cases of master and servant, * * * * * * * and in the event of M. Darrac's perseverance in such encroachments measures will be taken in his removal from Dacca." The French factory was situated in Islāmpur, on the banks of the river Buri-Ganga, on a portion of the site now occupied by the palace of the successors of the late Nawāb Khwāja Sir Ahsanullah (called the Ahsan Manzil). Rennell's map shows the French garden at Tezgāon to be on the east side of the Dacca-Mymensingh road between Ambar's mosque and the Tezgāon Church. The Dutch garden lay opposite, on the other side of the road.

The Portuguese. The Portuguese also had a factory in Dacca which was in the quarter of the town called Sangat-tola, but nothing is known of their commercial transactions and history.

Dacca under British Rule. In 1765 the East India Company succeeded to the Diwāni of Bengal. At that time the administration of the Province was divided into two departments, *viz.*, the *Huzuri* or Revenue and the *Nizāmat* or Judicial. The former was very soon taken over entirely by the English but the latter was allowed for a long time to be conducted in the old way subject only to a general control. Orme tells us that "the administration of the Province was now settled in the manner following:—Mahummud Reza Khān, the Naib Navob, conducted affairs at the Capital * * * * * and Jessaurut Khān at Dacca, in conjunction with a member of Council at each city, as Chief on the part of the English. Two days weekly the Naib communicated to his English colleague his transactions, plans, disbursements and receipts in every department, for his satisfaction and the information and approval of the presidency. Two days in each week were also set apart in which the Naib and Chief received appeals from the courts of justice and confirmed or reversed their decisions by the assistance of the Chief Magistrate. By these means Government was properly conducted and the English became informed of the laws, revenues and customs of the country."

Dacca during the Mutiny. The district did not altogether escape from the trials of 1857, though fortunately there was comparatively little loss of life. Two companies of the 73rd N. I. were stationed at Dacca, the rest of the regiment being at Jalpaiguri. From the month of March, when the Barrackpore mutiny broke out, it was for eight long months the aim of the authorities at Dacca to prepare for similar happenings there and at the same time avoid harsh measures with the sepoys, which, it was felt, would result in disaster to small European communities in surrounding districts who were not so able to protect themselves. In June a hundred men of the Indian Navy, under Lieutenant Lewis, arrived; and in the following month two companies of volunteers were raised which did excellent work during the Muharram and the Janmastami processions. Many false rumours reached the town, but in November alarming news was received both from Chittagong and from Barrackpore and it was determined to delay decisive action no longer. The following extracts from Lord Canning's final minute describe what was done :—

"At a meeting of the officers, civil and military, including Lieut. Lewis, it was after some discussion unanimously decided that the sepoys must be disarmed. Accordingly, the seamen under Lieut Lewis, and Volunteers assembled at daylight next morning (*i.e.*, 22nd November) and having disarmed the different guards in succession and without any attempt at resistance, they advanced on the lines which were situated in a strong position at a place called the Lāl Bāgh. Here they found the sepoys and a detail of native artillery, with two guns, drawn up ready to receive them; as the party advanced fire was opened upon them and a sharp engagement, lasting for half an hour, ensued. It is sufficient to say that the sepoys were driven out of their barracks and the guns carried with great gallantry. The rebels left 41 dead on the ground; whilst three were drowned in attempting to cross the river and a large number were more or less severely wounded; nor was the victory unattended by loss on our side: fifteen were severely and three slightly wounded. Of the former three died of their wounds. Dr. Green, Civil Surgeon, who, in the absence of other medical aid, attended the attacking party, was shot through the thigh, and Lieut. Lewis also received a slight wound. * * * Twenty persons were subsequently taken, ten of whom were sentenced to be hung, the remainder to transportation for life. The main body, thoroughly panic-stricken, made a hasty retreat from the division, passed by the stations of Jamalpur and Mymensingh, without attempting any attack, and reaching the Brahmaputra crossed near Bhagwa Ghāt and entered the district of Rangpur. * * * As soon as a steamer and flat could be prepared three companies of H. M.'s 54th were sent off to Dacca to act as circumstances should dictate. With them went a party of European seamen and a second party followed the next day * * * The detachment of H M.'s 54th having reached Dacca left the seamen to proceed to their destination in the Rangpur and Dinajpur districts. * * *

Mr. Carnac, Officiating Collector and Magistrate of Dacca, has acted with great vigour and promptitude throughout the whole course of the disturbances. On the occasion of the actual outbreak at Dacca he took a prominent part in the attack on the sepoys and he brought forward very favourably the conduct of his two assistants, Messrs. Bainbridge and Macpherson. Dr. Green, the Civil Surgeon, who accompanied the body of sailors on this occasion and, as has already been recorded, was severely wounded, is entitled to very honourable notice; and I must make special mention of the admirable behaviour of the Rev. Mr. Winchester, Chaplain of the Station, who in the service of the wounded men fearlessly exposed himself in the midst of the fight. Mr. Carnac has made a special report of the assistance he has received during the past year from his Nāzir, Jagabandhu Bose, whose services have received acknowledgment and reward. I take this opportunity of repeating my appreciation of the loyalty of the two Mohammedan gentlemen, Khwāja Abdul Ghani and Abdūl Ahmad Khan."

Such is the official account of what happened then in Dacca. We have a narrative from another point of view in the diary of Mr. Brennand, then the Principal of the Dacca College. The following extracts supplement the above:—

"*10th June.*—The troops appear excited on account of the rumour that European troops are to be sent to Dacca.

"*12th June.*—A panic spread among the Europeans in consequence of a report to the effect that the two companies of the 73rd which had left the station about the beginning of the month had met with some disbanded men from Barrackpore and had mutinied: that they had returned to Dacca and had been joined by the men at the Lal Bagh: that they were looting the bazar and setting free the prisoners at the jail. A number of Europeans assembled at the house of Mr. Jenkins,* the Magistrate: others resolved to defend themselves at the Bank.† Some of the ladies went on board boats on the river: arms were collected: the whole town was in a state of excitement: the *Bund* was crowded with natives in a state of wonder and curiosity.

"Lieuts. McMahon and Rhynd, the officers in command of the troops, started for the Lal Bagh where the sepoys were located. On their return they reported

* On the day of first panic Mr. Jenkins was the Magistrate and Mr. Carnac the Collector; subsequently the latter was appointed to be both Magistrate and Collector.

† This was the Bank of Dacca subsequently taken over by the Bank of Bengal. The present Bank building was then the Assembly Rooms, and is not that referred to.

that their men were all quiet and in their quarters: that the alarm was groundless.

"On the evening drive the natives who were collected in knots along the road seemed surprised to see us after the report that we had all fled and left them to their fate.

"*13th.*—Between the 19th and 23rd June the Government sent up 100 men of the Indian Navy under Lieut. Lewis for the protection of the town. They were located in the house on the opposite side of the road to the Baptist chapel.

"*5th July.*—The Metcalfes came in from Comillah in a fright: they had heard that the sepoys at Chittagong had mutinied and that they were on their way to Dacca. The report was, however, without foundation.

"Dacca has been comparatively quiet since the arrival of the sailors. Lieut. Lewis has his tars out frequently in the morning to practice with the guns in the space near the Racquet Court* and in front of the College.
* * *

"To-day there was something of a panic among the sepoys. Dowell, who is in command of the station, sent up to the Lal Bagh for the screws used in elevating the guns and the men there supposed that there was some intention of disarming them.

"*30th July.*—A meeting of European and East Indian inhabitants capable of bearing arms was held at the College: nearly 60 people present. It was resolved to form two corps of Volunteers—one of Infantry and the other of Cavalry. Major Smith to command the Infantry and Lieut. Hitchins the Cavalry.

"*1st, 2nd and 3rd August.*—The three days of the Buckereed. The Volunteers all on the alert: patrols out all night on each of the three days. * * * The 2nd being Sunday a party of the Volunteers stationed at the College to protect the people who were at church.

"*11th August.*—Many of the Armenians are leaving for Calcutta. The Europeans are thinking of fortifying the Mills.† The Volunteers are on parade for several hours daily and are making good progress in drill.

"*14th and 15th August.*—The festival of Junmostomee. There was as usual a large crowd of people. The Cavalry Volunteers were mounted on elephants and well armed * * * but all passed off quietly. * * * It has been decided that if

---

* The old Racquet Court was situated on the space now called Victoria Square.

† East of the Dholai Khal: afterwards the Military Police Barracks and then the Police Training School: still called the "Kalh Ghar".=The Factory (or Mill) house.

the men at Julpigoree do mutiny, the sepoys here shall be at once disarmed.

"*22nd August.*—The fortification of the Mills is going on. * * * There are 200 men at work digging a ditch.

"*27th August.*—The fortifications are progressing and it is supposed that, should there be occasion for it, we should be able to make a stand against 5 or 6 thousand men. * * *

"*30th August.*—Yesterday, Sunday, was the great day of the Mohurrum. The Cavalry Volunteers were out all night patrolling. * * *

"*14th September.*—Some alarm here in consequence of a report that the sepoys in Assam are in a state of great excitement and that they had become very insolent. The Government has sent off a number of sailors in the Horungatta by way of the Sunderbuns: they are expected to arrive here to-morrow and are intended for Assam.

"The 73rd at Julpigoree still quiet. We have hopes it will prove staunch. Should it not, we shall be involved here: but we shall be quite a match for the sepoys. * * *

"*4th October.*—To-day has been fixed upon by the Bishop as a day of humiliation. Winchester away in Sylhet. The service was read by Abercrombie and the sermon by Pearson. * * *

"*12th October.*—The Cavalry Volunteers gave a ball to the Infantry. The gathering was not so great as was expected: about ten ladies present. Of the Infantry Volunteers only about twenty attended in uniform. The party was on the whole a very pleasant one.

"*1st November.*—Something like a panic occurred on Sunday last, caused by the removal of the sailors to the house near the church, recently occupied by the Nuns. The sepoys got ammunition out of the magazine and it was thought that an outbreak was imminent. It is reported that they have written to their brethren at Julpigoree asking whether they should resist if an attempt were made to disarm them. We believe that the disarming could be effected with little danger to ourselves, but it is feared the effect on the troops at Chittagong, Sylhet and Julpigoree might be disastrous. It is supposed that if we can preserve order in Dacca the other places will remain quiet. The men are very civil, but with the example of their "bhaibuns" before us, we cannot put much trust in them.

"*9th November.*—The Infantry Volunteers gave a dinner to the station * * * upwards of fifty sat down to dinner.

26th November.—The storm that has been passing over India has just passed over Dacca, happily without any of the disastrous effects that have attended it in its course elsewhere. Up to Saturday last we were going on just as usual. There was a party out at cricket in the afternoon and the Volunteers were at their usual exercise with ball cartridge. In the evening we had our usual drive on the course. The dawk, however, brought bad news from Chittagong, and an express was received with intelligence that the remnant of the 34th, the regiment disbanded at Barrackpore at the beginning of the Mutiny, had broken out; that they had looted the Treasury, taking with them about three lakhs of rupees and that they had also killed several Europeans. It is now believed that the Europeans escaped. At about six o'clock in the evening it was determined that the sepoys here—the detachment of the 73rd—should be disarmed: their number, including the artillerymen under the command of Dowell, was 260. They had possession of two field pieces and in their lines they held a strong position. It is reported that they threatened to resist any attempt at disarming them and they affected to despise our sailors, who are generally of small stature. The sailors were about ninety in number, fit for duty. It was therefore necessary that they should use great precautions in dealing with a body of armed men nearly three times their number.

"The Volunteers were warned to be ready at 5 o'clock the following morning, Sunday, 22nd and they were enjoined to assemble quietly, so as to excite no suspicion.

"At the time appointed, there were assembled the Commissioner, the Judge, and some other Civilians, and from 20 to 30 Volunteers. It was still dark and we waited a short time for the signal. The plan was to begin by disarming the Treasury guards, to place the disarmed men in charge of the Volunteers: the sailors would then proceed with their whole force to the Lal Bagh: and it was hoped that the men there would have given up their arms without opposition. Everything appeared to go on well: the guards at the Treasury were disarmed before the signal was given for the Volunteers to advance. There were about fifteen of the sepoys standing or sitting outside their quarters, and the rest of them, making altogether about 36, were supposed to be inside the building. They appeared to be very much dejected and they reproached their officers for subjecting them to such disgrace, protesting that they would have given up their arms at once to their own officers had they only been asked to do so. In the meantime, the sailors, on reaching the Lal Bagh, found the sepoys drawn out, prepared to make a resistance; they had evidently been apprised of our intention to disarm them. The sentry fired his musket and killed one of our men: his example was followed by the others and a volley was fired on the sailors as they advanced through the broken wall near the southern gateway. The guns had been placed in position in front of Beebee Peri's tomb, so as to command the entrance, and they opened fire upon our men with grape. As soon as the sailors had got well into the place they fired a volley. Lieut. Lewis then led them up the ramparts to the left, charging the sepoys and driving them before them at the point of the bayonet. The sepoys took shelter in their quarters but were driven on from building to building by the sailors, At this time Mr. Mays, a midshipman, at the head of eight men who were under his command, made a gallant charge from the ramparts down upon the sepoy guns; they were soon taken and spiked, and the sepoys began flying in every direction. There was a severe struggle at the end of the rampart: many of the sepoys were driven over the parapet. Mr. Bainbridge had also a fall over the parapet as he stepped back to avoid the thrust of one of the sepoys. The sailors obtained a complete victory: the sepoys fled and concealed themselves in the jungle, leaving about forty of their number killed. Many of those who escaped were severely wounded. Our loss was one killed on the field, four severely wounded, since dead, nine more or less severely wounded. Dr. Green, who accompanied the sailors, was wounded in the thigh. He was kneeling down at the time attending to one of the sailors who had also been wounded. He is getting on well, but complains of numbness in the lower part of the leg.

" *12th July.*—Three companies of the 19th Europeans have arrived: the greater number will be located in the College, the others will occupy the Faujdari Court.

"The public garden south of the College has been made over to a Joint Stock Company for the purpose of building assembly rooms, a library, theatre, billiard room, etc.

" *5th November.*—The proclamation of the transfer of the Government of India to the Queen was read in English and Bengali on Monday last. The military were drawn up in line and the European residents were upon a platform erected for the purpose. Between two and three thousand people present. Some of the houses were lighted up in the evening in honour of the occasion and there was a dinner given by the Civilians and the Military to the station.

"The students had an illumination at the College with fire-works the following evening: they seemed quite enthusiastic in the display of their loyalty."

For nearly half a century after the Mutiny the history of the district was one of peaceful progress. The most noteworthy events were the tornadoes of 1888 and 1901 and the earthquake of 1897 which are described in Chapter VIII.

Dacca after the partition.

With the partition of Bengal in 1905 Dacca became once more the capital of a province. The scheme had been warmly supported by the Nawāb of Dacca and was welcomed by the Muhammadan community, but it was resented by a considerable section of the Hindu population. A boycott of British goods was proclaimed as a sign of their displeasure and conflicts arose between Muhammadans who desired to use Liverpool salt and Hindu patriots who endeavoured to enforce the sale of the Swadeshi product. On the whole, however, the district was more peaceable and orderly than its neighbours Bakarganj and Mymensingh. But all the while a society was being consolidated in its midst which aimed at something more than mere brawling in the market place. The authorities regarded this organisation with considerable misgiving, but for more than a year its members sedulously abstained from action which would expose them to a prosecution in the courts. In September 1907, on the occasion of the Janmastami procession, two incidents occurred which revealed its dangerous character. One of its members stabbed another Hindu in the back near the Victoria Park, while a gang of miscreants attacked two men who were sitting under a lamp post near the Shaheen Medical Hall and stabbed them, killing one and seriously injuring the other. A Muhammadan by-stander subsequently reported that he recognised the murderers as members of the Anusilan Samiti, but not a single Hindu shop-keeper in the vicinity would admit that he had witnessed anything, though the murder occurred at 7 P.M. when the streets and shops alike were crowded; and when the police went to arrest the persons named by the Muhammadan they had fled. In the following December Mr. Allen, the District Magistrate, when proceeding on leave to England was shot through the body at Goalundo railway station and narrowly escaped with his life. In 1908, the district was startled by a dacoity carried out by Hindu *bhadraloks* in a singularly open and audacious manner. A gang of these young desperadoes surrounded a house at Barrah in the Nawābganj thana, shot dead a chaukidar, who opposed them and made off with about Rs. 25,000 worth of booty. They were followed by the villagers right through the district, past Sābhār police station and Dhāmrāi, finally disappearing into the Madhupur jungles, but the people were unable to arrest them as they fired without hesitation at any one who approached, killing one man who was braver than his fellows and wounding others. Within the next three years seven murders and five grave dacoities, two accompanied by murder, were committed under circumstances which left little doubt that the perpetrators of these outrages were members of the anarchist or extremist party. A Sub-Inspector of Police was shot in the streets of Dacca, fortunately not seriously, and a member of the Anusian Samiti was sentenced to ten years' transportation for preparing bombs. After months of strenuous work a prosecution for conspiracy was launched against the most prominent members of this organisation and many of its members were sentenced to long terms of imprisonment by the Sessions Judge. On appeal to the High Court some of the convicts were released but the conviction of the principal members of the society was upheld.

On April 1st, 1912, the district was transferred once more to the Government which has its head-quarters at Calcutta.

CHAPTER III.

THE PEOPLE.

Early estimates of the population.

The first synchronous census of the district was taken in 1872, but the first estimate of the population was framed in 1792, exactly eighty years before. The Collector of that day, Mr. Douglas, calculated that Dacca and Faridpur, which then formed one administrative unit, contained 938,712 inhabitants. In 1824, the population of the Dacca district alone was estimated to be 512,385, and in 1851 it was officially returned at 600,000. At the time of the Revenue Survey (between 1857 and 1861) a further attempt at enumeration was made and the population was reported to be 904,615, the calculation being based on the recorded number of houses and the assumption that from three to five persons lived in each house. The last estimate issued by the Board of Revenue for 1868-69 showed 215,915 houses and a total population of 1,019,928.

The censuses of 1872. 1881, 1891.

The first regular census showed that these estimates fell far below the truth, for in 1872 the population returned was 1,827,931 or more than three times the estimated population of twenty years before. The density even then was high and amounted to 657 to the square mile. During the next nine years the number of the inhabitants increased by 14·3 per cent and the population in 1881 was 2,090,877, which showed a density of 751 to the square mile. Substantial though this increase was it is not sufficiently large to suggest that the census of 1872 had fallen far below the truth,* and the Census Superintendent ascribed it to natural causes aided by the development of the jute trade. It was in fact less than the increase which occurred in the intercensal period 1881—1891, which amounted to 14·5 per cent., the population in the latter year being 2,395,430 and the density 861 to the square mile. The increase in the Nārāyanganj thāna was enormous, it was no less than 33 per cent; in Rūpganj and Munshīganj it was over 20 per cent and in three thānas which lie wholly or partly in the Madhupur jungle, *i.e.*, Kāpāsia, Rāipura, and Sābhār, it was 18 per cent or more. The extraordinary increase in Nārāyanganj must have been largely due to the expansion of the jute trade, and the growth of population in the Madhupur jungle is easily explained by the extension of cultivation in that jungly tract which is even now in progress, but it is not quite clear why there should have been such a great advance in Munshiganj. It is true that this portion of the district suffers little from malarial fever, but the population was already quite phenomenally dense and epidemics of cholera are frequent and severe. In Mānikganj conditions were

* The increase in Mymensingh in 1881 was no less than 30 per cent.

quite different, the increase in the subdivision as a whole was only 4·6 per cent while in the Harirāmpur thāna there was a positive loss of population.

The census of 1901.

The census of 1901 disclosed an increase of 10·6 per cent, the population being 2,649,522, and the density 952 to the square mile, a density which was greater than that of any district in the province of Bengal, with the exception of the two which include a considerable portion of the suburbs of Calcutta. The whole of the Nārāyanganj subdivision again showed a very large increase (15 per cent) and the increase of 22 per cent in the Kāpāsia thāna indicated the extent to which immigrants were pouring in to open up the jungles of Bhowal. The Munshīganj subdivision showed an increase of 9·9 per cent, a noteworthy result in view of the fact that in the Srīnagar thāna the density reached the enormous figure of 1,787 to the square mile while in the Munshīganj thāna it was 1,526. The *Sadr* subdivision outside Kāpāsia maintained a steady rate of progress, and even in Nawābganj, which adjoins the unhealthy Harirāmpur thāna there was an increase of 9·1 per cent. Mānikganj, however, continued to be unhealthy and the rate of increase in that subdivision was only 4·5 per cent. The Harirāmpur thāna which lies in the south of Mānikganj has suffered from diluvion as well as from malarial fever and cholera and affords a most striking contrast to the eminently progressive district of which it forms a part, for during the twenty years ending 1901 the population only increased by 1·25 per cent. The high death-rate in the Mānikganj subdivision was one of the reasons why the census of 1901 showed a lower rate of increase than its predecessor, but another factor was the increasing loss due to migration. In 1901 the net loss from this cause was about 36,500 greater than it was in 1891, and, had the migration figures remained the same, the growth of the population in 1901 would have been 12·1 instead of 10·6 per cent.

The census of 1911.

In spite of the great density of the population the census of 1911 disclosed an increase of 11·7 per cent, the returns showing that there were no less than 2,960,402 persons living in the district. There had been no check in the development of the Bhowal jungles, and large increases were reported from all the thānas which contained waste land; Kāpāsia showing 26 per cent, Rāipura 19 per cent and Keraniganj 17 per cent. Much of this increase was probably due to migration from the three thānas lying along the south-west border of the district, for Nawābganj only increased by 1¾ per cent in the decade, Harirāmpur had a decrease of 7 per cent, and Sealo a decrease of more than one per cent. Nārāyanganj thāna, though the density was already high, showed an increase of nearly 19 per cent and Rūpganj immediately to the north had a gain of more than 16 per cent. The most noteworthy results were however obtained from Srīnagar. Even in 1901 this thāna had a density of 1,787 to the square mile, a density higher than that returned in any other rural area in India. But in spite of this, during the ten years ending 1911, the population increased by more than 11½ per cent, and the density was only four less than 2,000 to the square mile.

The district as a whole is very thickly peopled and in 1911 it had a density of no less than 1,064 persons to the square mile. Population is most congested in the south-east corner where the thānas of Nārāyanganj, Munshiganj and Srīnagar had densities of 1,618, 1,600 and 1,996 to the square mile. Technically the whole of the population of the Munshīganj subdivision for census purposes is rural, but in this portion of the district there are a large number of flourishing bāzārs along the banks of the rivers and khāls, and the inhabitants are to a great extent supported by trade and by the remittances of members of the middle classes whose homes are situated in Bikrampur but who earn their living elsewhere. Population is fairly evenly distributed over the remainder of the island lying between the Dhaleswari and the Padmā and ranges from 875 to the square mile in Harirāmpur to 1,086 in Nawābganj. The Madhupur jungle still contains considerable areas of waste land and in the Kāpāsia thāna there were only 524 persons to the square mile. The same conditions prevail in the north of the Keraniganj thāna and to a lesser extent in the east of the Rāipura thāna and in parts of Sābhār; but in the southern portions of these thānas and in Rūpganj the density probably did not fall short of a thousand to the square mile. Outside the Madhupur jungle there is in fact practically no spare land remaining, and it is hardly likely that the high rates of increase that have hitherto prevailed can be maintained. Density.

As is only natural in so densely peopled an area the balance of migration is against the district. In 1901, 85,299 persons were enumerated in Dacca who had been born outside its boundaries, but on the other hand 128,487 persons who had been born in Dacca were living elsewhere at the time of the census and the net loss of population was thus 43,188. The greatest interchange of population takes place with the contiguous districts and is largely due to the transfer of permanent settlers crossing the district boundaries, and to intermarriages. Considerably more than a fourth of the total number of immigrants came from the single district of Mymensingh, and as the females exceeded the males in numbers, we may safely assume that the majority of these people were cultivators who had moved across into the still undeveloped forests of Madhupur. The emigration from Dacca to Mymensingh is also large, but as females formed less than one-third of the whole, it is clear that many of these migrants were only temporary visitors. After Mymensingh the largest contributions to the district population were received from the Patna and Bhagulpur divisions (14,547), and the United Provinces (10,648). The great majority of these persons do not settle in the district but come to work in the jute presses, as Migration.

coolies employed on public works, as peons, durwans and constables, as boatmen and as servants. They do not bring their families with them and amongst the immigrants from Bihar there were only three females to every 26 males. There is also a considerable influx from Tippera, Pabna, and Faridpur, about two-thirds of the immigrants being in all probability cultivators who had moved with their families across the district boundaries. The number of persons who moved from Dacca into Faridpur or Tippera was, however, much greater than the number received from those two districts, and in their case, too, about two-thirds had left their native district for good. There is a noticeable flow of population from Dacca into Bakarganj during the cold weather, but this migration is only temporary and the men return to their families in the rains. The number of natives of Dacca in Calcutta was considerable (15,141), but Calcutta has numerous attractions for the middle classes of Bikrampur. Many of them go there for their education, and when they have passed through school and college they stay on in some one of the various professions affected by the educated classes or they embark in trade. Of emigrants to other provinces there were in 1901 13,401. Of these no less than 12,755 were found in the neighbouring province of Assam. The Assamese have not hitherto paid much attention either to trade or education and the natives of Dacca have succeeded in obtaining a large share of the clerical appointments in Government offices, on tea gardens, and on the railway. There are also a large number of Dacca Muhammadans engaged in the sale of miscellaneous goods while others go up as dealers in grain and hides, boatmen and professional fishermen. Many of the middle classes have settled in Assam, and in 1901 2,535 females who had been born in Dacca were enumerated in that province.

Towns. Of the two towns Dacca has suffered from marked vicissitudes while Nārāyanganj has enjoyed continuous growth. The city must certainly have been a large and populous place when it was the capital of Bengal and Dr. Taylor states that in 1800 it had a population of 200,000 souls.* It is not stated how this figure was arrived at and the decrease to the population of 68,038 found at the census of 1838 seems very large. The lowest ebb was reached about 1867 when the population was estimated to be only 51,636, but this estimate was probably too low as at the census of 1872 it was found to be 69,212. Since then there has been a steady increase and the population in 1901 was 90,542. At the time of the formation of the new province of Eastern Bengal and Assam, Dacca was constituted the capital and in 1911 the population had risen to 108,551. Nārāyanganj was an important mart at the beginning of the nineteenth century, but at the census of 1838 it only had a population of 6,252 persons.† In 1872 the

* Topography of Dacca, p. 366

† Taylor's Topography of Dacca, p. 99.

population was 11,377 and in 1881 it was 13,508. During the next twenty years it nearly doubled and in 1901 was 24,472, rising to 27,876 in 1911. This is the cold-weather population and in the height of the jute season when the river is packed with boats and all the mills are full there are probably another six thousand persons in the place.

Villages.

The district contains only two towns and the census returns for 1901 would by themselves suggest that the population is of a much more Boeotian character than it really is. Not only were 96 per cent of the people living in villages but only 10 per cent of the rural population were living in villages containing more than 2,000 inhabitants as compared with 46 per cent in Chittagong and 28 per cent in Noakhali. The village of Bengal is, however, a very indeterminate entity, and though it is a fact that towns and even very large villages are rare, it would be a great mistake to assume, as in other places may generally be done, that the great bulk of the villagers are agriculturists. It would be barely possible for agriculture alone to support so astonishingly dense a population as is to be found in the Munshīganj subdivision, and as a matter of fact 53 per cent of the population of the Srīnagar thāna were dependant upon non-agricultural means of subsistence for their support and 39 per cent in Munshīganj. In Kāpāsia which is a fair type of a really rural area in Bengal the corresponding figure is 13 per cent. Along the banks of the rivers and *khals* there are a great number of bāzārs which are centres of a thriving trade, and though each individual bāzār may not be large they make up by quantity for their lack of size. The houses and godowns in these places are generally made of reeds and plaster in a wooden framework and roofed with corrugated iron and there is an utter absence of all the amenities of urban life. There is no conservancy, drainage or water-supply, other than that provided by the river or *khal*; the paths leading from one shop to another become veritable quagmires in the rains and no attempt is made to clear away the mud or rubbish. On the other hand the sun and air have more opportunity of exercising their purifying effect than they do in the narrow streets of a native town, and this is a factor which makes much for health. There are one or two places such as Sābhār and Dhāmrāi which contain a certain number of houses built of brick or dried mud and which have a distinctly urban aspect, but their number is not large and most of the mofussil traders live in the small but flourishing bāzārs described above. The agricultural villages are also small but the census village is a very elusive thing. The Superintendent of the Bengal Census of 1901 states that the character of a Bengal village is so indeterminate that it is hardly necessary to waste much time in discussing the statistics relating to them, and it may well be that the difference in size between the villages of Dacca and Chittagong corresponds not to an actual difference in the facts but to a difference in the point of view from which they are regarded. In the flooded tracts the villages are built in an almost continuous line along the high land fringing either side of the *khals* and here the boundary between one village and the next must clearly be extremely arbitrary. In the lower land at the back the houses have to be built on artificial mounds and here the hamlets are small and scattered. Any naturally raised site such as the hillocks at Birulia or Dhāmrāi is eagerly appropriated and densely packed with houses. In the Madhupur jungle where high land is not so scarce the villages are more scattered. Whenever circumstances admit the people surround their homesteads with dense groves of bamboos and of fruit trees such as the mango, jack, and areca palm which afford, it is true, a pleasant shade but exclude most necessary light and air.

Marriage.

Hindus and Muḥammadans alike marry early, the former obeying the dictates of their religion, the latter adopting a custom which to Western ideas is neither natural nor attractive. Early marriages are quite as common amongst Muhammadans as amongst Hindus, and in 1901 there were over 7,000 Muslim wives who had not attained the age of 10. Outside the community of Kulin Brahmans, polygamy is rare amongst Hindus. With Muhammadans it is more in favour, but the custom can never be one of general observance as the supply of women fails. The natural growth of the Hindus is checked by their aversion to widow marriage, whereas attractive Muhammadan widows of tender age are rare. The most striking feature in a Hindu marriage is the procession *(chalan)* in which the bridegroom goes to fetch the bride. In Dacca such processions usually go out at night and wealthy persons are followed by long trains of musicians, torch-bearers, mounted men and persons carrying the wedding bed and the ornaments and utensils given to the bride.

Prostitutes are to be found in every bāzār and in considerable numbers in Dacca city, but they are not so common as in the neighbouring district of Mymensingh. In 1901 there were only 2,164 of these women and as there were 487,000 males between the ages of 15 and 40 it is clear that the proportion of men habitually resorting to them is not large. A house for the rescue of fallen women has been established at Dacca by the Brahmo Somaj community, but it is doubtful whether prostitutes as a whole are really discontented with their lot. The life of an orthodox and respectable Indian woman is hedged round by innumerable restrictions which must be exceedingly irksome to the more adventurous spirits among them, and there seem grounds for supposing that those who have once been placed outside the pale enjoy the wider interests and greater variety of their lives. They at any rate show little inclination to abandon it. Drink and disease are, however, unfortunately prevalent among them.

Cricket, football and hockey are now common even in the villages. *Haddo-goodoo* is a kind of prisoners' base, the players being ranged in two parties, the object of one party being to touch a player on the opposite side and escape 'home' without being caught. In the south of the district boat races are sometimes held and kite-flying is a common amusement everywhere. Cards, chess and draughts are also popular and the people generally are very fond of music and theatricals. Amusements.

Unlike most of the districts of Eastern Bengal the number of females enumerated in Dacca was considerably in excess of the number of males. This is principally due to the large number of persons who leave their families in the district and go elsewhere to earn their living, for if the figures are taken for those born and enumerated in the district, women are found in a small minority. The excess of females is especially pronounced among the Kayasthas, so many of whom have taken service in other districts; but it is also to be found amongst a humble cultivating caste like the Namasudras, and, in this district at any rate, there is nothing to show that caste has anything to do with the distribution of sex. There are only two age periods of life in which men are in a majority, 10—15 and 40—60, and it is probable that the advantage there has no real connection with facts, but is due to some objection entertained by females to those ages. Some of the deficiency at the age of 10—15 may be due to casualties in child-bed, but this cause would be even more in operation at the 15—20 period and at that age women largely outnumber men. The proportion of children to the total population was considerably above the average for the old province of Bengal. This is due, not to a higher death-rate amongst the middle aged but to the greater fecundity of the people. Sex and age.

Ninty-eight per cent. of the population of the district in 1901 spoke Bengali and one and a half per cent, Hindi. The only other language used by any considerable number of persons was Koch Mandi, which was returned by 10,131 people living in the north of the Madhupur jungle. Koch Mandi closely resembles Garo and the Koch are thought to be either Garos with a slight veneer of Hinduism, or members of the great Koch tribe which was at one time the ruling race in North Bengal. The dialect of Bengali used is known as Eastern Bengali and is thus described by Dr. Grierson:— Language.

"It exhibits well-marked peculiarities of pronunciation—a cockney-like hatred of pre-existing aspirates and, in addition, the regular substitution of an aspirate for a sibilant. While standard Bengali is unable to pronounce sibboleth, except as shibboleth, Eastern Bengali avoids the sound of sh and has 'hibboleth.' On the other hand, the Eastern dialect cannot pronounce the letters ch, chh, and j, but substitutes ts for the first, s for the second, and z for the third."*

* Linguistic Survey of India, Vol. V, Part I, p. 201.

For a further account of the peculiarities of Eastern Bengal, a reference should be made to Dr. Grierson's work. A list of words said to be peculiar to Dacca was published in the Principal Heads of the History and Statistics of the Dacca Division, Calcutta, 1867, but it is hardly of sufficient general interest to warrant its reproduction here.

Dacca has not been a centre of literary activity and the only well known Bengali writer native to the district was the late Rai Bahadur Kali Prasanna Ghose, C.I E, whose books enjoy a great measure of popularity in both Bengals. His best known works are *Bhaktir Jay*, the Triumph of Pious Devotion; *Nishita Chinta*, Night Thoughts; *Jankir Agni Pariksha*, or the Ordeal of the Empress of Oudh; and *Bromode Lahirai*, Thoughts on Marriage. The late Babu Dinesh Chandra Bose also enjoyed some reputation as a poet and Babu Dinesh Chandra Sen has written a voluminous history of Bengali literature. Babu Umesh Chandra Bose is the author of the Exile of Sita and several other works, and Mahamohopadhaya Prasanna Chandra Vidyaratna has compiled a very good Bengali grammar. Amongst Muhammadans Maulavi Aghla Ahmadali who died in 1876 was a Persian scholar of high repute. He was the Persian teacher of that great Oriental scholar Henry Blochmann and was the author of several works on Persian grammar and prosody. Saiyid Mahmud Azad who died in 1907 was considered in his day to be the most eminent Persian scholar in Bengal and was the author of numerous poems.

Newspapers.

The following is a list of the papers published in the Dacca district :—Dacca Gazette, published weekly, circulation about 5,000; Dacca Prakas. weekly, circulation 100; The East, bi-weekly, circulation 600; Eastern Bengal and Assam Era, bi-weekly, circulation small; the Santikana, monthly, circulation 500; the Sebak. monthly, circulation 500; the Siksha Samachar, weekly, circulation 1,000; and the Dacca Review, monthly.

Religions.

62·3 per cent of the population in 1901 were Muhammadans and 37·3 per cent Hindus; the Christians, who numbered 11,556 souls made up practically the whole of the remainder. In 1801, and again in 1857 – 60 it was estimated that the population of the district was equally divided between Hinduism and Islām, but in the absence of a regular census such estimates are of no practical value. In 1872 it was found that the Muhammadans formed 56·5 per cent of the whole and each successive enumeration has shown a marked increase in the Muhammadan element. The rate of growth amongst the Muhammadans between 1872 and 1901 was in fact nearly twice as great as that amongst Hindus, the former increased by 57 per cent in the 29 years, the latter by 24 per cent. Originally no doubt conversion played a large part in swelling the ranks of the Muhammadan community. Hinduism had little to offer to the cultivating and labouring classes and they were doubtless ready enough to accept th religion of their conquerors under which they could rise to social heights utterly unattainable in the Hindu system to a low caste Hindu. But whatever may have been the case in the time of the Mughals it is doubtful whether conversion has much to do with the growth of the Muhammadan population at the present day. Changes of faith no doubt take place, but they are generally due to a Hindu having fallen in love with a Muhammadan and to his having been expelled from Hinduism on that account. Such cases usually occur in the humbler orders of society, but some years ago a high class Kayastha Zamindār in the Mānikganj subdivision, annoyed at the criticisms to which he was subjected for his neglect to observe the minutiæ of his own religion, deliberately adopted the faith of Islām and married his daughter to a well-born Musalman gentleman. The principal reason for the great Muhammadan increase is no doubt to be found in their superior fecundity, which again is largely due to the more liberal use they make of the reproductive power of their widows by allowing them re-marriage. In 1901 16 per cent of the Hindu women in Bengal between 15 and 40 were widows, whereas amongst the Muhammadans the number was only 12 per cent. The Muhammadan dietary is also more nutritious than that of the Hindu and is likely to increase his fertility and the difference in age between husband and wife is less pronounced.

Muhammadans.

The Muhammadans are found in large numbers in every part of the district, but their proportions are highest in the north, in the Rāipura and Kāpāsia thānas, lowest in Dacca city and the Srīnagar thana, where they are positively outnumbered by the Hindus. The immense mass of the Muhammadans in the district belong to the Sunni sect and in 1881 there were only 4,231 Shiahs, most of whom were living in the city of Dacca. A certain number of the Sunnis belong, to the two reformed sects which are collectively known as Hidayati, 'Guide to Salvation,' or Ahl-i-Shara, 'followers of the precepts of Muhammad, as distinguished from Sabiki, 'old'; Berai, 'without a guide'; and Bedayati or Beshara, the terms applied to the unreformed Muhammadans. One of these sects was founded by Hāji Shariat Ullah, who in 1820 A.D. returned from Mecca to Eastern Bengal and preached the Wahhabi tenets in Dacca. He was opposed to all association with Hindu rites and ceremonies, to the preparation of tazias and to the adoration of Pirs. He also held that India was Darul-harb, (the mansion of War) where the observance of Friday prayers is unlawful and the waging of war against infidels is a religious necessity.† His work was carried on by his son Dudhu Miyan who made a determined stand against the levy of illegal cesses by landlords and died in 1860 after a somewhat tempestuous career during which he was repeatedly charged with criminal

* Report on the Census of Bengal, 1872, p. 133.

† The followers of the sect at the present day assert that they do not hold this view.

offences. His followers are often referred to as the Farazi and are to be known by their non-observance of the Muharrum and of the Friday and the two Id prayers in congregation. For many years they declined to submit to vaccination but their scruples were overcome in 1889. The other reformer was Karamat Ali who was opposed to the Wahhabi. He strongly denounced the growth of Hindu superstitions and prohibited the use of tazias but he held that India under British rule was not Daru-l-harb. His followers are known as Taizunis. The Rafizadain are the followers of Mizanur Rahman of Sylhet and raise their hand to their ears each time that the words Allah-o-Akbar are pronounced in prayer whereas the other sects do so only at the beginning of the invocation. The principal strongholds of the reformed sects are the Bangsal, Nāzirir Bazār and Shamsabād quarters of the city; and Dhāmrāi, Panchgāo, and Mirpur in the interior. Most of their adherents are traders.*

Mr Gait in his report on the census of Bengal in 1901 divides Muhammadans into three main classes—the *ashraf* or better class; the *ajlaf*, corrupted into *atraf* or lower class; and the *arzal* or degraded class. The *ashraf* include Saiyids, Shaikhs of wealth or of foreign descent, Mughals and Pathans. The Saiyids claim to be descendants of Fatima, Muhammad's daughter, and Alī, the fourth Khalifa. Many of them are Shiahs and in 1901 they numbered 3,472. Of Pathans there were 10,797 and of Mughals 447. The Pathans are the descendants of settlers of pre-Mughal days. They were overthrown by the Mughals in a great battle near Dhāmrāi, and the Sābhār, Mānikganj and Harirāmpur thānas are now the principal centres of the Pathan population. The immense mass of the Muhammadans describe themselves as Shaikhs. The functional caste of greatest numerical importance is that of the Jolahas or weavers (59,380). The term is a corruption of Johala (the ignorant) and is therefore rot in favour with those to whom it is applied. It is a strict caste, the traditional occupation being weaving or dyeing, but its members have also taken to cultivation and clerical service when they can get it. The Jolahas rank higher than most of the other functional castes and the poorer cultivating Shaikhs will eat with them. The Kulus or oil-pressers (7,511) are also strictly endogamous even when they have ceased to practise their traditional occupation. The Bediyas (1829) are a gipsy caste who are described at length in Sir Herbert Risley's Tribes and Castes of Bengal. The Kuttis (deriy. *kutna* to husk) are a community who originally earned their living by husking paddy. Many of them now trade in hides and are fairly well-to-do, but they rank low in the social scale. Most of them live in the Bangsal, Shamsabād and Rahmatganj quarters of the city.

* For further information on the Muhammadan sects of Eastern Bengal see Dr. Wise's paper on the Muhammadans of Eastern Bengal contributed by Mr. Risley to J. A. S. B. for 1894.

Restrictions on intermarriage and social intercourse are found amongst Muhammadans as amongst Europeans and the main difference between their caste system and that of the Hindus lies in two facts, firstly, that it is much less rigorous, and secondly, that the immense mass of the population belong to one caste and therefore approach the condition where there is no such thing as caste at all.

Muhammadan shrines.

The principal sacred places of Musalmans in the district are:—

1. The Shrine of Qadam Rasul in Nārāyanganj erected over a stone slab containing a footprint said to be that of the Prophet. It was built by Diwān Manuar Khān, grandson of the famous Isa Khān, the last real independent Pathan ruler of this part of Bengal during the reign of Shāh Jahān.

2. The tomb of Shāh Langar at Muazzampur in Thāna Rūpganj. The date of his death is not known but the adjoining mosque was built during the reign of Ahmad Shāh who ruled in Bengal from 1409 to 1426 A.D.

3. The tomb of Shāh Malik west of the Dilkosha gardens in Dacca. The year of this saint's death is not known.

4. The tomb of Shāh Ali Baghdadi at Mirpur. This saint died in the year 1577 A.D. and was interred in the mosque at that place which was built in 1480.

Hindus.

Although the Hindus are numerically inferior to the Muhammadans, they form the bulk of the upper and middle classes and wealth, learning and influence are largely centred in their hands. The number of Muhammadan zamindārs is very small and, though Muhammadans deal in hides and to some extent in jute, the wealthy trading families are nearly all Hindus. A large number of the petty shopkeepers are Muhammadans but they have not the capital to enable them to compete with the Hindus in wholesale and quasi-wholesale trade and the cream of commerce passes into Hindu hands. Of Hindu influence and predominance at the bar it is hardly necessary to speak. The proportion of Hindus is, as is only natural, highest in the Munshīganj subdivision and lowest in the subdivision of Nārāyanganj. No statistics have ever been collected to show the distribution of the Hindus under the different sects into which the followers of that religion are divided but Saktism is the variety that is most in evidence.

Hindu festivals.

Sāktas and Vaishnavas alike have their special festivals, but the one which creates most stir in the city itself is the Janmastami, in honour of Krishna's birth, which is celebrated in August. There are two special objects of worship, one a Salagram, from the Gunduck river called Lakshī Nārāyan, which was brought to Dacca about 250 years ago and the other an idol called Morli Mohān. In honour of these idols two processions are organised by the weavers—one party taking their name from Nawābpur, the other from the Tanti Bāzār. The cost of the latter procession is largely met from an endowment, but the

Nawābpur display is the result of co-operation and its promoters are therefore less under the control of their nominal leaders, than are the men of Tanti Bāzār. The spectacle is really most remarkable. The narrow streets of the city are packed with so dense a crowd that it would be impossible for the procession to advance at all without the assistance of a strong body of police. The line is headed by elephants lent by the zamindārs of the district covered with richly ornamented trappings: then come various side-shows many of them of a rather scurrilous character, burlesquing the current topics of the day and often making somewhat scandalous allusions to the *vie intime* of the members of the opposite party. The most beautiful parts of the procession are the gold and silver shrines some of which are worth from Rs. 15,000 to Rs. 20,000, which are dragged along on bullock carts, and at night are illuminated with Bengal fires. Thousands of people come from the interior to witness this display and every house-top and window is packed. On this auspicious occasion the restrictions of the purdah are to some extent relaxed and ladies, who in ordinary life never appear from behind the veil, are to be seen at their windows richly clad and decked with heavy ornaments of gold and silver.

A large proportion of the Hindus in the city are Vaishnavas and the Jhulan Jatra, or swinging of Krishna, in August and the Huli in February or March are observed with much punctilio. The Rath Jatra, when Krishna in the form of the idol Madhab is dragged to visit the house of his father-in-law and is brought back again on the eighth day, is observed in Dacca and other places, but nowhere with so much ceremony as at Dhāmrāi. The idol at this place is believed to possess peculiar sanctity and thousands of pilgrims attend to see it dragged down the wide street of the village on a car which is of absolutely colossal dimensions and is adorned with rude carvings. The Durgā pujā is celebrated with much pomp in every part of the district. Great idols are constructed, representing Durgā supported by a lion with Lakshmī and Sarasatī her daughters standing on either hand. Kārtik and Ganesh, her two sons, sit beside her and her husband Siva is resting on her head. The pujā is performed for four days and on the fourth night the idols are thrown into the river. The huge gaudily painted images are placed on boats and accompanied by musicians assemble at central places such as Dacca, Mirkādim, Bhāgyakūl and Bahar. Here there is a very pandemonium of noise and jollification kept up the whole night through. Boat after boat arrives with its great staring figures lit up with blazing magnesium wire and the air is filled with the din of cymbals and tom-toms and shouts and songs. It is not till the sky is once more growing grey and the magnesium wire is paled by the rising sun that the revellers consent to immerse their images in the river and to retire for a little badly-needed rest.

The success of these pujās naturally depends to a great extent on the support accorded to them by the wealthy zamindārs, and from the point of view of the poorer members of the Hindu community it is a matter for congratulation that different families have devoted special attention to different pujās. The Jagadhatrī pujā, in honour of Durgā in her character of holder of the universe, is not observed very generally throughout the district but is celebrated with much pomp by the zamindārs of Jaydebpur, on the sixth day after the Kāli pujā, while the zamindārs of Kasimpur and Srinagar concentrate all their efforts on the Durgā pujā. The Baliati Babus, the Pāl Babus of Lohajang and the Bāghyakul family specialise on the Rāsh, Dol, and Janmastami pujās, the Kartik pujā is specially affected by the wealthy money-lenders of Dacca and the Lakshmi pujā by the Nāg Babus of Kalakopa.

Nāngalband near Nārāyanganj is hallowed by memories of Parasu Rām and a great bathing festival is held at this spot in the month of Chait (*vide* article on Nāngalband). Other shrines which stand high in the estimation of Hindus are the temple of Dhakeswari near Dacca city and the temple of Kāli at Chachartala. The temple of Chachartala stands on the bank of the Padmā and has so long withstood the erosive action of the river that the Hindus think that its survival must be due to supernatural agency. The Dhakeswari temple is situated about two miles to the west of the Magistrate's cutcherry. Tradition states that it was founded by Ballāl Sen and rebuilt by Rājā Mān Singh, but no traces of these buildings are left and the present temple is said to have been erected about two hundred years ago by one of the Company's servants. The following account of the temple was given in 1867 :— Hindu shrines.

"It was in olden times a most famous place of resort. Every stranger coming to Dacca was expected to lose no time in presenting himself before the goddess with an appropriate offering of a goat, buffalo, or other animal according to his means The number of daily sacrifices is said to have been from 25 to 50 goats and from 5 to 10 buffaloes.........the temple is still an object of reverence to devout Hindus and religious ceremonies are still performed within its precincts; but its ancient glories have departed; it is comparatively deserted, the buildings are buried in jungle and being utterly neglected are gradually mouldering and falling into decay."*

Since this was written the pendulum has swung back once more and the Hindu religion has profited by the growth of national feeling and the tendency to reject the teachings and influences of the West. The Dhakeswari temple is no longer buried in jungle and its clean white-washed buildings receive their decent modicum of worshippers and their offerings of goats, black and

* Principal Heads of the History and Statistics of the Dacca Division, Calcutta, 1868.

occasionally white. Another temple which has also profited by the Hindu revival is the Kālibāri on the Ramna race-course.

Hindu castes.

By far the most numerous Hindu caste in the district are the Nāmasudras, a humble cultivating caste who are believed to have been the autochthones of the Bengal delta. Till recent years they have been regarded with great contempt by the higher Hindu castes, and as a result they resolutely declined to take any share in the agitation against the partition of Bengal. Having been treated as pariahs and outcastes they refused to listen to the invitation of the higher caste Hindus to join in a movement directed against the established Government. Nāmasudras are numerous throughout the district but especially so in the Srīnagar, Keraniganj, Sābhār and Nawābganj thānas. After the Nāmasudras the caste most strongly represented is that of the Kāyasthas, though it is but a bad second as they are out-numbered in the proportion of almost three to one. The Kāyasthas are very evenly distributed throughout the district but they are scarcest in Bhowal, and most numerous in the island lying south of the Dhaleswari. The Shahas numbered 71,000 in 1901, the Sābhār and Mānikganj thānas being the great centres of the caste. By tradition liquor-sellers, they have become the traders and bankers of the district and some of the wealthiest zamindārs of Dacca are members of this caste. The Munshiganj subdivision is the great stronghold of the Brahman population, but outside this area they are distributed very evenly over the district. The only other caste with more than 50,000 members is the Kaibarttas of whom there were a large number in Srīnagar and the thānas bordering on the Lakshya river.*

Hindu omens and superstitions.

Some of the Hindu superstitions of the district deserve notice. Death or misfortune is portended by the screech of an owl, the cawing of crows, the howling of jackals, the vision of a buffalo in a dream, the flowering of bamboos and the sight of a tortoise or an ass when setting out on a journey. A person who when leaving a house is summoned from behind must immediately turn back unless he wishes to enjoy bad luck, though this would seem to be a very natural proceeding on his part, quite apart from any sanction conferred by superstition. Deaths which occur on Saturday or Tuesday are thought to be particularly unfortunate for the survivors, and if one of these days is the Amabasya day there is risk that the spirit of the deceased may haunt the village and give rise to epidemic diseases. It is thought that a person's life is shortened if he is touched by the fan when he is being fanned, and the evil effects of such an accident must be averted by striking the fan thrice against the ground. It is unlucky to hear weeping when a man is taking food or rising from the bed; in the latter case the trouble can be best averted by returning to bed and remaining there

* For an account of the manners and custom of these castes reference should be made to the Tribes and Castes of Eastern Bengal by the late Sir Herbert Risley, K.C.I.E.

till the weeping stops. If a man enters a tank by one ghat and ascends by another he will shorten his mother's life, and it is said that a man who sits on the threshold of the entrance door of his hut is likely to fall into debt This is a superstition that can easily be explained on rationalistic lines, as a man who contents himself with looking on at the work of the world is likely to grow poor. A person who has a bad dream will not tell it to any one but goes to the bank of the river and takes the river into his confidence. Bad dreams are unpleasant but a good dream is almost a worse infliction as the percipient must rise the instant that he wakes and sit up for the remainder of the night.

CHRISTIANITY. The Roman Catholics.

In 1901 the total number of Christians in the district was 11,556, of whom 11,131 were Roman Catholics. Two missions from this church are now labouring in Dacca—the Portuguese, who are subject to the Bishop of Madras, and the missionaries of the Congregation of the Holy Cross, an American Order, whose chief now fills the Roman Catholic See of Dacca. It is stated in some old papers in the possession of the Portuguese priest in charge of the Hosnabād church that the first Christian missionary to Dacca reached Hosnabād about three hundred years ago. The local zamindār, enraged at his success amongst his tenants, ordered the holy father to be bound hand and foot and thrown into a well or ditch, declaring that he would thus put to the test the real character of the new religion. To his surprise the priest survived and, overcome with repentance, the zamindār made him a grant of land. The oldest church now existing in the district is however the Portuguese church at Tezgaon about four miles north of Dacca, which was originally erected in 1679 and rebuilt in its present form in 1779. The church was however rebuilt on the same site and the stone floor is covered with inscriptions to the memory of the dead who lie beneath, the oldest one that is still decipherable recounting the virtues of one Choy Daviates, who died in 1714. In addition to Tezgāon there are churches maintained by the Portuguese at Dacca, Hasnabād, Nagari and Panjorah. The mission is a fairly wealthy one as the landed property it owns yields an income of upwards of Rs. 49,000 a year.

In comparison with the Portuguese the connection of the Order of the Holy Cross with Eastern Bengal is a thing of recent date, as the first missionaries did not arrive till 1852 and the diocese of Dacca was not created till 1886. In 1908 there were twelve missionaries of this Order stationed in the district, two at Bandurah, two at Tumuleah, one at Solipur and the remainder at Dacca. The mission maintains a school for Europeans and Eurasians at Dacca, which is affiliated to the University of Calcutta, and here and at their schools in the interior they have more than 1,200 children under their instruction. In addition to the cathedral at Dacca (built 1898) there are churches at Bandurah (built 1852 and rebuilt in 1888) and Solipur (built 1860). It is reported that there are about 8,100 adherents of this mission and 6,150 members of the Portuguese church, but as the total number of Roman Catholics in Dacca in 1901 was only a little over 11,000, it is clear that a considerable number of these persons must be living outside the district or else that conversion has been proceeding with usual rapidity in recent years.

Protestant missions.

Baptist missionaries first visited the district in 1805 from Serampur, but they were ordered by the Collector to return, partly because they had no passports and partly because the pamphlets they distributed "had caused great uneasiness among the people." In 1816 a missionary was, however, definitely posted to Dacca, and no less than seven schools were opened. In 1825 work was commenced among women and girls and the mission extended its labours, not only to the neighbouring districts, but even to Assam. Other workers then came forward to assist and Assam was handed over to the American Baptist Mission and the Welsh Calvinists, while the out-districts were surrendered to the Australasian Baptist Mission At the present day there are 7 European and 35 Bengali workers in the district; but though the number of Baptists in other parts of the division is considerable there were in 1901 only 114 in Dacca itself. The other Christian mission is the Oxford Mission, who first visited Dacca in 1902. The principal object of this mission is to bring a heathy moral influence to bear on students, and for this purpose they have erected a fine hostel with 41 separate rooms in which they are prepared to lodge boys who are reading at the schools and colleges in the city, irrespective of the religion they profess. Native Christians are reported to live on terms of peace and amity with their Hindu and Muhammadan neighbours, but the change of social customs that it entails is a serious obstacle to the extension of the faith. Between 1872 and 1901 the Christian population increased by 41 per cent. and as the total population increased by nearly 45 per cent it is clear that the number of conversions was not very large. The Anglican communion numbered 157 in 1901. There is a good Anglican church in Dacca which was consecrated by Bishop Heber in 1824. There are also Greek and Armenian churches in the city. The Christian cemeteries are described in the article on the city of Dacca.

The Sikhs.

Guru Teg Bahādur visited Dacca, and there is a Sikh temple at Shujatpur near the Ramna. The Sangat at Sangatolla close to Sutrapur is now the chief place of worship but pious Sikhs still visit the ruins at Jafarabād where there is a well whose waters are thought to have curative powers.

CHAPTER IV.

PUBLIC HEALTH.

The present system of recording vital statistics was introduced in 1869 when the duty of reporting deaths was imposed on Chaukidars. In 1876 the system was extended to births, but the returns received were so inaccurate that it was soon abandoned outside the towns, for which special provision had been made in 1873, and births were not recorded again till 1892. Vital occurrences are reported by chaukidars when they attend at the police-stations for their parades and a monthly return is submitted from each station to the Civil Surgeon. These returns are tested by touring officers and more particularly by the officers of the Vaccination Department and, judged by this standard, their inaccuracy is not very great. The Inspecting Staff itself is not, however, entirely above suspicion and there can be little doubt that a large number of occurrences escape registration. A detailed examination of the records of nearly every police-station shows that at certain seasons and in certain unions there is an absence of vital occurrences that can hardly be in accordance with the actual facts, while the recorded rates fall far short of those calculated by Mr. Hardy, the well known Actuary, after a most careful examination of the census figures for 1881 and 1891. Mr. Hardy calculated that in 1891 the birth-rate in Bengal was 51·8 and the death rate 44·8 per mile. For the nine years ending 1900 the average recorded rate was—births 35·8, deaths 31·8, while in the Dacca district the average recorded annual birth rate for the decade 1893—1902 was 33·32, the death rate 29·03. VITAL STATISTICS.

Table VI of the Statistical Tables which gives details for thānas shows how far removed the reported figures are from accuracy. There is no very material difference between the conditions prevailing in the Sābhār thāna and those to be found in Nawābganj, yet in the former the average birth rate for the decade ending 1902 was 51·98, the death-rate 41·15 per mille, and the corresponding figures in the latter were 28·90 and 22·02. It would be idle therefore to lay claim to accuracy in the returns and as the degree of inaccuracy may vary materially from year to year and from place to place, it is clear that the figures must be used with caution. The general tendency is, however, for the recorded births to exceed the recorded deaths, and in areas and years in which this is not the case it is safe to conclude that public health has been unduly bad

Taken as a whole the district is one of the healthiest in Bengal. The enumerations of 1881 and 1891 both disclosed an Healthiness of district.

increase of over 14 per cent and in 1901 there was an increase of 10·6 per cent, which was more than double that recorded for the province of Bengal There is also a continuous and satisfactory surplus of recorded births over recorded deaths. The salubrity of the district is generally ascribed by its inhabitants to the beneficial action of the great rivers. The floods that sweep over the country during the rains cleanse the lowlands of all impurities and leaves them clean and sweet and the cool breezes blowing over these vast stretches of water fortify the constitution against disease. In parts of the district, however, conditions are less favourable. The forests in the north are thought to have a prejudicial effect upon the health of persons who have not become thoroughly acclimatised to them, and public health has for many years been bad in the Mānikganj subdivision. In the decade ending with 1902 the recorded deaths actually exceeded the births in the Sealo Aricha thāna and in Harirāmpur the excess of births was very small. The marked inferiority of Mānikganj is clearly shown in the census returns, though census figures are of course to some extent affected by migration. In the last three census decades the increase in the district as a whole was 14·5, 10·61, and 11·7 per cent; in the Mānikganj subdivision it was only 4·6, 4·46 and 1·2 per cent. The probable causes of the unhealthiness of Mānikganj are discussed in the following paragraph:—

Fever.

More than half the recorded deaths are assigned to fever, but fever, it need hardly be said, is an expression that is very loosely used. Most mortal diseases are accompanied by a rise in temperature; the diagnosis is performed not by a medical man but by an ignorant rustic, and if the patient has not succumbed to cholera, small-pox, dysentery, or one or two other well recognised causes of mortality, it is fairly certain that he will be registered as a fever victim. The Madhupur jungle is generally considered to be a most malarious tract and this view is borne out by the recorded vital statistics. In the district as a whole fever during the decade ending with 1902 accounted for 542 out of every thousand deaths. In the Kāpāsia thāna which lies in the Madhupur jungle 813 deaths out of every thousand were put down to fever, while in the Rāipura thāna which adjoins it on the east the corresponding figure was 731. The death rate from fever in Mānikganj is also very high. The special unhealthiness of Mānikganj is no doubt due to the high subsoil level of the water and the obstruction of the drainage. There is a general tendency towards deterioration of the rivers of the delta, and the effects of this tendency in Mānikganj are especially pronounced. The principal rivers in the west, the Dhaleswari and the Ichhāmati, have been silting up, and in this portion of the district there is an impervious layer of blue clay about two feet thick which is only about thirteen feet below the surface at the river banks, and is probably only three or four feet below the surface in the interior.

This was the explanation offered by the Civil Surgeon in 1882 and it has received the endorsement of successive Sanitary Commissioners.

The rest of the district is comparatively free from malarial fever, and in 1907 less than 11 per cent of the patients in the Dacca dispensaries were treated for this complaint. The corresponding figure for the province as a whole in that year was over 15 per cent and in the neighbouring district of Faridpur it was over 19 per cent.

The connection between fever and drainage being undoubtedly extremely intimate it is only natural that the disease should be most prevalent in the autumn when the floods are beginning to subside.

Cholera.

Dacca is rather liable to cholera, the average annual recorded death-rate from this cause during the decade ending 1906 being 3·12 per mille, a figure which was only exceeded by one other district in Eastern Bengal. The tract of country lying between the Dhaleswari and the Padmā is the part that suffers most.

Population in the Munshiganj subdivision is extraordinarily dense, the rivers and channels in the interior are drying up and considerable difficulty is experienced in obtaining good drinking water. The main channel of the Padmā now flows along its western bank and in the dry season there is very little current in that portion of the river which washes the shores of the Mānikganj subdivision. The people if left to themselves are completely indifferent to the most elementary sanitary precautions. In 1886 the Civil Surgeon wrote as follows:—"In my experience it is hopeless to expect villagers to adopt any prophylactic measures whatever. They will persist, in spite of all our efforts, in drinking foul water, even if they are in a position to obtain river water, and to expect them to boil or filter water, to clean a drain, to leave an infected spot temporarily, even to drink prophylactic doses of acid sulphuric dilute if given them is utopian."

Latrines are erected in close proximity to or even actually in tanks from which drinking water is drawn, and the banks of the rivers are habitually used for the purposes of nature. At Aricha there were till recently rows of latrines erected in the slack water of the Padmā which acted both as the receptacle of the night-soil and as the source of the water-supply of that large and prosperous bāzār. The people do not understand that if a well is sunk in close proximity to accumulated filth and ordure it is liable to contamination, for which perhaps there is some little excuse, but they do not even realise, that the same place cannot with impunity be used as a receptacle for sewage and a source of water-supply. The villages are packed in close proximity to one another along the banks of water-courses and rivers, and when cholera once breaks out it quickly spreads from one centre to another. No precautions are taken with the soiled clothing and evacuations of the patient and infection is in many cases carried by flies. The extent to which the prevalence of cholera depends upon the neglect not only of proper sanitary precautions but even of the ordinary rules of decency is shown by the fact that even when cholera is raging in the Munshīganj subdivision but few cases occur at the Kārtik Bāruni fair. At this fair there is a large population living in boats and in temporary shelters and were it not for the enforcement of proper rules epidemic disease would most certainly be rife.

Prior to 1877 when Dacca city was first supplied with filtered water cholera used to be very prevalent in the city and bad outbreaks continued to occur from time to time as the water-works at first were only able to supply about one-third of the population. In 1876, 305 persons died from cholera in the city, and in 1882, 527, which was equivalent to a death-rate of 6·57 per mille. A peculiarity of this outbreak was that it occurred between July and September at a time of year when the whole district is under water and true cholera is hardly known. The unusual character of this visitation produced an absolute panic. "All who were able to do so left Dacca or lived in boats on the river. The colleges and schools were deserted and the streets obstructed by processions fervently propitiating the responsible deities." The widespread character of the epidemic was doubtless due to the fact that the milkmen's quarter was infected at the very commencement. An even worse outbreak occurred in 1893 when there were 581 deaths, and 1904 and 1905 were also years of high cholera mortality, 493 deaths occurring in the former year and 506 in the latter. In 1909 there were 334 deaths from cholera in the city, but the extension of the water-works was completed in March 1910 and in that year there were only 141 deaths. Nārāyanganj town has also been very subject to the disease and in no less than eight years between 1891 and 1906 there were more than 100 cholera casualties. The opening of the water-works in 1908 has, however, done much to relieve the town of this dreadful scourge though there were 82 deaths from this cause in 1909.

In the district as a whole the two worst epidemics which have occurred of recent years were those of 1893 and 1895. In the former year the death-rate from this cause was no less than 7·27 per mille. The tract that suffered most severely was the island lying between the Dhaleswari and the Padmā, the death-rate per mille from cholera being Munshiganj 9·83, Srīnagar 11·35, Nawābganj 8·16, Mānikganj 9·58, Harirāmpur 3·12, and Sealo Aricha 8·86. The total number of deaths registered was 17,610, 80 per cent of which occurred in the last three months of the year. In 1895, 16,970 deaths were registered which was equivalent to a death-rate of 7·08 per mille, the highest district death-rate recorded in Bengal that year. The disease was again most prevalent in that portion of the district which it punished most severely in 1893.

Dysentery and diarrhœa are rather common, the average annual death-rate from these causes during the decade ending 1906 being 1·27 per mille as compared with 0·75 for the province as a whole. The remaining districts of the division suffer but little from these diseases and their prevalence in Dacca must probably be ascribed to a larger proportion of urban population. They are particularly in evidence in the towns of Dacca and Nārāyanganj, the average annual death-rate from this cause in the former city being no less than 4·30 in the decade ending 1902, and the Munshiganj subdivision is also much affected. The whole of this tract is very densely populated and many people are living in conditions that are practically urban. Dysentery and diarrhœa.

Small-pox is not a serious cause of mortality and in the decade ending 1902 the average annual death-rate from this disease was only ·05 per mille. A staff of nearly 100 vaccinators is employed almost all of whom are licensed vaccinators, *i.e.*, not salaried servants of Government but persons permitted to charge two annas for every operation. Till recently arm to arm vaccination was common in the district, but the practice is now dying out. Small-pox.

Like the rest of Eastern Bengal the district has been almost entirely free from plague. In 1899 there was an outbreak in the thānas of Munshiganj and Nawābganj, 81 persons being attacked, of whom only nine recovered. One death from plague also occurred in 1907. The causes of the immunity of the district from this terrible disease are still obscure. Plague.

Elephantiasis and bronchocele, enlarged spleen and rheumatism are fairly common as are also skin diseases and worms, the principal varieties being the common round worm, Ascarides, Tænia and Distoma Intestinate. Croup and laryngitis are comparatively rare, but catarrh, bronchitis, and asthma are common. Leprosy is more prevalent than in Faridpur and Bakarganj, where it is extremely rare, but it is not of very common occurrence. The proportion of male lepers to every 100,000 males in 1901 was only 39 as compared with 72, the ratio returned for the whole of Bengal. Other diseases.

No provision seems to have been made for the medical attendance of the sick in the days of Mughal rule, but a Lungur Khānā or poor-house was maintained. In 1803 a native hospital was opened, but Taylor, writing in 1838, described it as being small, ill-ventilated, capable of containing only 40 patients and altogether ill-adapted to the purpose for which it was erected. The lunatic asylum was at that time in existence, but no provision had been made for lepers, and none indeed has yet been made even at the present day. Medical Institutions.

The most important medical institution not only in Dacca but in the whole of Eastern Bengal and Assam is the Mitford Hospital. This hospital owes its existence to Mr. Robert Mitford of the Civil Service who served in Dacca for many years and died in Europe in 1836. He left the bulk of his property to the The Mitford Hospital.

Government of Bengal to be employed in works of charity and public utility in the city of Dacca, but the will was disputed and the decision of the final Court was not pronounced till 1850. The hospital was opened in 1858 and in 1867 had accommodation for 92 in-patients. Since that date it has been considerably enlarged and in 1907 there were 139 beds for men and 42 for women, while the Lady Dufferin Hospital which stands in the same compound has four beds more. In addition to the main ward of the hospital, there are lecture and dissecting rooms, an outdoor patient department and accommodation for European in-patients.

The Mitford Hospital is a source of immense good. In a large city like Dacca there are many poor persons who gladly avail themselves of the opportunity of receiving medical treatment in a hospital and in 1907 there were nearly 4,000 indoor patients, while outdoor patients numbered nearly 31,000. Well-to-do persons come to the Mitford Hospital even from other districts for surgical treatment and in 1907 the number of operations performed was 3,515.

The total income in 1907 was Rs. 33,727. Of this Rs. 10,000 represents the annual grant from the Municipality, Rs. 3,604 the subscription from the District Board, and Rs. 7,164 the interest on investments. There is a medical school attached to the hospital which is fully described in the chapter on Education.

The Victoria Hospital at Nārāyanganj.

The Victoria Hospital at Nārāyanganj was opened in 1892 and contains 20 beds for men and 10 for women. There is a large foreign element in the population of that town employed in jute mills and in other ways, and in 1907 the hospital received 540 male and 111 female in-patients, while the number of out-patients was nearly 17,000. The total income of the hospital in 1907 was Rs. 5,600, of which Rs. 3,300 was received from the Municipality and Rs. 600 from the District Board.

Dispensaries.

In addition to the hospitals at Dacca and Nārāyanganj there are in the district 22 dispensaries, 13 of which are assisted by the District Board while nine are entirely maintained by private persons.

The District Board dispensaries are situated at Baldhara, Bankhuri, Mūlchar, Mahādebpur, Teghuria, Churain, Rāipura, Monohardi, Narsingdi, Tilli, Joinsher, Mānikganj and Munshīganj, and the Mission dispensary at Nāgari.

The first of these dispensaries was established at Mānikganj in 1864. Then came Jaydebpur and Joinsher in 1866, Bhāgyakul in 1868, Kālipara in 1870, and Māluchi in 1872. The last named dispensary was erected in accordance with the instructions laid down in the will of Babu Ishan Chandra Roy who left certain property for its support. This property now yields an income of about Rs. 3,000 per annum which is considerably more than is required for the maintenance of the institution and it is proposed to devote the surplus funds to the endowment of a new dispensary at Harirāmpur. All the appointments and equipment of the Māluchi dispensary are of the very best, as is only natural in an establishment in which no considerations of economy need intervene.

Only five of these dispensaries have any provision for indoor accommodation and the total number of beds available is only fifty-nine. This is not, however, a matter for regret. Indigent strangers are the only persons who would consent to become in-patients at a dispensary and the number of these people in the interior is not large. Eight beds are maintained at the Māluchi Eye Dispensary, but the average daily number of indoor patients is less than two.

Judged by the standard of population the number of dispensaries in the district is not large, as even after including private non-aided institutions there were in 1907 only eight to every million inhabitants as compared with thirteen in the province as a whole and 24 in a large district like Sylhet. Distances are not, however, great and communications are fairly good, so that in Dacca the sick have greater facilities for obtaining access to medicine than in many other places. Public dispensaries are, moreover, not so urgently required in Dacca as in other portions of the province, as the number of private medical practitioners is unusually large. In 1901 there were in the district no less than 164 doctors with diplomas or certificates. A figure like this requires some standard of comparison, and this standard may be found in the remaining three districts of the division which had only 34 between them! It is perhaps doubtful whether uncertificated doctors are not more of a danger than of a help to the patients whom they treat, but of these persons Dacca had in 1901 no less than 2,627, a figure which was only exceeded by one district in Bengal. Most of the trained private doctors are, however, living in the towns and the southern part of the district, and an increase of medical facilities is called for in the north.

The experiment was recently tried of requiring doctors in charge of dispensaries to attend the bāzārs in the vicinity on market days with a stock of medicines, but it did not prove a success and was soon abandoned. There is, however, little doubt that much still remains to be done to bring medical relief to the doors of the people. The population of the towns of Dacca and Nārāyanganj is only 4 per cent of the population of the district as a whole, yet in 1907 the patients treated in the medical institutions of those two towns formed nearly 50 per cent of the total number of patients treated in the 15 institutions for which returns are published. There is of course a larger proportion of indigent foreigners in the towns than in the interior and persons sometimes come from other districts to be treated in the Mitford Hospital, but these two facts are not in themselves sufficient to account for such a very marked difference in the figures.

The following rough abstract taken from the returns for 1907 gives a good idea of the class of diseases most commonly treated at these medical institutions:—Total number of patients 112,000; ulcers and other diseases of the skin 30,000; dyspepsia, diarrhœa and other diseases of the digestive system 16,000; malarial fever 12,200; diseases of the eye and ear 8,200; injuries 6,000; rheumatism 4,200; worms 4,000; dysentery 2,800; venereal diseases 2,700. In 1907 the total income of the 15 institutions which accepted public aid was in round figures Rs. 55,800. About 4 per cent of this was received from Government, about 20 per cent from the District Board, about 24 per cent from the two Municipalities, about 17 per cent from endowments and about 9 per cent from subscriptions.

Lunatic Asylum.

The Dacca Lunatic Asylum was founded in 1815 and has accommodation for 217 males and 45 females; it receives patients from the Dacca and Chittagong divisions and from the districts of Sylhet and Cachar. The average number of insanes admitted annually is 52 and the average daily strength 232; nearly half the inmates are criminals. The annual cost is about Rs. 26,000.

Sanitary condition of Dacca.

The sanitary condition of the district leaves much to be desired. In 1867 the Collector wrote as follows of Dacca city:—"Dacca has long been famed for its filth, and in this respect undoubtedly bore away the palm even from that town of odoriferous celebrity—the ancient city of Cologne. In 1713 it is described by a Jesuit priest in the following terms:—'*Pour ce qui est de la ville, rien de plus sale et de plus mal-propre.*' He says the streets are full of dirt and ordure which *s'y rassemblent* after the slightest shower. More than a century and a half has elapsed since the priest wrote and considerable improvement has been made. Much, however, remains to be done. At present the sanitary condition of the town varies in different localities. The main thoroughfares and places of public resort are, as a rule, clean and well kept, as are also the streets in the neighbourhood of the river; it is in the back streets and unfrequented by-lanes and alleys in the centre of the town that nuisances are still rife; and here many very objectionable localities are still to be found. In many places the proprietors of houses have built masonry drains, totally regardless of the fact that they have no outlet. As a natural consequence these drains become stagnant channels filled with rubbish. . . . The houses of the wealthy are not much better than those of the poorer classes as regards conservancy arrangements. In most spouts may be seen in the outer wall from which the sewage and filth from the upper storeys dribbles down to the ground below, leaving in its passage down the wall a horrible coagulated mass of abomination, often more than an inch thick." *

* Principal Heads of the History and Statistics of the Dacca Division, p. 80.

Much has been done to improve the sanitary condition of the city during the 43 years that have elapsed since these words were written, but unfortunately even at the present day they still hold good in the main. Through the liberality of Nawāb Abdul Gani of Dacca the city was endowed with a supply of filtered water in 1877 and this has done much to check the ravages of cholera which formerly exacted a heavy toll from the inhabitants. The Conservancy Department has been developed and improved, and considerable sums of money have been expended in opening up passages through which the sweepers can gain excess to the privies. But this work is very costly, and it is calculated that there are still five thousand private latrines which cannot be approached and which must therefore of necessity be left uncleared from year to year, a mass of festering ordure in the midst of a congested population. The principal streets are swept, but there is no system of drainage in the city, and in the by-lanes there is often an offensive stench from the accumulation of sewage and decaying garbage not only in the lane itself but in the adjacent premises.

The streets and lanes are very narrow, and are in consequence both dark and stuffy. One quarter, indeed, the Sankhari Bāzār, is quite phenomenal. The houses are extraordinarily narrow, but run back for an enormous distance forming a curious warren of tiny rooms and passages into which neither light not air can enter. Even the conditions of the bāzārs in which food is exposed for sale are most insanitary. Steps have recently been taken to extend the water-supply and to improve the conservancy arrangements and the question of introducing a drainage system is under consideration. Dacca is, however, an old city, constructed at a time when the laws of sanitation were unknown in India and nothing short of demolition and re-building would bring it into accordance with the requirements of the twentieth century. The following description of the conservancy arrangements in Dacca city is taken from the Sanitary Report for 1905:—"The population of Dacca is over 90,000. There are 13,000 private and 12 public latrines on the registers, and it is estimated that about 22,000 people are not provided with conveniences of any sort. The soil of 8,000 privies is more or less removed and the remainder from one cause or another is inaccessible. The custom in Dacca is to build houses in blocks back to back with a courtyard in the centre. At the back of the courtyard the privies open on to a central channel by means of which they are served. In some cases 50 or 100 latrines open on to a single passage, and it is frequently so narrow that it is hardly possible for a man to crawl along by placing his feet on the slippery ledges on either side between the wall and the drain, and the ends of the passage may even be closed up by houses so that there is no possible entrance. It is needless to say that the sewage from these latrines has never been removed and has in the course of years collected until it stands considerably above the level of the courtyards. I have seen some of these unopened passages from the roofs of the adjoining houses. Their condition is indescribably filthy even in the cold season. The people complained to me that in the rainy season the sewage flows back into their houses."

Nārāyanganj.

In Nārāyanganj affairs are very different. Standing as it does on a site, the greater part of which is much below flood-level its natural disadvantages are very great. But it is a comparatively young town and from the first has enjoyed the advantage of a large community of European businessmen connected with the jute trade. These gentlemen have taken a close interest in municipal affairs, and it is doubtful whether in East or West Bengal there is another town of its size in which a Sanitary Inspector could find so few subjects for criticism. The construction of the new water-works has removed the one defect, as prior to their erection the mortality from cholera was high.

Sanitation in the interior.

The sanitary condition of the villages is far from satisfactory, and matters can hardly be put on a proper basis until the villagers themselves realise how important it is to improve the surroundings of their dwellings and are willing to devote the time and labour required for the purpose. In the flooded tracts there is one valuable asset on the side of health; the annual flood washes the country every year and at the beginning of the cold weather leaves the surface clean. But indirectly it is a source of serious trouble. The houses have to be built on mounds raised above the surface of the water and to create these mounds holes are dug in close proximity to the house. When the floods fall these holes are left, mere stagnant pools filled with decaying vegetation and garbage, the breeding grounds of mosquitoes and disease. Considerable sums have been expended in Mānikganj town in making tanks and using the earth so obtained in filling up these holes, but the cost of carrying out this very desirable reform over the district as a whole by paid labour would be beyond the means of any Government and the only hope of improvement lies in the voluntary effort of the people themselves. There are, however, other sources of disease which admit of easier remedy. The sun and air are alike purifying agents and much good would be done if the villagers would content themselves with providing their houses with a reasonable amount of shade instead of, as is often the case, burying them in a dense jungle of bamboos and palms.

Much disease is also caused by the reckless and insanitary disposal of excreta. Rows of privies are often to be seen standing in the shallows along the edges of the Padmā where there is no wholesome current to sweep away impurities, and the result of this disgusting practice is to be found in the high death-rate from cholera recorded in these villages. The banks of rivers and streams are freely used as latrines; when the waters rise they absorb this filth and the people who drink this diluted sewage not infrequently suffer from bowel complaints. The District Board is taking steps to improve the water-supply in the interior and by the end of 1908, 274 wells had been sunk. Money will also be granted for the repair of tanks, provided that the owners will give reasonable guarantees that they will be strictly reserved for the provision of drinking water, but in Bengal landowners are very jealous of their rights and, up to date, they have declined to allow the Board that modicum of control which alone would justify them in expending public money on the property of a private individual. This is the more to be regretted in that there are grounds for supposing that in the alluvial tracts tanks are a better source of water-supply than wells, as in the opinion of some authorities, the water is exposed to such contamination from decaying vegetable matter during its percolation through the soil that it requires to be thoroughly oxidised by exposure to sun and air in a tank. Wells are, however, satisfactory in the higher parts of the district. It has sometimes been asserted that the retting of jute has a prejudical effect upon the health of people living in the neighbourhood. Water in which jute has been steeped is rendered unfit for drinking and the rotting jute diffuses a most noisome stench, but it is difficult to trace any connection between jute and fever, and in 1897 the Civil Surgeon pointed out that in some of the healthiest thānas in the district the cultivation of jute was very widely practised.

CHAPTER V.

ECONOMIC CONDITION OF THE PEOPLE.

SOCIAL ORGANISATION OF THE PEOPLE.

Broadly speaking, the inhabitants of the district fall into the following main classes—the great landlords, the professional classes, the traders, the agriculturists, the artizans and weavers and the boating and labouring classes. The great landlords are few in number and, as in England, their ranks are from time to time reinforced by men who have made money in trade and the learned professions. The proportion of the district population included in the category of professional classes is unusually large, for Bikrampur is the stronghold of the Bengali middle class and there are a great number of people living there who are largely dependant for their maintenance on the remittances received from fathers, husbands, and brothers who are earning their livelihood in other districts of Bengal and in Assam. In the professional classes are included an army of clerks, many of whom draw but slender salaries and whose families accordingly suffered considerably from the higher prices of 1906. The Shāhās and to a lesser degree the Telis are the great trading castes and several of their members have amassed very considerable fortunes from money-lending and commerce and have purchased important zamindāris. More than three-fifths of the population of the district still derive their sustenance from the land, and the condition of the agricultural industry, the relations between the landlords and the tenants and the rates of rent are therefore matters of great importance.

Rents: different classes of land.

The following are the classes into which land is commonly divided for the purpose of assessment to rent—*bhiti* or homestead, *nal* or culturable land which is divided into the following three classes: first class *awal*, second class *doiam* and third class *chaiam*, culturable waste (*laik patit* or *patit*), and *jola* or *doba* which is low-lying marshy ground. With the increase of population these distinctions are tending to disappear and villagers agree to pay the highest rates even for inferior land. Special rates are generally charged for *pan* and vegetable gardens and for land under thatching grass.

In Bhowal the higher land is divided into two main classes, *baid* and *challa*, and each of these classes again into three grades, *pardor*, *kamdor*, and *chedor*. The most fertile land in this part of the district are the *baids* or shallow depressions which intersect the higher land and which closely resemble a formation in the Golaghat subdivision of the Sibsagar district known as *hoolas*. No special rate is charged in Bhowal for homestead land as much of the *nal* land lies above flood-level, but higher rents are sometimes paid for land cultivated with *karolas* (a species of cucumber) and jute. When this pargana was still largely under jungle special leases with a rent-free period were granted for the reclamation of the land. Brahmottar and other rent-free tenures were also offered to men of respectable family who were prepared to settle there. These concessions have been now withdrawn.

Rents, as is only natural, are highest in Bikrampur where the rural population is extremely dense. The old-established rates per bigha ranged from Re. 1-4-0 to Rs. 2 for cultivated land and was Rs. 4 for homestead; but as much as Rs. 4 a bigha is sometimes paid for cultivated land and Rs. 8-12-0 for homestead. In Mānikganj 12 annas a bigha is a not uncommon rate for cultivated land, and from Rs. 2-8-0 to Rs 3 for homestead. In Nārāyanganj the rent for culturable land is from Re. 1 to Re. 1-4-0 per *kani*, but in the khas mahals it ranges from 6 annas to 9 annas. It should be explained that the *kani* in Nārāyanganj is a little less than a bigha. Rents.

In Bhowal the customary rates are as follows:—

	Pardor.	Kamdor.	Chedor.
	Rs.	Rs.	As.
Bioe	2 to 2-4	1-2 to 1-4	8 to 10
Challa	0-8 to 0-10	0-5 to 0-6	3 to 4

Near the city the rates of course are higher, and land used for market gardens in the outskirts of Dacca fetches from Rs. 8 to Rs. 12 per bigha.

These rents in themselves are probably not more than the land can well afford, but the landlords add to their incomes in other ways. In cases of transfer the landlord usually exacts one-quarter of the purchase money as his fee. The right to settle on a piece of land is often put up to auction and seldom fetches less than ten times the annual rent, while as much as Rs. 75 a bigha is sometimes paid. Illegal cesses are also occasionally imposed. Road and Public Works cesses are sometimes realised from the raiyats at double the authorised rate—and the *tahori*, a cess of one anna or more in the rupee of rent, which is distributed amongst the collecting staff, is almost universal. *Marocha* is an *abwab* occasionally paid to the landlord when a marriage takes place in his tenant's family and in some estates *abwabs* are collected to defray the cost of dispensaries and schools. These cesses are usually paid by the cultivators without much demur and the relations between lordlords and tenants are, generally speaking, good. Other cesses.

Prices. It is doubtful whether it is of much use to carry an enquiry into prices back too far, as few things are more liable to mislead the casual reader than the market rates of a hundred years ago. They apply these rates to the conditions of the present day and infer that the people were prosperous because the prices of the necessities of life were low, forgetting that money then was very scarce and that the people had not much to spend. Taylor states that between 1810 and 1836 the average price per maund was for best rice Re. 1—0-15½ and for the cheapest quality Re. 0-13—12½. This suggests a land flowing with milk and honey, but that the suggestion is fallacious can be gathered from the fact that in 1784, when rice was what we should now consider very cheap, *i.e.*, 17 seers to the rupee, "the distress of the inhabitants exceeded all description." The statistics published by the Government of India show the retail price of rice at Dacca since 1861. The cheapest year since that date was 1862 when 31·58 seers could be purchased for a rupee. In 1866 the Orissa famine sent the price up to 10·63 seers, but two years later it was back again to 28·86 seers. The market varied considerably from year to year and in 1869 it was up again to 17·55. In 1873, it was 23·2 and in the following year up to 12·31. Between 1878 and 1880 it averaged 12·06 seers and in the next triennium the average was as low as 23 seers. This was the last of the really cheap rice and never since then has the average price for the year fallen to 20 seers. In 1889, the price rose to 14 seers and in the quinquennium ending 1895 it averaged 13·31 seers. The famine of 1897 sent the price up to 9 6 seers, but 1899 was a year of abundant harvest and rice sold at the rate of 17·91 seers to the rupee. In 1904 rice was again cheap at 15·26 seers, but in 1906 and 1907 it was extremely dear at 8·11 and 8·06 seers to the rupee. This was due to the exceedingly unfavourable conditions prevailing in those years. In 1906, there was the highest flood on record, the railway to Goālando was breached, and the price of rice in Dacca suddenly rose from Rs. 5½ to Rs. 8 per maund, while in parts of the interior it touched Rs. 9 per maund. The restoration of communications and the importation of cheap rice from Burma sent prices down from this famine level but for some time they continued to be very high. Fairly normal conditions had, however, re-established themselves by 1910 and in January of that year common rice was selling at the rate of 13¼ seers to the rupee.

Apart from individual bad seasons several causes have contributed to send up the price of grain. The increase in population has brought the less fertile land under cultivation and the average yield per acre has decreased. The great extension of jute cultivation has not only displaced a considerable area of rice, but by putting an enormous amount of money into circulation, has increased the power of the consumer to pay, and the consumer's capacity for payment is probably a considerable factor in the local price of rice. The difference between the normal price of the present day and the normal price of a hundred years ago is principally due to the increase in the quantity of money in circulation, but though the great output of gold from South Africa during the nineties may have helped to send up the price of rice, other factors were, no doubt, contributory causes. There has been a considerable increase in the amount of rice exported from India and the raiyat now tends to sell his crops and hoard money instead of grain. But the handling of money is a thing which is not learnt in a day, and while grain cannot very easily be frittered away, money can.

Salt has been for centuries in India an article on which taxation has been regularly levied and the price of the commodity largely depends upon the rate of the tax. In the decade ending 1838 the average price was Rs. 4-15-8 per maund.* Between 1861 and 1881 the price was usually between 8½ and 9½ seers to the rupee. In 1882 on the remission of taxation it fell to 12·38 seers, but six years later when it was found necessary to raise the tax again it rose to 9·24 seers. In 1905 when the tax was again lowered it fell to 12·75 seers and further remissions brought the price in 1907 down to 16·2 seers per rupee or about half of what it was some eighty years before.

The rise in prices has naturally been accompanied by a rise in wages. In 1803, a farm labourer received from Re. 1 to Re. 1-8 a month and a cooly from 8 annas to Re. 1 and his food. By 1837 the rate of wages had risen to from Rs. 2-4 to Rs. 4 for a farm labourer and from Re. 1 to Rs. 2-4 with food for a cooly. In 1867, the daily wage of a cooly was 3 annas. Wages tend to rise with the rise in the price of food but, if the returns can be relied upon, they reflect the variations of the market much less rapidly than the grain-dealers do. In 1873, the wages of an agricultural labourer were Rs. 6 per mensem and they remained at about that figure till 1886 though the period included several years of scarcity when the price of rice was up to less than 12 and 13 seers to a rupee. In 1886 and 1889, they were returned at from Rs. 6 to Rs. 10 per mensem, and in 1893 at from Rs. 8 to Rs. 10. This was, however, a year of scarcity when rice rose to 10·24 seers to the rupee and they are said to have subsequently fallen to from Rs. 5 to Rs. 7. The high prices at the beginning of the century sent wages up again and they touched their highest level in 1905 at from Rs. 10 to Rs. 12 per mensem. Wages, however, vary considerably in different parts of the district and at different seasons of the year, and for jute weeding it is not uncommon to pay from 8 to 10 annas a day. Wages.

A large number of the houses in Dacca city are built of brick and some of those along the river bank are of considerable size. They hardly, however, comply with European standards of comfort, as the rooms though numerous are very small and dark. Dwellings.

* Topography of Dacca, p. 291.

There are also a considerable number of masonry houses in the interior, especially in the south of the district where so many families of the middle classes have their ancestral homes. Poorer houses in Dacca generally have mud walls with a roof made of kerosene oil tins beaten flat and stretched over bamboo rafters, but there are some in which the walls are made of split bamboo and the roof of thatch. The peasants' cottages in the interior have walls of split bamboo or reeds plastered with mud, roofs of thatch or corrugated iron. The centre of the ridge pole in thatched houses is very much higher than either end, as it is found that curved roofs are less likely to be injured by storms. In the flooded tracts the houses have to be raised on high mounds, and the cost of preparing the site leads to the construction of small and uncomfortable dwellings. In the north, where the demand for land is less acute and a lower plinth suffices, the cultivator plans his homestead on a more liberal scale and each steading consists of three or four cottages surrounding a small courtyard which is regularly plastered with mud and cowdung and kept scrupulously clean. In certain villages, where suitable earth is found, the walls of the houses are made of mud, and the building, especially if inhabited by a wealthy Shāhā, presents quite an imposing appearance. Good examples of this mud architecture are to be found at Murāpāra, Sābhār, Birulea, Dhāmrāi, Bhabla and Gotasia in Manohardi. The cost of preparing a cultivator's hut in the flooded tracts, including the cost of raising the plinth would be about Rs. 400, of a good steading with three or four different houses in the north of the district about Rs. 100 and of a mud house such as is to be found at Murāpāra Rs. 300.

Furniture is a commodity which has comparatively small attractions either to rich or poor. Even the wealthiest zamindārs have little furniture in the rooms appropriated for their own use and what there is, is of the simplest character. There is a wooden platform (*takta posh*) with a carpet (*satrangi*) and a few big pillars on which visitors of good position sit, with low benches and mats for humbler folk. But wealthy men also have rooms furnished in European style for the reception of European visitors.

Cultivators even when well to do have still less. A box or two to hold their clothes, a wooden stool, some mats on which they sleep on the mud floor and that is all.

The bedding of the ordinary villager consists of a patch-work quilt made of clothes too old to be any longer worn, but the well-to-do use sheets and a cotton quilt in the cold weather. All classes of the community use mosquito curtains which are generally made of cloth woven in Tippera and Noakhali. Till recently the well-to-do used ordinary European mosquito curtains, but under the influence of the Swadeshi movement, many Hindu gentlemen sacrificed their comfort to their enthusiasm and reverted to the thicker and stuffier native cloth. For cooking and eating they use brass and bell-metal pots and pans, plates and bowls of enamelled iron and cheap but ugly imported pottery. Enamelled ware is cheaper and easier to clean than brass but is denounced by advocates of Swadeshi. For lamps the cultivators use little tin pots filled with kerosene or earthenware saucers with the wick floating in the oil, but in the winter they go early to bed and are generally satisfied with the light afforded by the fire at which they cook their food.

Dress.

The most advanced section of the community appear in public either in full European dress or in trousers and the neat and decorous *chapkan*, which resembles a cassock reaching to the knee more than anything else known in western lands. But in private rich and poor alike amongst Hindus wear *dhuti*, shawl, and *puggaree*, though ready-made jackets are coming into favour even amongst the poorer classes. Muhammadans in place of the *dhuti* wear a *lungti* or petticoat of coloured cloth reaching to the ankles and a fez or cap. Well-to-do Muhammadans often spend a good deal upon their wardrobe, but fortunately the villagers have not yet become imbued with any desire to squander money on dress and an old man whose clothes would disgrace a scarecrow will sometimes admit that he has sold his jute for as much as Rs. 500. The ordinary dress of a woman, whether Hindu or Muhammadan, is the *sari*, a long piece of cloth fastened round the waist so as to form a petticoat and also a covering for the upper part of the body. It has the great advantage of being cool but at times leaves little to the imagination, and it is no matter for surprise that men should not like their womenfolk to appear too freely in public in quite such exiguous attire. The *saris* worn by ladies of the upper classes are often very beautiful garments and they also wear bodices and jackets.

Jewellery.

The jewellery worn falls into the following classes :—

Head ornaments.—*Jhapta* weight 3 tolahs; flower for the hair knot weight 2 tolahs. Forehead, *shitri* weight 1½ tolahs. Nose, *lalok* weight 1 anna; ear-rings weight 1 to 5 tolahs, necklaces weight 3 to 6 tolahs; armlets weight 3 to 5 tolahs, bracelets, anklets and waist chains.

Economic condition of the people.

It is difficult to speak with much precision with regard to the economic condition of the people. The permanent settlement allows a large margin of profit to the zamindārs, but the number of big estates is not great and some old families have been impoverished by the subdivision of their properties and by expenditure in excess even of a very considerable income. The upper middle classes are comfortably off, but the great body of persons who hold ministerial appointments have suffered severely of recent years from the high prices of food. They feel themselves compelled to keep up the outward appearances of gentility, but in many cases this can only be done at the price of abstinence from real necessaries. The trading and money-lending classes are wealthy and the district as a whole is undoubtedly a very rich one. This is shown by the fact that in 1906 when rice was selling at between four and five seers for the rupee there was never anything in the shape of famine. The cultivating classes are, as a whole, well off and would be still more prosperous had they fully learnt the art of managing money. At present a considerable portion of the golden harvest reaped from jute is frittered away in unnecessary and unproductive expenditure. Artizans, such as potters and weavers and fishermen and boatmen, are, as a rule, poorer than the class directly supported by the land.

The great majority of the cultivators are said to be in debt, the ordinary rate of interest being in the neighbourhood of Rs. 3-2-0 per cent per month. Where the demand is great and the security poorer than usual, the rates rise to 6¼ and even 12½ per cent per mensem. Small sums are often lent on the personal credit of the borrower, sometimes without any documentary evidence, but these loans are seldom repudiated. When more money is required the holding is hypothecated, though *jotes* are not usually held to be transferable without the consent of the zamindār. Cultivators seldom mortgage or sell their crops before harvest time, except in the case of jute when they occasionally take an advance on the understanding that the whole of the crop will be sold to the creditor either at current bāzār rates or at a price agreed upon beforehand.

Intelligent observers whose acquaintance with the district extends over more than a quarter of a century affirm without hesitation that the standard of comfort amongst the peasants has risen in a very noticeable manner and they are much more prosperous than they used to be. No small part too of the sense of poverty amongst the clerical classes is due to their increased desire for luxuries. Gramophones and bicycles command a large sale and the young *bhadralok* of the present day ask much more of life than did their grandfathers. There was much that was reprehensible in the *swadeshi* movement, but as far as it represented a desire to revert towards a simpler form of life, to eschew foreign luxuries which were really beyond the purses of the people and to open up means of livelihood to young men who had outgrown the profession of their fathers, it was wholly good.

CHAPTER VI.

AGRICULTURE.

GENERAL CONDITIONS.

It has already been explained that the district falls into two main divisions, the high land known as Bhowal or the Madhupur jungle and the low land that surrounds it. Along its western and south-western face the boundary of the Madhupur jungle is for the most part clearly marked and drops steeply to the alluvial flats. But on the east the slope is much more general and the level gradually falls as one proceeds from the north of the district towards Nārāyanganj so that in many places it would not be easy to lay down a fixed line and say here the high land ceases and the low land begins. Even within the limits of Bhowal it would be a mistake to suppose that there is nothing but high land for there are considerable differences of level ranging from land that is so high and dry as to be almost unfit for cultivation to land that is too low to grow even long stemmed rice. Outside the Madhupur jungle the staple crops are wet rice and jute. The whole of the surface is flooded in the rains and near the *bils* the depth of the flood is such that only *boro* or spring rice can be grown before the water rises. On the high lands in the north the staple crops are *aus* or summer rice, jute, hemp, safflower, sugarcane, tobacco, mustard, pulses and vegetables. The *baids* or stretches of lower land in the Madhupur jungle are planted out with *sail* or transplanted winter paddy, while *aman* or long stemmed winter rice is grown in the lower lands. Barley, wheat, mustard and millet are sown in the lower parts of the district during the cold weather and sugarcane is raised both in the dry and flooded tracts. The really essential factor which determines the value of any given field is not so much the soil of which it is composed but the depth of the water which stands on it in the rains and it is the height and duration of the flood even more than the local rainfall which decides whether the harvest in Dacca will be good or bad. These floods serve a double purpose for they not only supply the crop with the moisture it requires, but they restore fertility to the soil by the rich deposits of silt which they bring down.

Soils.

The soils of the district fall into three main classes—the red clay of the Madhupur jungle, the ordinary *bil* clay and the newly-formed alluvium. The red clay contains an excess of iron and lime but is deficient in silicious matter. When dry it is extremely hard and like the red clays of the Khasi Hills it becomes slippery rather than soft when exposed to rain. On the surface it has in many places been enriched by the formation of a vegetable mould. The *bil* clay is a stiff clay deposited on the bottoms and edges of *bils*. It is most common in the southern and western parts of the district where the main channel of the Ganges used to flow and has in many places been mixed with the decayed remains of aquatic plants. This clay is stiff and difficult to prepare as it cakes into large clods which resist the plough and have to be broken with the hammer. The new alluvium consists of sand and loam mixed in varying proportions The alluvium of the Meghnā where the current is less rapid has a finer texture, is richer in vegetable matter and is more retentive of moisture than the alluvium of the Ganges. These three classes of soil are styled by the cultivators *lal mati*, *maithal mati* and *dorosha mati*. *Aus* paddy and the jack fruit tree alone do really well on *lal mati* and though the villagers sow mustard. pulse, and tobacco the outturn is poor. The *bil* soil is however very rich and yields fine crops of jute and rice. A fourth term used by the peasants is *chhaiya mati*, a name which is applied to any poor class of soil.

Rainfall.

The mean rainfall at Dacca is 71·71 inches, but the variation from year to year is not infrequently considerable, and though the total rainfall of the year is seldom insufficient it is occasionally ill distributed. The character of the spring rain has a great effect upon the harvest. If it is too heavy the seed is liable to be washed away, if it is too late the seed cannot be sown in time to allow the young plants to grow high enough to overtop the floods when they come. When once the rivers have spread over the land it is they who dominate the situation much more than the local rainfall. If the water is too deep the rice is liable to be drowned outright or to be swept away or the vital force of the plant is exhausted in growing a stem long enough to keep its head above the water and there is not sufficient vitality left to form good grain in the ear. If, on the other hand, the floods drain off too rapidly, the stalk collapses from want of proper support and the ears are injured by falling in the water. In the north of the district there is, however, a considerable area of unflooded land and this requires seasonable rain throughout the summer and especially in September and October. So great, however, is the difference in the levels of the cultivated land that it is hardly possible for every part of the district to produce a bumper crop. In seasons when the highest rice fields receive sufficient moisture, the lowest lands almost of necessity receive too much, and when the flood is not too high in the south of the district the transplanted rice fields in the north have generally to go a little short.

Population supported by agriculture.

In 1901 65·3 per cent of the population were declared to be supported by agriculture which was 6 per cent less than the proportion returned for the whole of old Bengal. This is partly due to the fact that the famous Bikrampur pargana in Munshiganj is the great home of the Bengali middle class and in the densely populated Srinagar thāna no less than 53 per cent of the population were non-agriculturists. In fact the proportion of the population supported by industries, commerce and the professions is not approached by that recorded in any other district of the two Bengals. The proportion of agriculturists to the total population is highest in Bhowal and lowest in Munshiganj

The only form of irrigation which is required in the lower parts of the district are the water-lifts used in the cultivation of *boro* or spring rice. These lifts, called *dunis*, are of a very simple character and are used to raise the water from the centre of the *bil* to the fields round the edge on which the *boro* has been sown. Wells might, perhaps, be usefully employed in the north of the district, but the supply of subsoil water is not large and it is doubtful whether the cost of sinking a well would be recouped. Well irrigation is, at any rate, only practised by the up-country men who have settled down as market gardeners near the city of Dacca. Irrigation.

The staple food crop of the district is rice, which falls into three main species—*boro* or spring rice, *aus* or summer rice and *aman* or winter rice which is again subdivided into two distinct kinds—the long stemmed *aman* sown broadcast on the lower lands and the transplanted *aman* (*roa*) which is grown on the higher land in the north of the district. Under each of the main species there are, moreover, numerous varieties ripening at different seasons of the year, and there is hardly a month in which some form of rice is not coming under the sickle. Rice.

Boro paddy is grown on the sides of *bils* and streams and on the churs and along the banks of the Meghnā and to a less extent of the Padmā and the Dhaleswari. At Mirpur, a little to the west of Dacca, there is a great expanse of *boro* land near the confluence of the Turāg and Buri Ganga and much *boro* is grown along the banks of the Turāg all the way from Mirpur to Kāliākoer. As soon as the rains are over the seed is sown on a piece of soft land which has been worked into puddle by treading it up, or, in exceptional cases, by from three to five ploughings Before it is sown the seed is moistened and hung up in a damp basket in the cultivator's house till it begins to germinate. When the plants are about 9 inches high they are moved from the nursery to the field, though on the banks of the Meghnā and in other places where they are exposed to a strong tide they are often allowed to grow to double that height. The fields are as a rule not ploughed and the seedlings are simply planted in the soft mud left behind when the floods recede; but unless the plants are exposed to the action of the river tides the fields have to be irrigated by water-lifts. The seed is generally sown in November transplanted in December or January and harvested in April or May. The grain is coarse but the outturn is larger than that of the other varieties, and the cost of cultivation is less as there is as a rule no ploughing to do. There is another system of *boro* cultivation, known as Boro paddy.

lepi, which really entails the minimum of time and trouble. The seed is simply sown broadcast on soft mud flats near the big rivers and the mud is then smoothed over it, to protect it from the action of the tides. There is no ploughing, harrowing, transplanting, or weeding, simply the sowing of the seed and the reaping of the harvest. It must, however, be admitted that the sowing is a little troublesome as the mud is so soft that the cultivator has to seek a precarious footing on the trunk of a plantain tree or a couple of bamboos to prevent himself from sinking in.

Aus.

Aus paddy is grown on high land and is usually found in the more elevated parts of the Madhupur jungle and on high land near the rivers. It can, however, only be grown on land on which the depth of water does not exceed two feet at the beginning of the rains, as the crop is only from three to three and a half feet high and the stalk does not grow fast enough to keep pace with the rising of the flood. The fields on which it is grown are generally sown with pulse and mustard, and as soon as the winter crop has been carried they are ploughed and harrowed with all speed to prepare them for the *aus*. The date of sowing depends upon the time when the floods may be expected to rise in the locality. On the churs of the Meghnā the seed is sometimes sown in the middle of February while in the north of Munshīganj it is often left till two months later. As soon as the tiny shoots appear the field is harrowed with a ladder and when the plants are about six inches high the operation is repeated with a rake. Weeding is a very troublesome process and hired labour is occasionally employed. Harvesting takes place between July and September, but in the *diaras* if the rivers rise too soon the cultivators have to cut the crop while it is still green and only fit for fodder. The principal varieties of *aus* are the *puki*, *gorfa*, *surjomukhi* and *shaita*, the last, as its name suggests, being supposed to ripen in sixty days.

Aman; long stemmed aman.

Long stemmed *aman* is grown in those parts of the district where from five to fifteen feet of water accumulate during the rainy season. It possesses the power of growing to keep pace with the rising of the flood to a remarkable degree and has been known to shoot up as much as 12 inches in a day and night and to attain a total length of twenty feet, though the average length is from ten to twelve feet. This is, however, prejudicial to the proper development of the plant, and if it has had too severe a struggle to surmount the rising flood, there is not enough strength left for the proper formation of the ear. At harvest time only about a foot and a half of the stalk is cut off with the ear and the remainder is gathered into heaps and burnt upon the field. The land is then ploughed two or three times and left till the middle of March when the clods are broken with the mallet and there are one or two more ploughings and harrowings. Sowing takes place in April and after the seeds have germinated a ladder is dragged over the field. When the plants are four or five inches high the soil is loosened with a rake, and then all that remains to be done is to weed, and this is an operation which is often omitted. The principal danger to which this rice is exposed is too high and sudden a rise of water which may either drown the plants altogether or wash them bodily away. *Aus* is sometimes sown in conjunction with long stemmed *aman* in the hope that if one crop fails the other may prove successful. In these cases the sowing takes place a few weeks earlier and the *aus* is reaped towards the end of July.

Transplanted aman or sail. Transplanted *aman* is generally grown in the Madhupur jungle and in the higher land in the north-east corner of the district. In April a small plot of land is reduced by numerous ploughings to a fair tilth, and is thickly sown with seed which has been soaked in water for twelve hours and kept till it has germinated. While the seed is growing the fields are ploughed up into a rich puddle and the embankments intended to retain the water are repaired. The plants are transplanted between August and October when they are from a foot to eighteen inches high and harvested in December. Late transplantation often injures the crop as if the rain stops early it fails to obtain sufficient moisture and lazy and impecunious raiyats often allow it to be partly choked by weeds. *Sail* paddy is sometimes sown after jute or *shaita aus* has been harvested but in such cases seldom yields a good return.

Wild paddy. When the same variety of paddy is sown too often on the same field it degenerates into a plant which sheds its grains at the slightest touch. This paddy is known as *jhara* and often appears self-sown in the fields where it has to be destroyed to prevent it from choking the crop.

Accidents of cultivation. Apart from the vital question of the suitability of the supply of water, the crops are exposed to other incidents of fortune. Monkeys sometimes do much damage, specially in the *baids* of the Madhupur jungle, where wild pigs are also troublesome. In this locality in 1904 and 1905 considerable areas of rice were destroyed by a mysterious blight called *dak* which the villagers described as a vapour issuing from the ground but which appears to have been an obscure form of blight. Insects also attack the crop, the most troublesome being the small black beetle, known as the rice *hispa* (*hispa ascuesceus*). Other pests are known to the cultivators as *echi, manjura, chhagla, biccha*. A satisfactory method of dealing with these insect plagues has still to be discovered.

Wheat and barley. The area under wheat is small, the principal centres of cultivation being at Pāthargbāta at the junction of the Ichhamāti and Dhaleswari, near Roail, and near Teota. Ploughing begins as soon as the waters recede, as the seed must be sown before the middle of November if a full crop is to be secured. From four to eight ploughings and harrowings are given and weeding also is necessary. The crop is harvested towards the end of March and difficulty is sometimes experienced in threshing out the grain owing to the dampness of the atmosphere. Wheat was originally introduced from Behar and unless fresh seed is periodically obtained it rapidly deteriorates in these uncongenial surroundings. Barley is grown on the high lands fringing the Padmā, Meghnā, and Dhaleswari. Four or five ploughings are required but weeding is not necessary. The beginning of November is the proper seed time.

Millet. *China* is a fairly common crop in the Nawābganj thāna but is not extensively cultivated elsewhere. The soil most favoured is a rich clay loam which is prepared with about ten ploughings, care being taken to retain as much moisture as possible. The seed is sown in the middle of February and is harvested about the beginning of June. The crop is said to be a heating one and after it has been carried the soil is allowed to fallow. *Kaon* is also grown on rich sandy loams on high, well-drained river banks. The crop is very sensitive to standing water, and if rain water remains on the field for but twenty hours it will be lost. Sowing time extends from the beginning of February till the middle of March and the crop takes about four months to mature.

Sugarcane. Several varieties of sugarcane are raised in the district but they fall into two broad classes—*Khagri*, a cane that, like jute, will grow in standing water, and the other kinds which succumb at once to water-logging. *Khagri* is a thin hard cane and though the juice is of good quality the yield is poor. The *deshi* is thicker than *khagri* and has a soft rind; the yield of juice is poor, less than that of the *gendari*, which has long joints, a soft rind, and a large supply of sweet juice, qualities which render it much in favour as an eating cane. The *sharang* has much the same qualities but is a larger cane than the *gendari*. The *kali* or *kajli* is a hard red cane with sweet juice. Sugarcane is generally grown in small plots as, though the crop is a very paying one, it entails much labour on the cultivator. It is much in favour with up-countrymen who plant it in the environs of Dacca and on the banks of the Dolai Khāl, and it is also freely grown on the banks of the Lakshya river. The *khagri* variety is cultivated near Rāmpal and on alluvial lands which are not too deeply flooded but much of the district lies too low for the purpose. The method of cultivation varies with the soil. On the red clay near Dacca city the plough is seldom used and the soil is merely hoed up. Along the Dolai Khāl seven or eight ploughings are generally allowed, but on the alluvial flats and on the high land near the Meghnā the cane is generally planted on fields from which a crop of mustard has been taken and a smaller number of ploughings will then suffice. The plants are raised from shoots put out from the joints of the mature cane after it has been cut into suitable lengths. Near Dacca almost the whole of an old cane is used for the purpose with the exception of about two feet at the lower end but elsewhere only the tops of the canes are generally used. The shoots are planted in holes or trenches which are from one to three feet apart and have been well manured with cow-dung or, less often, oil-cake. During the rains the field is well hoed and weeded and the plants are well earthed up. While the crop is growing the withered leaves are either stripped off or are tied up round each cane and care must be taken to protect the patch from the ravages of jackals and other animals. December and January are the months in which canes intended for the sugar-mill are cut, but canes sold in the market to be eaten raw are harvested much earlier. The canes are exposed to the attacks of other pests besides wild animals. The *manjura* is an insect which eats up the central shoot and is treated with powdered turmeric and borers also damage the plant. Cracks sometimes appear and should be treated with kerosene oil, though care must be taken that no oil reaches the root In former days wooden mills were employed to crush the canes but they have been superseded by the iron Bihia mill. The juice is collected in earthen pots and is now generally boiled in large iron pans. for, though they have some drawbacks, they are free from the risk of breaking over the fire and spoiling their contents. When the *gur* has been sufficiently boiled it is transferred to a large vessel and churned to clarify it, after which it is stored in pots of convenient size.

Three varieties of mustard are raised in Dacca district—*maghi* or early mustard that is harvested in the month of Magh, white mustard, and black mustard. *Maghi* is only sown on *diarah* lands. White mustard is sometimes sown broadcast on soft land but is generally sown as a mixed crop with peas. Black mustard is the commoner variety and is grown on the high land in the north and east, generally on fields from which a crop of jute or *aus* paddy has been taken. The land receives from six to ten ploughings, the seed is sown about the middle of November and the plants pulled in February and March. The only variety of *til* raised in the district is the *kat* or white *til*. It is generally grown in conjunction with *aus* or *aman* paddy on high and well drained land, for stagnant water is most injurious to it. Linseed is also a crop of some importance. Oilseeds.

Khesari is grown on the low lands of the district and forms the principal pulse of Munshīganj. It generally follows *aus* or *aman* paddy. In the former case two or three ploughings are required but in the latter the seed is sown broadcast on the soft soil before the rice is cut. Khesari straw affords some of the best fodder available in the district. Two varieties of *maskalai* are known—common *kalai* and a *kalai* with white seeds known as *thikra*. It is grown on the alluvial flats, after the water recedes, when no ploughing is required and also on the higher ground. Of *mung* there are three varieties—*sona mung* which has golden seeds of medium size, *ghasi mung* which has seeds of grass colour and *ghora mung* which has large Pulses.

golden seeds. *Mung* is not extensively cultivated and is seldom seen except in the Mānikganj subdivision and near the old Brahmaputra. A rich sandy loam is required and it is never grown on unploughed land.

Two varieties of pea are raised in the district, the chick or small ash coloured pea and the large white pea known as the Kābuli or Patna pea. The tract of land that stretches from Sunghar on the Dhaleswari to the north of Tāngail in the Mymensingh district grows particularly good peas. The soil is a black clay and all that is required is to broadcast the seed on the soft mud when the water recedes. The plants are pulled in March and the seeds threshed out by bullocks.

Fibres.

Excellent cotton used at one time to be produced in the Dacca district. Mr. John Taylor writing in 1800 stated that a tract of land about 40 miles long by 3 miles wide in the parganas of Bikrampur, Kārtikpur, Kedirpur, and Rājānagar, produced some of the finest cotton then known. Cotton was also grown in the north of the district as the name of the Kāpāsia thāna clearly indicates. Mr. James Taylor has given a full account of the system of cotton cultivation in his Topography of Dacca (1840) which has been reproduced in Sir William Hunter's Statistical Account of the Dacca District (pp. 84 and 85), but at the present day the cotton crop is not of sufficient importance to warrant more than the most summary of notices. It is, in fact, only raised in small plots by aboriginal tribes in the forests in the north of the district, and the total area under this fibre probably does not exceed a few acres. Cotton is still found by the hillmen of Assam to be a very paying crop, so its disappearance from the district must be due to the fact that the cultivators find that they can use their time and land to better account.

Jute.

But, if cotton has disappeared, its place in the agricultural economy of the district has been more than filled by another fibre—jute. Estimates of the money worth of a crop to the actual cultivators are dangerous things, but in 1906 when the price of jute was exceptionally high the amount paid for the Dācca crop by the big jute dealers was probably over 450 lakhs of rupees.* Jute is said to have been cultivated for many years in Dacca but first came into importance as a commercial crop in 1865, when indigo was falling out of favour. According to Mr. Sen a maund of fibre could originally be bought for 8 annas,† in 1855 it was Re. 1-8 a maund and in 1868 about Rs. 2-4. Thirty years later it was only Rs. 3-8 per maund but then ensued a period of rising markets, which reached their height in 1906 when the average

* Estimated area under jute 295,000 acres, estimated yield 18 maunds of fibre an acre, average price Rs. 8-12 per maund.

† Agricultural Report of the Dacca District by A. C. Sen, Calcutta, 1885, p. 50.

price was Rs. 8-12 per maund.* Jute is, however, subject to even more marked fluctuations than other staples and over production met its usual reward, the price falling sharply in 1908. Two varieties of jute are in cultivation but both belong to the same species, *Cannabus capsularis*. One has a light green stalk and yields a large amount of fibre, the other has a red stalk and though the fibre is of good quality the yield is smaller. The following different varieties of jute are recognised in the Nārāyanganj market. Good qualities—Bhawalia, Uttoria, Belabo, all from the northern part of the district, poor qualities Bikrampuri, which loses its colour and lustre very soon and comes from Munshiganj, and Lamjaor which comes from the other side of the Meghnā.† Jute, like rice, is a very accommodating crop. It is grown on high land where it depends upon rain alone for the moisture it requires, on the *diarahs* which always retain much moisture in the soil, and on low land where it stands in three or four feet of water. It is grown all over the district but more towards the north and east than towards the south and south-west. The crop is an exhausting one and where the land is not enriched by deposits of silt the raiyats not unfrequently use manure. The cost of cultivation is high. From six to twelve ploughings are required, where the soil is stiff the clods have to be broken with the hammer, and weeding is a troublesome and essential operation. The crop, too, has to be carefully thinned out, for if too many plants are left they become sickly, while if there are too few they branch too soon and are stunted in their growth. Seed time varies with the level of the field. On low land it is scattered as early as the latter half of February to admit of the plants attaining sufficient growth before the rising of the waters. On high land it is not put in before the middle of April. When the seed has formed, which is generally about five months after sowing, the crop is ready for the sickle. The plants are cut about two inches from the ground, the tops cut off at the point where they bifurcate, and the sticks tied up in bundles. They are then placed in a heap in the water, covered with the tops and a layer of earth, and left to rot from ten days to a month. If the jute is lying in the inundated fields the fibre is stripped from each plant separately. If it has been collected in a pond or ditch a handful of plants are taken up and the stalks broken close to the lower end. The operator then removes the stalks from this portion, and wrapping the fibres round his hand drags off the outer covering of the remainder of the stalks. The fibre is then well washed, dried in the sun for two or three days, and made up into

* This is the average price shown in the official returns. Messrs. Ralli Brothers, however, state that the average price in 1906-07 was Rs. 10-2-9 per maund.

† The following classification of jute has also been received from Nārāyanganj. Good quality—Bhowal, Pubail, Mirzapuri, Lakhpuri. Medium—Lamjoari, Belalia, Baktabali, Bhabanathpuri, Ballispara. Low quality—Bhatial, Chaura, Bikrampuri.

bundles. Apart from the injury caused by insufficient or excessive rain much harm is occasionally done by the cricket *(urchenga)* which bites through the plants near the ground and the *chenga*, the caterpillar of a kind of ait worm. The commercial aspects of the jute trade is discussed further in Chapter IX. Hemp *(sanpat)* was formerly raised in considerable quantities and in 1806 the district produced 10,000 maunds of hemp fibre. At the present day little is grown for export and most of the fibre is consumed locally in the manufacture of nets. The seed is sown in autumn, generally on the banks of rivers, and the plants are gathered in February. They are then soaked and macerated for ten days till the fibre has been sufficiently softened to admit of its being gathered in bundles at the centre of the stalks. In that state it is exposed to the sun, and, when dry, is stripped off and twisted into hanks. The tops of the plant make good fodder and are sometimes pressed into a kind of hay. Rhea *(Urtica nivea)* also thrives in the district but the difficulty experienced in decorticating the fibre has been a bar to any wide extension of cultivation.

Grass and fuel crops.

Ulu grass (*Saccharum cylindricum*) and *kaola* are grown for thatch. *Ulu* grass is planted on high land which has been ploughed up into a good clayey surface. The first year's crop will not be more than 18 inches long and after it has been cut the field is burnt and covered with rice straw. *Kaola* is grown in the Madhupur jungle. *Lataghas* is grown on river churs and alluvial flats and is used for the walls of huts. A number of plants are cut into small pieces and stuck in the soft mud, and after this nothing further is required. The grass yields a crop for three successive years before the field needs to be broken up again. *Khaliya* grass is also grown on churs and submerged land and makes excellent fodder for cattle. *Dhainche* is a leguminous plant largely grown on churs and newly formed alluvial land. It grows with extraordinary rapidity and is thus useful for fuel and it serves as a hedge to prevent cattle trespass and to check the flow of water on to the fields.

Vegetables and garden crops.

Tobacco is generally grown on land from which a crop of jute has been taken but it is not often raised on a commercial scale and the requirements of the districts are to a great extent met from outside. Several varieties of the plant are recognised such as the *bilati, deshi, kattabogi, siberjata, bilaikani, bangala,* and *hingli.* When the plants have been cut they are left for three or four days on the ground and are then collected in a heap and allowed to ferment for 48 hours. After this they are spread for three days on the roof of a house and then hung up inside for a fortnight more. Three days' pressure in a weighted heap completes the process. Sweet potatoes are grown in the sandy soil along the banks of the Meghnā and the old Brahmaputra and ordinary potatoes do well though they are only grown to a very small extent. Chillies are raised in considerable quantities especially in the eastern part of the district, but the local supply has to be supplemented by imports from Chittagong and Rangoon The Dacca brinjal is of a rather unusual variety, the fruit being in the shape of a crescent about one and a half inches thick and from six to twelve inches long. Both brinjal and chillies require transplantation and careful cultivation. Ginger and turmeric are raised near Rāmpāl and in the Madhupur jungle, but the supply of the latter spice does not meet the local demand and has to be supplemented by imports from Patna, Jessore and other places. Onions are grown in the Nawābganj and Harirāmpur thānas along both sides of the Ichhāmati from Chhatea to Jhitka. The best onion fields are entirely reserved for that crop and are manured with rice straw. The plant requires careful cultivation, with plenty of ploughing, harrowing and weeding. Garlic is also a well known garden plant especially near the Ichhāmati river. Three or four varieties of *kachu* are in cultivation of which the *narikeli* is the best known variety. The *Gimi kumra* is grown as a garden crop in Munshiganj in betel gardens which have a good clayey soil. The seeds must be taken from the plant not more than a day or two before use and sown at distances of six feet apart on land which has been well ploughed and harrowed. Near Teota the *Gimi kumra* is grown as a field crop. The water-melon (*tarmuj*) is grown on the same kind of soil in much the same way but the seeds are steeped in water for two days and allowed to germinate before they are sown.

The *karola* (*Cleome pentophylla*) is grown in the Madhupur jungle especially near Mīrpur and Pubail. It is a rains crop and is sown in April and gathered from July to September. The seeds are washed before they are put in the ground and the plants are trained over bamboo platforms. Plantains (*Musa sapientum*) are grown all over the district, but near Munshīganj they are treated as a field crop and are planted in rows six or seven feet apart with ginger and turmeric in between. The plantains of Munshīganj have a great reputation in Bengal but are rather too highly scented for European taste. The principal varieties recognised are the *kabari, sabari, chinichampa, kanaibansi, amrita-bhog, martaban, agniswar,* and *bichikala.* The pan vine (*Piper betel*) is grown by Baruis and pan gardens are a conspicuous feature in the landscape seen from the Buri Ganga, and the Ichāmati. Jack fruit trees are common in the Madhupur jungle and the datepalm in the west of the district in the Mānikganj subdivision. Cocoanut palms and the areca palm are met with all over the district but the cocoanut is not very common. Pine-apples, lychees, pepayas and mangoes form the best table fruit.

Dye crops.

Indigo was at one time extensively cultivated, and in 1840 there were thirty-three factories in the district. The ruins of these buildings are still to be seen in various places, melancholy records of a vanished industry, for indigo has now entirely disappeared. Safflower was also once an important crop and in 1824 the safflower exported from the neighbourhood of Dacca was valued at about two lakhs of rupees. The industry has, however, been almost killed by aniline dyes, and the plant is seldom seen outside the Nawābganj, Mānikganj and Sābhār thānas.

Extension of cultivation.

No figures are available to show the actual extension of cultivation, but it is clear that the cultivated area must have grown with the growth of the population and outside the Madhupur jungle there is no longer any culturable land available. The churs that are thrown up in the great rivers are a fruitful source of bloody quarrels and raiyats will gladly take settlement of land that has not yet emerged above the water even in the dry season. A subdivision like Munshīganj that has a rural population approaching 2,000 to the square mile must clearly be cultivated up to the highest limit, and there can be little doubt that for many years there has been no culturable waste land in the district outside Bhowal.

This great extension of cultivation is apparently a development of British times. In 1786 the Collector, Mr. Day, stated that in his opinion there was no district in the three provinces of Bengal, Bihar and Orissa which had more waste land and jungle in it than Dacca. In 1802 the Collector estimated that one-fourth of the southern, one-eighth of the eastern, three-eighths of the western, and five-eighths of the northern division of the district was uncultivated. Dr. Taylor in 1839 estimated that one-third of the area of the district was still uncultivated and under jungle. Estimates are dangerous things, but there can be little doubt that at the time when the Hon'ble Company took over the *diwāni* there were still considerable areas of waste land lying idle in every quarter of the district, whereas at the present day there is hardly a square foot of land outside Bhowal which has not been pressed into the service of man. In Bhowal, however, the condition of affairs is rather different. The population of the district as a whole increased by 25 per cent in the twenty years ending 1901, but the population of the Kāpāsia thāna, the whole of which lies within the Madhupur jungle, increased by 46 per cent. The construction of the Dacca Mymensingh railway has helped to open up this tract and every year raiyats are moving into it from the more congested areas that surround it on all sides. The want of water is the most serious obstacle to an even more rapid enlargement of the cultivated area, for much of the land lies high and is only fit for rice cultivation in years of abundant rainfall. More, however, could probably be done for the cultivation of dry crops, for the great bulk of the inhabitants of this tract are very simple people with little initiative or enterprise. Communications still leave much to be desired, there are few schools or shops and the interior of this tract forms a pronounced contrast to the more progressive and advanced low lands which surround it.

Improved methods of cultivation.

The natives of the district are not as expert or diligent cultivators as the natives of Bihar, but so little attempt has as yet been made to introduce new varieties of crops or improved agricultural methods that it would not be fair to stigmatise them as too unenterprising or conservative. They are certainly free from that restless craving for something new which drives men into rash and ill-considered enterprises, but when once it has been proved that a crop will really pay they are ready to take it up. The cultivation of jute has extended enormously of recent years, and the iron variety of sugar-mill has ousted the less efficient country-made machine. Iron ploughs of European pattern were tried at Teota in 1885 but they proved too heavy for the small undersized bullocks and too costly for the purses of the raiyats. The zamindārs of Teota have also tried to introduce potatoes and new varieties of sugarcane, but the cultivators are still disposed to regard all innovations with indifference. In 1906 a model agricultural farm was opened a little to the north of Dacca city, and there are grounds for hoping that new agricultural methods of proved merit will not be rejected by the people. The most hopeful field for development is to be found in the high land of Bhowal and here much might still be done. Mr. Sen, who examined the agricultural resources of the district in 1889, declared that this tract was admirably adapted for the cultivation of the following crops—sugarcane, cotton, ginger, tobacco, sorghum, turmeric, plantains, rhea, mulberries and lychees. At the time of the scarcity of 1906 the District Board distributed potato seed to raiyats who would undertake to sow it, but few persons could be induced to make the experiment. An attempt was made to grow tea in Bhowal but it was abandoned in 1890. It is doubtful whether the rainfall is sufficient there to make tea a paying crop. No advantage has yet been taken of the Land Improvements Loans Act. The Agriculturists Loans Act, however, proved very useful during the periods of high prices from 1906 to 1908 and the total amount advanced in those three years was over three-quarters of a lakh.

Chemical manures and bone-meal are very seldom used but the cultivators are by no means indifferent to the advantages of manure. The straw of the long stemmed paddy is invariably burnt in the fields and cow-dung, ashes and house sweepings freely used. High land jute is always manured with cow-dung where it is available, and in Mānikganj a kind of green manure is applied by growing khesari and feeding it off the land. Fields in which plantains are grown are top-dressed with pond mud, while if onions and radishes are to be sown straw is first ploughed in. Tobacco and brinjal are not manured direct as such applications are said to spoil their flavour, but cow-dung is applied to the preceding crop of jute. Oil-cake is also used but sparingly as it is far from cheap, and it is the question of expense which militates against a more extended use of manure. The cultivators recognise that it is to their advantage to use such materials as are ready to their hand but they are not satisfied that chemical Manures.

manures are a good investment for their money. Much of the land of the district, too, has its fertility renewed by rich deposits of silt and on this account is less dependent on artificial appliances.

Cattle. The indigenous cattle are undersized and poor milkers but they are fairly hardy and do not require much fodder. Efforts have from time to time been made to improve the breed by the importation of Hissar bulls, but the lack of good grazing ground or suitable fodder crops soon produces a deterioration in their descendants. The Teota zamindārs have been more successful with Nagara bulls which are small and hardy but get offspring capable of yielding from four to seven seers of milk a day. In Dacca itself the big white Hissar bullocks are sometimes used for traction, but though there are a large number of carts in the north of the district, it is very seldom that anything more than the small country bullock is employed in them. In the lower parts of the district there is no grazing ground above water in the rains and the cattle are tethered on mounds, often up to their knees in water, and stall fed. In the Madhupur jungle there is generally grazing land available but the grass is poor. In addition to what they can pick up on the grazing grounds or the stubble of the rice fields, milch cows are fed on *dal* grass, *khalia* grass, oil-cake, bran and occasionally boiled rice. An ordinary country cow seldom gives more than two quarts of milk per diem. An up-country cow will yield as much as ten quarts but the milk is of inferior quality. The following different preparations are obtained by the Goalas from their milk. *Dadhi* is milk which has been boiled till it has lost one-fourth of its volume and has then been fermented by the admixture of a small piece of *dadhi* left over from the preceding brew. Butter is of two kinds—*nani*, which is made from fresh milk, and *makhan* which is made from *dadhi*. *Khir* is milk which is boiled and stirred till it has thickened. *Chhana*, ordinary curds, and *ghi*, clarified butter, need no explanation. A seer of milk will yield ¾ of a seer of *dadhi*, 4 chittacks of *chhana*, 3 chittacks of *khir* and one chittack of butter. Dacca cheese is prepared from buffalo milk treated with rennet and salt, but most of it is manufactured outside the district in Sylhet and Mymensingh. Buffaloes as a rule are finer animals than cattle, but they are not kept in large numbers. Sheep and goats alike are undersized, so also are the ponies bred in the district, and well-to-do people generally use Australian animals. Pack ponies are fairly common in the western part of the district, where the people have been very slow in taking to the use of bullock carts, but they are very sorry little beasts as are also the ponies driven in the *tikka gharis* of Dacca. Pigs are reared by the aboriginal tribes in the Madhupur jungle and are much in evidence round the sweepers' lines in Dacca. Elephants are kept by the wealthier zamindārs and in parts of the Madhupur jungle they afford practically the only means of locomotion by land as the beds of the streams are so soft as to be unfordable.

There is a veterinary dispensary in the city of Dacca and a travelling veterinary surgeon is also employed by the District Board. The diseases most prevalent are foot and mouth disease, rinderpest, tympanites, dysentery, diarrhoea and fever. The principal centres for the purchase and sale of indigenous cattle are the markets held at the following places:—Madhobdi in Rūpganj thāna, Bāradi in Nārāyanganj, Chalakchur in Manobardi thāna, Putia in Raipura thāna, Alī Panchdona in Keraniganj thāna, and Jhitka in Harirāmpur thāna.

CHAPTER VII.

TRADE AND INDUSTRIES.

EARLY TRADE OF DACCA.

The muslins of Bengal are mentioned as an article of commerce as early as the second or third centuries of the Christian era, with pearls, which are still found in mussels in the rivers, malabathrum and spikenard; and there can be little doubt that Dacca contributed its share to the shipments of merchandise to the West. Business no doubt was brisk in the capital of Rājā Bikramāditya but the first authentic reference to the trade of the Dacca district as distinguished from the trade of Bengal in general occurs in the sixteenth century. Ralph Fitch describes Seripur, a town about 18 miles from Sonārgāon, which was entirely washed away by the river at the beginning of the seventeenth century, as being a great mart for cotton goods, while Sonārgāon was a centre of the rice trade. Many of the residents of the latter place were reported to be very rich, but if they had wealth they were afraid to avail themselves of the advantages it confers as they still lived in huts and wore nothing but a cloth about their loins.

When Dacca became the capital of Bengal in 1608 it soon became the principal centre of trade in that locality. Tavernier who visited the place in 1666 describes it as "a city of great trade."* The "great trade" does not, however, seem to have brought to those engaged in it great wealth, or, if it did, they were not disposed to invest their profits in their houses for Tavernier has but a mean opinion of the city.

"These houses (those of the carpenters along the river bank) are properly no more than paltry huts built up with bamboos and daubed over with fat earth. Those of Dacca are not much better built. The governor's palace is a place enclosed with high walls in the midst whereof is a pitiful house built only of wood. He generally lodges in tents which he causes to be set up in the great court of that enclosure. The Hollanders finding that their goods were not safe in the ordinary houses of Dacca have built them a very fair house, and the English have another which is reasonably handsome." At that time Dacca was a mart for cotton cloths, rice, sugar, salt, betel-nut, tobacco, shell bracelets, and ornaments of coral, amber, and tortoise shell. Wheat, pulse, raw cotton and woollen cloths were imported from Upper India and silk and lac from Assam.†

---

* Tavernier's Travels in India, Part II, Bock I, p. 55.

† A Descriptive and Historical Account of the Cotton Manufacture of Dacca—London, 1851, p. 123.

Both the Dutch and English had factories in Dacca in 1666 at the time of Tavernier's visit. The total amount of the English investment was not, however, large, amounting in 1681 to only £16,000 and trade was not allowed to proceed without frequent unpleasant interruptions. *Dutch and English factories.*

In 1688, the Company's agents were confined in their factory by the Nawāb and were not released till July in the following year. During this period the Company are said to have lost Rs. 40,000 at Dacca. The factory was again closed between 1696 and 1699, but matters gradually improved and in 1724 a new factory was founded at Dacca by Mr. Stark, where business was carried on till 1756. In that year the factory was occupied by the Nawāb's troops when Calcutta was captured by Sirāj-ud-daula, but it was soon restored again to the factors and in 1757 they were lending 50 of their Buxis to the Nawāb who was threatened by one Amani Khān and had very little confidence in the bulk of his military forces.

Peace, however, did not last long and in October 1762 the factors placed the following minute on their records :—"The various rumours that prevail in the country and the general insolence of the natives with the interruption put upon trade in general giving us reason to suspect that we shall be engaged in troubles when the season shall permit of carrying on operations in the field—agreed to put factory in state of defence and get sepoys from Chittagong."* The troubles which they anticipated did not arrive in the next open season but were deferred to a more unpleasant time, for in July 1763 the factory was captured and its occupants compelled to fly from Dacca by night. The tide, however, soon turned and in the same month the factors were back again, not merely as the agents of a trading institution but as the administrators of the district, burdened with newly acquired responsibilities. Of the weight of their responsibilities they were fully conscious as they pathetically remark: "The collecting of the revenues of so large a district is an important business which we are not much acquainted with."†

The French trade with Dacca dates back to 1726 when they sent an agent to represent them, and about 1740 a factory was founded there by Messieurs Devewz and Chameuz.‡ In 1778 the English took possession of this factory, restored it in 1783, occupied it once more ten years later and restored it again at the peace of Amiens. In 1803 it was again taken and held till 1815 when it was returned to the French who finally sold it in 1830. *The French factory.*

Under the Mughal Empire establishments for the manufacture of the finest muslins for the use of the Imperial Court were maintained at Dacca, Sonārgāon and other places. The most *Trade in cloth in the days of the Mughals.*

* India Office Archives.

† India Office Archives.

‡ Account of the district of Dacca by Mr. John Taylor in a letter dated November 30th, 1800. India Office Archives.

expert weavers in the province were selected to work here; their names were registered and they were compelled to attend daily at the appointed hours, until the different tasks assigned to them were finished. "The incessant inspection of the darogahs and their people," says the Resident, "and the fear of incurring punishment for any deviation of the duty expected of them must have effectually deterred the weavers, while manufacturing the cloths, from attempting any improper practices." Guards were placed over any weaver who showed an unwillingness to work and corporal punishment was inflicted on them if they attempted to abscond. Besides being thus oppressed they were defrauded of a considerable portion of the wages allowed them by Government. Speaking of the condition of the Dacca weavers at this time the Abbé Raynal remarks (Raynal's History of the Settlements and Trade of the Europeans in the East and West Indies, Vol. II, p. 157): "It was a misfortune to them to appear too dexterous, because they were then forced to work only for the Government which paid them ill and kept them in a sort of captivity."*

In the middle of the eighteenth century the establishment of the Dacca factory consisted of two or more European factors, a considerable number of domestic and factory servants engaged on sorting, marking and packing the cloths and a company of sepoys. The goods were procured through brokers who drew money from the factory and travelled through the country making advances to the weavers. When the cloths were delivered at the factory they were classified and valued by an arbitrator and a commission on the total value varying from 8 to 4½ per cent paid to the brokers, in addition to incidental expenses incurred by them which amounted to about 71 per cent of the value of the cloths.

Decline of trade in cotton goods.

In 1747 the estimated value of the cotton goods exported from Dacca was 28½ lakhs of rupees†. During the last ten years of the eighteenth century the average annual value of the exports was about 17 lakhs, nearly two-thirds of which represented the property of private merchants. By 1813 the amount of the Company's export had fallen to the small sun of 3½ lakhs and in 1817 the factory was closed. Much has been written of the departed glories of the trade of Dacca, but it seems doubtful whether the weavers of those world-famed fabrics personally derived much benefit from the practice of their art. The Abbé Raynal draws but a dreary picture of the life of a skilled worker in the days of the Mughals, and even in 1754, many years before the manufacture of muslins was commenced in Britain, the profits of weaving had fallen very low. Mr. Hyndman writing in that year to the Chief at Dacca describes the miserable condition of the weavers at Chandpur. They were deeply indebted to *dalals* and *pāikars*, many had left their homes, those who remained had little desire

* A Descriptive and Historical Account of the Cotton Manufacture of Dacca in Bengal, London, 1851, p. 83.

† Report of Mr. John Taylor in 1800.

to work seeing that the fruit of their labours passed into the hands of others and they alleged that at the ruling prices weaving did not even afford them a living wage. In 1800, Mr. Taylor, the Resident, reported that in 1760 a weaver earned from 1 to 1½ Arcot rupees per mensem. Salt at that time was a rupee a maund, rice 2½ maunds the rupee, and oil 2½ rupees a maund so that the weavers' wages clearly only sufficed to provide him with the barest necessities of life.

British yarn was first imported into the district in 1821 and soon displaced the hand-made product. One of its chief attractions was the fact that it was uniform in size and that no difficulty was experienced in obtaining any quantity of a particular quality. This entailed an enormous saving of time and labour as it was estimated that two-thirds of the time occupied in preparing the fine muslins was spent in visiting the different marts to search for thread suited for their manufacture. There was also a very marked difference in the price. Native yarn of the same quality as the best imported yarn (No. 200) cost 13 annas per $\frac{5}{4}$ of a hank as against 3 annas, while the price of the lowest grade was 2 annas as compared with 1 anna 10 gandas.* Kasidas or embroidered cotton cloths were another article of trade which fell into disfavour. They were used as a head-dress by soldiers in the Turkish army, but on the uniform being changed the sales in Calcutta fell from Rs. 4,00,000 in 1835 to Rs. 1,00,000 in 1838.†

When the business of weaving became no longer profitable more attention was paid to the production of raw staples, an industry to which the abundance of culturable land allowed full scope. Safflower became an important product, and indigo, for which there were only two small factories in 1800, was manufactured in 33 factories in 1833, which produced 2,500 maunds of dye and distributed £30,000 amongst the cultivators.‡ At the height of the trade there were no less than 37 indigo factories in the district situated in the following places. All of them have now disappeared and crumbling ruins overgrown with trees alone remain to tell the tale of a once flourishing industry. Indigo.

List of Indigo Factories:—

Keraniganj Thāna.

Ati.

Sābhār Thāna.

Fulbaria—Duligram.

Nawābganj Thāna.

Joypāra—Galimpur.

Kāpāsia Thāna.

Shaorati—Ekdala—Burmi.

* Taylor's Topography of Dacca, p. 171.
† Taylor's Topography of Dacca, p. 308.
‡ A Descriptive and Historical Account of the Cotton Manufacture of Dacca, p. 135.

Mānikganj Thāna.

Burrarea—Tilli—Kinjinkhara—Mānikganj—Sanacel.

Ghior Thāna.

Mirzāpur—Nathpur—Pāikara—Goalkhali—Mawacel—Bogla or Khetapara.

Harirāmpur Thāna.

Azimnagar—Machain—Maloochi—Kubeerpoor.

Munshiganj Thāna.

Serajabaj—Balasia—Bhaberchar.

Srīnagar Thāna.

Char Ramanud—Deguli—Lobajang.

Rūpganj Thāna.

Rāmchandradi—Ladoorchar—Petulganj—Hoshunkata.

Rāipura Thāna.

Guzareea—Mamdabad—Burhibari—Kamalpur.

Trade in 1839. In 1839, Taylor gives the following list of exports—cloths, indigo, betel-nut, safflower, pāt, soap, skins, shell bracelets, jewellery, copper utensils, cheese and preserved fruits. The imports were mustard and til seed, sugar, lime, timber, tobacco, cotton, rubber, ivory, pepper, arsenic, wax, gold and silver, silk, wheat, shoes and blankets, chank shells, English yarn and piece-goods, earthen and glassware, needles, country drugs, spices and cutlery.

Trade at the present day. At the present day the principal imports are cotton piece-goods and yarn, salt, kerosene oil, wines, shoes and umbrellas from Calcutta, lime and coal from Assam and timber from Assam and Chittagong. Rice is also imported in large quantities, with spices, molasses, and betel-nuts. The principal article of export is jute, Nārāyanganj being the great centre of the jute trade in Bengal, collecting the fibre that comes in from the neighbouring districts of Mymensingh, Tippera, and Faridpur and pressing it into bales. There is also a brisk trade in hides and some export of pulses, betel-leaf, oilseeds and pottery.

Trade routes and centres. A considerable volume of trade is carried by the Dacca-Mymensingh railway, which brings jute down from Mymensingh and carries goods imported through Nārāyanganj to Dacca and stations further up the line, but the bulk of the commerce of the district is water borne. Communication with Calcutta is kept up by large steamers plying between Nārāyanganj and Goalando or direct to Calcutta through the Sundarbans. Other steamers serve the Meghnā and in the rains smaller vessels with light draught ply up the Buri Ganga and the Dhaleswari. But within the district the bulk of the commerce is carried by country boat. When the rivers and creeks fill these great lumbering hulks can penetrate into almost every corner collecting jute and other produce and distributing salt, oil and sometimes rice. The distribution of the purely internal trade of the local products sold at the local market is carried on through the agency of smaller boats and in Bhowal carts are employed to carry timber and other articles from the interior to the railway or the marts along the Lakshya river.

As a result all the important centres of trade are situated on the banks of navigable rivers. With the exception of Dacca and Nārayanganj none of these places give any indication of their real importance. The ordinary shop is a building of no pretensions with corrugated iron roof and walls of bamboo mats or reeds daubed with mud, standing on a mud plinth, but at the large centres there are warehouses and godowns with walls as well as roof of corrugated iron. The houses are huddled together in close proximity and the lanes connecting them are, in the rains, little better than quagmires. In the centre of the bāzār there is generally an open space covered with tumble down sheds where the local market is held. There are no outward indications of wealth and nothing to suggest that this dirty, untidy, dilapidated village has a trade worth many lakhs of rupees a year and that not a few of its inhabitants are rich men.

The original germ from which all trade springs is the bāzār, market, or *hat* held once or twice during the week to which the neighbouring villagers bring their surplus produce for sale. Round this market place a few permanent shops spring up and if the site is a convenient centre for the collection and distribution of commodities these shops increase in number. Appended to this chapter is a list of the bāzārs and of the more permanent centres of trade. Fairs are also held at various places throughout the district, generally in connection with some religious festival. The most numerously attended fair is the great bathing festival at Nāngalband which is visited by as many as 100,000 people. Great numbers of people also assemble on the occasion of the Rath Jātra at Dhāmrāi, but more trade is actually done at the Kārtik Bāruni fair which is held in the cold weather on the banks of the Dhaleswari, about a mile to the north of the Munshīganj court-house. Before the introduction of river steamers this fair was one of the principal centres of trade in the whole district but it is rapidly losing its importance.

The jute trade.

If Dacca was famous for its manufacture of one kind of fibre two hundred years ago, it is almost equally famous for its output of another kind of fibre at the present day. The trade in Dacca muslins was no doubt a valuable one, but the amount received on their account was never in any way comparable with the sums paid for the bales of jute that left the district at the beginning of the twentieth century. As there has been no survey of recent years and as there is no machinery for the record of agricultural statistics, estimates of the area under a given crop are largely guesswork. Experience has, however, shown that the guess of the Agricultural Department with regard to the jute crop of any given year is generally in fairly close agreement with the figures of the crop as subsequently ascertained, and it would thus seem that these estimates are not so very much beside the mark.

Taking these estimates then for what they are worth, it appears that the jute crop of Dacca in 1906, a year when the area under cultivation was large and the price phenomenally high, must have been worth about 465 lakhs of rupees.*

Owing to the absence of regular agricultural statistics it is difficult to measure the growth of the industry by the area under cultivation. Figures for early years are not available, but in 1891 it was calculated that the area under jute was 104,000 acres. From that date onwards there was a general tendency upwards, but the figures, as they are only estimates, would hardly repay detailed examination. The highest on record was reached in 1907 with 312,000 acres under cultivation, but this increase in production was naturally accompanied by a fall in price and in the following year the area fell to 222,800 acres. Turning to prices we reach firmer ground. From the Report on the cultivation of and trade in jute in Bengal published in 1874, it appears that between 1856 and 1872 the price per maund in September ranged between Rs. 2 and Rs. 4, the average being Rs. 2-12. In 1872 the price was Rs. 2-4 per maund, in 1897 it was Rs. 3-8, by 1903 it had risen to Rs. 5 per maund, and three years later it was Rs. 8-12.† Prices could hardly be expected to remain at this high level and in 1908 they dropped to Rs. 7-4 per maund, but by June 1911 it was up again to Rs. 8.

The system of cultivation has already been described in Chapter IV. The cultivator generally sells to a petty trader or *farriah* who goes to the villages and markets with a boat. The *farriah* again sells to a *bepari*, who either deals direct with the jute merchants at Nārāyanganj or through an *aratdār* or broker who has advanced him money. The *bepāris* are usually Muhammadans, the *aratdārs* Hindus. The jute growers do not as a rule take advances on their crop and they generally receive only about eight annas less than the amount actually paid by the Nārāyanganj merchants. Their opportunities for gauging the market are naturally not great, but they try to do the best for themselves they can and hold up their fibre if they think prices are too low and that there are chances of a rise. Jute is not as a rule assorted before it is offered for sale in Nārāyanganj, but a bundle or two is opened and if, after the price has been determined, the quality is found on weighment to be below sample the purchaser insists on a reduction. There is no regular market but *bepāris* come with their boatloads of jute to the godowns of the different firms and try to deal. The jute is taken out of the boat and a bundle opened here and there, but

* Estimated area under jute, 295,000 acres. Estimated outturn per acre, 18 maunds. Average price Rs. 8-12 per maund. Messrs. Ralli Brothers, the great exporters, give the average price as Rs. 10-2 per maund in 1906-07, but to be on the safe side the official figure which is lower has been taken.

† This is the official average price. Messrs. Ralli Brothers, who are large exporters, give the price at Nārāyanganj in 1906-07 at Rs. 10-2-9 per maund.

if the price offered does not tempt him the *bepāri* has no hesitation in loading up his boat again and will sometimes visit half a dozen different firms before finally parting with his goods. In addition to purchasing at Nārāyanganj merchants have buyers at all the important mofussil centres and from July onwards their tugs are to be seen puffing up and down the rivers towing after them six or seven huge native boats, sometimes riding light in ballast, sometimes laden with their cargoes of the fibre. The boats of the traders are to be found on every river and stream and at every market and bāzār, and the whole countryside is full of life and bustle. After Nārāyanganj and Dacca, Lohajang, Aricha and Baira are probably the most important centres of the trade in Dacca district, but there are many markets where jute is bought and sold in large quantities which will be found in the list appended to this chapter.

When the jute is purchased it is assorted in the merchants' godowns into different qualities and pressed in hydraulic presses into bales, which are as hard as blocks of stone. Cutcha bales which are less tightly pressed and weigh from $3\frac{1}{2}$—4 maunds are sent direct to Calcutta ; pucka bales which weigh 5 maunds are sent to Chittagong *viâ* Chandpur and thence to Europe. Before the construction of the railway, pucka bales used to go direct to Chittagong by sea and sea-going brigs are still to be seen in the Lakshya river. In 1910 there were 47 haling houses in the district which employed daily on the average nearly 9,300 adult labourers.

For mills in Calcutta there are generally five grades or 'marks' of jute, but Messrs. David & Co., who do a large export trade to Europe, make up their pucka bales into ten different qualities. The points of fine quality jute are strength, good colour, good gloss and reasonable length. Jute from the point of view of the baler is divided into two main classes, highland and lowland, highland being considerably the better of the two. The best known classes of jute in the Nārāyanganj market are highland—Mymensingh, Serail, Fanduk and Cachar, which does not come from Cachar but from the neighbourhood of Brāhmanbaria, and Lamjoar, or lowland jute, in which is included the produce of Munshīganj and all low-lying country.

The maund with which jute is purchased is calculated at the rate of $84\frac{10}{16}$ tolas to the seer. Another curious custom is that when the *aratdār* and the merchant's clerk are bargaining they communicate to one another the prices offered and demanded by writing them with the finger on the palm of the other man's hand underneath a cloth.

The hide trade.

Dacca is also an important centre of the hide trade and a hide merchant calculated that in 1908 hides to the value of more than 42 lakhs of rupees were exported from the district. They are despatched to Calcutta and then shipped abroad, cow-hides going as a rule to the continent, buffalo-hides to Turkey and goat skins to America. A tannery has recently been opened at Dacca and is reported to be doing well.

Weaving. In 1901, 17,044 persons in the Dacca district were returned as actual weavers. The bulk of these people were Muhammadan weavers or Jolahas, who manufacture coloured *saris*, the *lunghis* or cotton petticoats which are worn by men, *gamchas* or napkins and *chaddars* or shawls. These articles are cheap and durable and still command a ready sale, the price of a *sari* ranging from Re. 1-8 to annas 12 and of a *lunghi* from Re. 1 to annas 8. The ordinary native loom and the method of weaving have often been described, and full accounts will be found in the Monographs on the Cotton Fabrics of Assam, by Mr. Samman, and in the corresponding work, by Mr. N. N. Banarji, on the Fabrics of Bengal. Descriptions of mechanical processes of this nature when condensed are generally unintelligible and dull, and those who are really interested in the subject should refer to the work of Mr. Samman, where it is discussed with a perfect wealth of detail, and where the obscurity of mere verbal description is to some extent dispelled by photographs. Tradition has it that the most expensive Dacca muslins were so fine that they had to be woven under water. This is, in all probability, incorrect, but it is a fact that vessels of water are sometimes placed underneath the loom to produce the requisite humidity in the atmosphere. Dr. Taylor states that he saw specimens of thread spun in Dacca which was on the scale of 160 miles to a pound of the staple.*

Even at that date, however, thread had been spun in England of the fineness of 167 miles to the pound though it was not used for manufacture. Cloth of very fine texture used formerly to be woven for the use of the Imperial Court. One variety, known as *jhuma*, is mentioned in an old Tibetan work, where it is said that a licientious priestess who appeared in public clad in it, appeared to all intents and purposes to be naked.†

Abrawan, or running water, is of an equally delicate texture. It is stated that, on one occasion, the Emperor Aurangzeb rebuked his daughter for exposing the charms of her person too freely, whereupon she urged in her defence that she was wearing no less than seven suits of *abrawan*.‡ *Shuldum*, or evening dew, takes its name from the fact that it is supposed to be invisible when spread on the damp grass. Other well known kinds of muslin were *mulmul khas*, *circar ali*, *nyansuk* and *buddun khas*. The finest muslins made of recent years were called *sogawadi*, *i.e.*, "fit for presents only." They were ten yards long by one wide, they generally weighed from 6 to 7 tolas and cost from Rs. 125 to Rs. 200. Muslins such as these are now only made to order.

---

* Topography of Dacca, p. 169.

† A Descriptive and Historical Account of the Cotton Manufacture of Dacca—London, 1851, p. 43.

‡ *Ibid*, p. 44.

Dr. Taylor asserts that in the time of Jahāngīr a piece of muslin five yards in length and one in breadth could be manufactured so as to weigh less than 1,600 grains.*

It is doubtful, however, whether the prudent man can attach any importance to Jahāngīr's weights. Inaccuracies in these matters readily creep in. Indeed Mr. Banarji, writing as recently as 1898, quotes Dr. Taylor as saying that the muslin was fifteen yards long instead of five.† At any rate in 1850, a piece of muslin ten yards by one yard was manufactured so as to weigh only 8½ siccas, whereas the commercial resident in the time of Aurangzeb gives ten siccas as the weight of a piece only 35 inches longer and 3½ inches wider.‡

At the present day the following fine cloths are manufactured:—

1. *Mulmul* prepared from British yarn, size 20 yards by 1 yard, cost from Rs. 5 to Rs. 60, exported to Upper India and Nepal for wearing apparel.

2. *Saris* with borders embroidered in gold thread, size 5 to 6 yards long by 44" to 50" wide, price from Rs. 5 to Rs. 40. The best *saris* which are only prepared to order cost from Rs. 50 to Rs. 150.

3. Ordinary *saris* with coloured thread borders of the same size sell for from Rs. 2 to Rs. 15 a piece.

4. *Dhutis* with coloured and white borders 5 to 6 yards long by 44" to 50" are generally sold for Re. 1-8 to Rs. 12. A superior kind adorned with gold borders and gollabottom fetch from Rs. 5 to Rs. 10.

5. *Urnis* of different sizes 5 to 7 cubits long by 1½ to 3½ cubits wide are sold for from annas 8 to Rs. 16 a piece.

6. Handkerchiefs 18 or 24 inches square are prepared and sold per dozen Rs. 3 to Rs. 8.

Coarse cotton goods are woven to a greater or less degree in almost every part of the district. Fine muslins are prepared at Nawābpur, Tānti bāzār, and Kalta bāzār in Dacca city and in the following villages:—Dhāmrāi and Sābhār in the Sābhār thāna, Mānikganj and Baliati in the Mānikganj thāna, Abdullāpur and Muriswari in the Munshīganj thāna, Demra, Matail, and Dogair in the Keraniganj thāna and Kachpur in the Nārāyanganj thāna.

Cloths are embroidered not only with the needle, but in the loom itself, the latter process, according to Babu C. C. Mitra, being as follows:—"The weaving is begun as in the case of a piece of ordinary cloth, and a pattern of the embroidery drawn on paper is pinned beneath. As the weaving goes on the workman continually raises the paper pattern to ascertain if the woof has approached closely to where any flower or figure has to be Embroidery.

* Topography of Dacca, p. 172.

† Monograph on the Cotton Fabrics of Bengal, p. 28.

‡ Descriptive and Historical Account of the Cotton Manufactures of Dacca, p. 57.

embroidered and when the exact place is reached he takes his needle (a bamboo splinter) and as each woof thread passes through the pattern, he sews down the intersected portion of it and so continues until it is completed. When the embroidered pattern is continuous and regular as in the usual *sari* border, the weaver, if a skilful workman, usually dispenses with the aid of a paper pattern. Two persons generally work together at a piece of *jamdani*, by which a great saving is effected."

These cloths which are embroidered in the loom are known as *jamdani*. A piece of ordinary workmanship costs from Rs. 5 to Rs. 15, but as much as Rs. 400 may be asked for one in which the pattern and materials are of exceptional excellence. *Kasidas* are cloths embroidered by hand with silk or coloured cotton thread. The embroidery is very roughly done, generally by poor Muhammadan females, and the cloths are exported to Bassora, Jiddah, Constantinople and Aden where they command a fair sale. There is also a considerable production of *chikan* work or muslin embroidered with cotton, for which there is some demand in Europe. The same term is applied to a kind of network formed by breaking down the texture of the cloth with a needle and converting it into open meshes. Tailors are common in Dacca, and in 1901 3,244 persons returned themselves as working at this trade. A special branch of the art is *rafugari* or darning. An expert *rafugar* is able to extract a single thread from a piece of muslin twenty yards long and replace it with another. This operation, which is known as *chunai*, is necessary when a coarse thread is discovered after bleaching.

Gold silver smith's work.

Some idea of the wealth of the district can be gathered from the fact that at the census of 1901, 6,426 persons reported that they earned their living by working as gold and silver smiths. The methods and products of these smiths are, however, somewhat primitive. A hole in the mud floor to do duty as a furnace, an earthenware bowl, a couple of dirty fans which serve as bellows, and a small box of hammers, pincers, chisels and other tools is their stock in trade.* Rings, bracelets, ear-rings, and other articles of jewellery, are their chief production, but these as a rule are only made to order and a Dacca jeweller keeps practically nothing in stock. Stone-setting and ring-carving are moderately well done and the filigree work is fair though not comparable with that of Cuttack. Some of the costliest specimens of the jewellers' art are to be seen on the occasion of the *Janmastmi* procession, when really fine shrines of gold and silver are dragged through the city on bullock carts.

Shell carving.

Shell carving is the industry which would be most likely to catch the eye of any visitor to Dacca, not so much because of its intrinsic importance as because the Sankhāris who follow this

* The curious will find a detailed list of tools on p. 7 of Mr. Mukharji's Monograph on Gold and Silver Work in the Bengal Presidency.—Calcutta, 1905.

profession all live in one bāzār, which deserves a visit owing to the peculiar character of its architecture. The Sankhāris are a hardworking community, and whether from living so much in the shade or whether it is due to their association with their white shells their complexions are much fairer than those of the ordinary Bengali. The shells are brought from Ceylon, Bombay, and the Madras coast. The Bombay shells, *do-anna pati*, *alla-billa*, and *surti* are the most expensive of all but they are rare, the *titkāwri shankha* and *pati* which come from Ceylon are much esteemed, while the Madras shells are cheaper. The tops of the shells are knocked off with a hammer and the shells sawn into widths suitable for bangles which are then polished and carved. The Sankhāris live in well built brick houses and are an industrious and flourishing community.

Other industries.

Other industries followed in the district are—the manufacture of brass, bell-metal, and earthen utensils, of buttons, socks and banians, biscuits, combs and *churis*, ink, penholders, shoes and caps, and musical instruments. Boat-building is an important industry, budgeroes or green boats, in which well-to-do persons pursue their leisurely but comfortable journeys, being constructed at Dacca. There is a steam oil mill a little outside the town on the road to Nārāyanganj and a soap factory, a tannery, and an iron foundry in the city, in addition to the railway workshops which employ over 400 men daily.

Weights and measures.

The local measures of time are as follows :—60 *anupal* = 1 *pal* ; 60 *pal* = 1 *danda* ; 2½ *dandas* = 1 *ghanta* (hour) ; 3 *ghanta* = 1 *prahar* ; 8 *prahar* = 1 *dibas* (day and night) ; 7 days = 1 *saptaha* ; 15 days = *paksha* ; 29 – 32 days = 1 *mas* (month) ; 365 days = 1 *batshar* or year. Gold, silver, spices, medicines, thread and fine cloth are weighed by the following standard :—4 *dhan* = 1 *rati*, *kuj* or *lal* ; ½ *rati* = 1 *pi* or *poa anna* ; 6 *rati* = 1 anna ; 8 *rati* = 1 *masha* ; 16 anna = 1 *tola* or *bhari* 180 grains Troy. The weights for heavier substances are 1¼ *tola* = 1 *kachcha* ; 5 *tola* = 1 *chhatak* ; 4 *chhatak* = 1 *powa* ; 16 *chhatak* = 1 *ser* ; 5 *ser* = 1 *pasuri* ; 8 *pasuri* = 1 maund equal to 82 lbs avoirdupois. Land measures are as follows :—1 *biggat* = 9 inches ; 1 *hath* = 18 inches ; 1 *aassi* = 120 feet. A *nal* is a measure of length varying from 9¾ to 11¼ feet. A *kani* in the Munshīganj subdivision is 24 *nals* by 20 *nals*, the *nal* being usually 11¼ feet in length and the area about 1 acre 1 rood and 23 poles. Elsewhere a *kani* or *pakhi* is only 12 *nals* by 10 *nals*. A *dron* = 16 *kani* ; a *khada* = 16 *pakhi*.

List of Bāzārs in the Dacca District.

The more important permanent centres of trade are marked with an *.

There is trade everywhere in grain, salt, oil and piece-goods; the principal centres for timber, hides and jute are also indicated.

Name of Thāna.	List of Bāzārs.
1. Keraniganj.	1. Ati.
	2. Baraid*(Hides and timber)
	3. Benjara.
	4. Dargar Bāzār.
	5. Demra.
	6. Golamrājā Bāzār
	7. Hāzāribag.*
	8. Kalatia.*
	9. Kander Baonia.
	10. Kaoran.
	11. Khagail.
	12. Konda
	13. Mirpur.*
	14. Rohitpur* (timber)
	15. Zenzira* (Hides timber).
2. Nāwabganj.	1. Amtā Barrah.
	2. Bagmara.
	3. Bandura
	4. Barua Khali.
	5. Bhatigovindapur.
	6. Charkighāt.
	7. Churian.
	8. Daudpur.
	9 Debinagar.
	10. Govindapur.
	11. Joypāra
	12. Kalākopa* (timber).
	13. Kamarganj.*
	14. Karimganj.
	15. Maghla.
	16. Maksudpur.
	17. Mamudpur.
	18. Nandirbāzār.
	19. Narisha
	20. Nawābganj.
	21. Nayābāri.
	22. Palanganj.
	23. Paragaon.
	24. Sikaripāra.
3. Sābhār.	1. Ashulia.
	2. Bagdhania.
	3. Balibhadra.
	4. Bathuli.
	5. Benopur Naihati.
	6. Biralia.
	7. Dhāmrāi* (Bell, metal, utensils, cloth.)
	8. Dhantara.
3 Sābhār—*(contd.)*	9. Earpur.
	10. Fulbāria.
	11. Goalbari.
	12. Kaiakhola.
	13. Kalampur.
	14. Kāsimpur.
	15. Konda.
	16. Kushuria.
	17. Nannar.
	18. Rowilo
	19. Sābhār* (Timber).
	20. Sadullapur.
	21. Shimalia.
	22. Suapur.
4. Kāpāsia.	1. Aral.
	2. Aralia.
	3. Baghia.
	4. Bamanagar.
	5. Baraber.
	6. Barabo.
	7. Baraid.
	8. Barishabo.
	9. Barami* (Jute), cloth and timber.
	10. Bholaiganj.
	11. Chandpur.
	12. Dardaria.
	13. Durgapur.
	14. Ghorshalo.
	15. Ghorsinga.
	16. Ikaria.
	17. Kaoraid.
	18. Kāpāsie.
	19. Karihata.
	20. Lohaid.
	21. Mamradi.
	22. Maona.
	23. Nainda Sangan.
	24. Nalgown.
	25. Nonia.
	26. Nayan Bāzār.
	27. Pabur.
	28. Raied.
	29. Rājābāri.
	30. Rājendrapur.
	31. Rāniganj.
	32. Shammania.
	33. Shingna.
	34. Singri.
	35. Sripur.
	36. Taraganj.
	37. Trimshimi.
	38. Ulushara.

List of Bāzārs in the Dacca District—(contd).

Name of Thāna.	List of Bāzārs.
5. Kāliā koer.	1. Amta.
	2. Bāraibāri.
	3. Bāraipāra.
	4. Barinda.*
	5 Benoopur.
	6. Chahut.*
	7. Dhaildi.*
	8. Fulbāria.*
	9. Kalikair.*
	10. Ulatpara.
1. Mānik-ganj.	1. Atigram.
	2. Ayanapur.
	3. Bainara.
	4. Bairā *
	5. Baldhāra.
	6. Bankhuria.
	7. Barail.
	8. Barandi.
	9. Basu Bamna.
	10. Betila.*
	11. Bharalia.
	12. Chandor.
	13. Dantia.
	14 Daragrām.
	15 Dāshāra.*
	16. Dhānkora.
	17. Gorpāra.
	18. Jagir Bāzār.*
	19. Joyara.
	20. Joymantab.
	21. Kathigram.
	22. Khuberpur.
	23. Lalitganj.*
	24. Lemubarihat.
	25. Mitara.
	26. Niltia.
	27. Rājārhat* (Jute).
	28. Rājnagar.*
	29. Rāmnagar.
	30. Sanka.
	31. Shaturia* (Jute).
	32. Singair* (Jute)
	33. Surupiahat.
	34. Tilli.
2. Hirarām-pur.	1. Andhar Mānik-nagar.
	2. Azimnagar.
	3. Baburhati.
	4. Bagmara.
	5. Bāhādurpur.
	6. Balarabāzār.
	7. Barmara.
	8. Bhagabanchar *
	9. Bukihati.
	10. Dhulsuon.
	11. Gangādhardi.
2. Harirām-pur—(*contd*)	12 Jhitka* (Jute).
	13. Kājikanda.
	14. Kaltā.
	15. Kānchanpur* (Jute).
	16. Kāntapara.
	17. Kutirhat.
	18. Lakshmikul.
	19. Lesraganj* (Jute).
	20. Lolakhola.
	21. Māniknagar.
	22. Mirjanagar.
	23. Rājkhara.
	24. Rāmkrishnapur.
	25. Shutanarihat.
	26. Timanarhat.
3. Aricha...	1. Aricha* (Jute).
	2. Araibari.
	3 Jāfarganj* (Jute).
	4. Nali.
	5. Rupsha.
	6. Teota* (Jute).
	7. Uthali.
4. Ghior ...	1. Baniajuri.
	2. Barangail.
	3. Bisunpur.
	4. Butani Bāzār.
	5. Daulatpur.
	6. Deorchar.
	7. Ghior Bandar* (Jute).
	8. Jabra* (Jute).
	9. Khalsibater Bāzār.
	10. Koryonahat.
	11. Mahadebpur.
	12. Mirjapur.
	13. Pacher Kanda.
	14. Rājairhat.
	15. Sridharganj.
	16 Uttararali.
1. Munshi-ganj.	1. Aiona.
	2. Antshahi.
	3. Bajrajogini.
	4. Banisai.
	5. Baonia.
	6. Bhitikandi.
	7. Dadhiaramal Bāzār.
	8. Feringi Bāzār.
	9. Gazāria.
	10. Gubākhali.
	11. Kalmā.
	12. Kāmārkhāra.
	13. Mākkuhati.
	14. Mirkādim Kamalā-ghāt* (Kerosene oil).

List of Bāzārs in the Dacca District—(contd).

Name of Thāna.	List of Bāzārs.	Name of Thāna.	List of Bāzārs.
1. Munshiganj—(*contd.*)	15. Munshīganj. 16. Munshirhāt* 17. Rekābi Bāzār.* 18. Sekherhāt. 19. Serajābād. 20. Siddhisadhab Bāzār. 21. Sonārang. 22. Tangibāri.	4. Lohajang—(*contd.*)	12 Kharia. 13. Lohajang* (Jute). 14. Maidhyapāra. 15. Nagerhat. 16. Naopāra.* 17. Shainbati. 18. Shimalia. 19. Teotia.
2. Rājābāri	1. Bahar. 2. Balasia 3. Bara Baghadi Bāzār. 4. Bidgaon. 5. Dighirpar* (timber). 6. Hashail. 7. Hāt Karimganj *alias* Hashail hāt. 8. Rājābāri.	1. Nārāyanganj.	1. Baidyer Bāzār.* 2. Bāradi. 3. Chaitpur. 4. Fatulla. 5. Gabtali. 6. Kachpur. 7. Kalāgāchia. 8. Madanganj.* 9. Manohardi. 10. Munshirail Bāzār. 11. Nārāyanganj.* 12 Rupsi. 13. Siddirganj. 14. Uddabganj.
3. Srīnagar	1. Bagra. 2. Baraikhali. 3. Baram. 4. Bashail. 5. Bejerhati. 6. Bhagyakul* (Jute). 7. Damla. 8. Hashara. 9. Ichhāpura. 10. Kamargaon. 11. Kathiapāra. 12. Kukulia. 13. Māizpara. 14 Rājānagar. 15. Rārikhāl. 16. Serājdigha* (Jute). 17. Shinjhara. 18. Sholaghar. 19. Srinagar. 20. Taltala* (Jute). 21. Tantra.	2. Rāipura	1. Amirābād. 2. Bashgari. 3. Belābohāt. 4. Dulalkandi. 5. Govindapur. 6. Hashnābād. 7. Hatu Bhanga. 8. Jossarhāt. 9. Joynagar. 10. Kacharikandi. 11. Kuthir Bāzār. 12. Latarbo. 13. Manipurhāt. 14. Marjalhāt. 15. Nārainpur. 16. Naodia. 17. Paratali. 18. Patiahāt. 19. Rahimābād. 20. Rāipurāhāt. 21. Shibpurhāt. 22. Srirāmpurhāt. 23. Talluk Kāndi.
4. Lohajang.	1. Bejgow. 2. Bhogadia.* 3. Birijkha.* 4. Dakhin Charigow. 5. Dhankunia.* 6 Gaupara 7. Gaodia.* 8. Hailda.* 9. Kalikal. 10. Kāmārpur. 11. Kanaksār.	3. Narsingdi.	1. Gopaldi Bāzār. 2. Narsingdi Bāzār* (Jute).
		4. Manohardi.	1. Bagadi. 2. Barachapa. 3. Bhaula. 4. Bhitichinadi.

List of Bāzārs in the Dacca District —(concld).

Name of Thāna.	List of Bāzārs.
4. Manohardi—(*contd.*)	5. Biramedpur.
	6. Chalabdiar.
	7. Chandandia.
	8. Doaigaon.
	9. Elduasia.
	10. Ghashari.
	11. Ghoshgown.
	12. Gotasia.
	13. Harisangan.
	14. Hasima Syampur.
	15. Hatiardi Nama Bāzār.
	16. Hatiardi Tan Bāzār.
	17. Lakhpur* (Jute).
	18. Lohapur.
	19. Manohardi.
	20. Naraindi.
	21. Pachbabandi.
	22. Paibon.
	23. Paluly.
	24. Paradia.
	25. Paratola.
4. Manohardi—(*contd*).	26 Rampur Barapachani.
	27. Rampur Chotapachani.
	28. Ruperbandi
	29. Sarippur.
5. Rûpganj	1. Denga* (Jute).
	2. Dhandi
	3. Madhabdi.
	4. Murapāra.
	5. Pakaria.
	6. Pānchdona.
	7 Sultanshahadi.
6. Kāliganj	1. Charsindur.
	2. Ghorasal.
	3. Jamalpur.
	4. Kāliganj.*
	5. Palash.
	6. Pubail.*

List of fairs and melas held in Dacca District.

No.	Name of Mela or Fair.	Situation.	Duration of Fair.	Number of people attending.
	KERANIGANJ THĀNA.			
1	Rājarbāg Mela ...	4 miles from Railway Station.	2 days in February and April.	1,000
2	Char Raghunathpur.	½ a mile from Steamer Station.	On the last day of the month of Paush.	400
3	Jinjira Mela ...	½ a mile from Dacca Steamer Station.	1 day during Dolpûrnima in March.	700
4	Demra Mela ...	½ a mile from Shorutia Steamer Station.	2 days in June...	200
5	Malibāg Mela ...	1 mile from Railway Station.	Every Saturday and Tuesday between January 15th and February 15th.	400

List of fairs and melas held in Dacca District.—(contd).

No.	Name of Mela or Fair.	Situation.	Duration of Fair.	Number of people attending.
	KERANIGANJ THĀNA—(*contd.*)			
6	Shunna Mela ...	1 mile from Shorutia Steamer Station.	On the day of Chaitra Sankrānti.	400
7	Dhitpur Mela ...	2 miles from Shorutia Steamer Station.	Ditto ...	600
8	Nainpara Mela...	3 miles from Dacca Railway Station.	Ditto ...	500
9	Rohitpur ...	8 miles from Dacca Steamer Station.	Do. and during Rathjātra in June and in Māghipūrnima in February.	500
10	Dharma Sar ...	Ditto ...	On the last day of Sraban (July).	500
11	Subhadya ...	1 mile from Dacca Steamer Station.	In the month of Paush and Baisākh and during Rathjātra.	500
12	Kāliganj Mela ...	½ a mile from Steamer Station.	On the Dasahra day.	400
13	Snān Ghata Mela	5 miles from Tangi Railway Station.	During Baruni Snan in Chaitra.	500
14	Keraid Mela ...	13 miles from Dacca.	On the 1st day of Baisākh.	1,500
15	Konda Mela ...	2 miles from Jajira Steamer Station.	Ditto ...	400
16	Sakta Mela ...	6 miles from Dacca.	In Baisākh and Magh.	400
17	Basta Mela ...	5 miles from Dacca.	On the Chaitra Sankrānti day.	300
18	Mirpur Mala ...	7 miles from Dacca.	In the month of Baisākh.	800
19	Basila Mela ...	5 miles from Dacca.	On the Māghipūrnima day.	400

List of fairs and melas held in Dacca District—(contd.)

No.	Name of Mela or Fair.	Situation.	Duration of Fair.	Number of people attending.
	KERANIGANJ THĀNA—*(contd.)*			
20	Paina Mela ...	5 miles from Dacca.	March and April	500
21	Baghair Mela ...	4 miles from Dacca	February ...	Between 200 and 250
22	Pubdi Mela ...	5 miles from Dacca	On the occasion of Jhulan in August.	About 400
23	Digaon Mela ...	10 miles from Dacca.	1st Baisākh and on the Dasahra day.	3,000
24	Amaya Mela ...	5 miles from Tangi Railway Station.	1 day in Baisākh (April).	400
25	Harirāmpur Mela	8 miles from Dacca.	Ditto ...	400
26	Golar Tek Mela	7 miles from Dacca.	During Rath-jātra in June.	1,500
27	Alinagar Mela ...	11 miles from Dacca.	On the last day of Chaitra.	600
28	Aksail Mela ...	11 miles from Dacca.	On the last day of Paush.	400
29	Badda Mela ...	4 miles from Dacca.	On the last day of Chaitra.	4,000
30	Syampur Mela ...	1 mile from Dacca.	In April ...	1,000
31	Kadda Mela ...	5 miles from Jaydebpur Railway Station.	2 days in April during Astami and Bāruni Snān.	500
32	Jaydebpur Mela...	½ a mile east from Railway Station.	2 days in June during Rath-jātra.	800
33	Jarur Mela ...	4 miles from Railway Station.	3 days on the 1st day of Baisākh, 1st day of Paush and Chaitra Sankrānti day.	300

List of fairs and melas held in Dacca District—(contd.)

No.	Name of Mela or Fair.	Situation.	Duration of fair.	Number of people attending.
	KERANIGANJ THĀNA—*concld.*)			
34	Hardabo Baj Mela.	3 miles S.-E. from Jaydebpur Railway Station.	2 days in Chaitra Sankrānti.	300
35	Bhadam Mela ...	10 miles from Jaydebpore Railway Station.	2 days in Chaitra Sankranti and 1st day of Baisākh.	300
36	Gutia Fair ...	10 miles from Railway Station.	1 day on the last day of Jaistha (May).	400
	KĀPĀSIA.			
37	Ghalaghat Snan Fair. ...	Close to Lakhpur Steamer Station.	1 day only on three occasions in Bāruni Snān and Astami Snān and in Kartik Purnima Snān in April and November.	2,000
38	Aralia Astami Snān Mela.	20 miles from Kaoraid Railway Station.	1 day only in in April.	2,000
39	Torgao Fair ...	9 miles from Rājendrapur Railway Station.	1 day only in April.	300
40	Rājābāri Fair ..	3 miles from Rajendrapur Railway Station.	Ditto ...	300
41	Paltamara Fair...	6 miles from Jaydebpur Railway Station.	3 days in April	300
42	Aral Dakshingao.	3 miles from Lakhpur Steamer Ghat.	Ditto ..	300
43	Barmi Fair ...	2 miles from Sat Khamair Railway Station.	1 day on 1st Baisākh (April .	300
44	Chāndpur Fair...	5 miles from Lakhpur or Rāniganj Steamer Station.	Ditto ..	200
45	Augabo Fair ...	Ditto ...	Ditto ...	20

List of fairs and melas held in Dacca District—(contd.)

No	Name of Mela or Fair.	Situation.	Duration of fair.	Number of people attending.
	KĀPĀSIA—(*contd.*)			
46	Boraid Fair ...	3 miles from Lakhpur or Rāniganj Steamer Station.	1 day on 1st Baisākh (April).	200
47	Kāpāsia ...	3 miles from Rājendrapur Railway Station.	1 day on 1st Jaistha (middle of May).	200
48	Dhāmrāi Rathjātra Mela.	About 6 miles north of Sābhār Thāna.	10 days in June and July.	About 30,000
	SĀBHĀR.			
49	Roail Siv Ratri Fair.	About 4 miles west of Sābhār Thāna.	3 days in March	About 200
50	Nāngalband Fair (Astami or Brahmaputra Snān).	4 miles N.-E. of Nārāyanganj town.	4 days in April or May.	100,000
	NĀRĀYANGANJ.			
51	Panchamighat Mela.	8 miles from Nārāyanganj.	1 day only in March and in June.	Between 400 to 500.
52	Baliapara Mela...	16 miles from Nārāyanganj.	Ditto. ...	300 per day.
53	Bāradi Fair ...	1½ miles Bāradi Steamer Station.	7 days from Chaitra Sankrānti.	1,000 each day.
	RĀIPURA.			
54	Manipura Mela...	Close to the Steamer Station.	3 days from the Chaitra Sankrānti.	300
55	Marjal Mela ...	1 mile west of the Steamer Station.	Ditto ...	800
56	Saiker Char Mela	3 miles south of the Steamer Station.	7 days from the Chaitra Sankranti.	500

List of fairs and melas held in Dacca District—(contd.)

No.	Name of Mela or Fair.	Situation.	Duration of Fair.	Number of people attending.
	RĀIPURA—(*contd.*)			
57	Dulal Kauda Mela	5 miles north of the Steamer Station.	3 days from 1st Baisākh.	800
	RUPGANJ.			
58	Kanchan Mela ...	5 miles from Rupganj P. S. Steamer Station.	3 days. The Mela sits from the Lakshmipūrnima day in October.	300 every day.
59	Golekandail Mela	3 miles from Murāpāra Steamer Station.	3 days. Paush Sankrānti day in January.	500 every day.
	KĀLIGANJ.			
60	Kāliganj Fair ...	Close to the Steamer Ghat.	1 day on Paush Sankrānti.	800
61	Chin Mela at Kanadi.	Ditto ...	1st Baisakh ...	200
62	Chin Mela at Baragow.	4 miles from the Steamer Ghat.	2 days. 1st Baisākh and 1st Juistha.	1,500
63	Chin Mela at Ghorasal.	Close to the Steamer Ghat.	Ditto ...	1,500
64	Chin Mela at Paltamāra.	12 miles from the Steamer Ghat.	Ditto ...	3,000
65	Chin Mela at Shekandardi.	6 miles from the Steamer Ghat.	Ditto ...	300
	MANOHARDI.			
66	Hatirdia Fair ...	6 miles S.-W. of Lakhpur Steamer Station.	From February to middle of April.	100 per day.
	MUNSHIGANJ.			
67	Kārtik Bāruni ...	On banks of Dhaleswari near Kamalāghat Steamer Station about one mile from Munshiganj town.	6 weeks from the beginning of January.	15,000

List of fairs and melas held in Dacca District—(contd.)

No.	Name of Mela or Fair.	Situation.	Duration of Fair.	Number of people attending.
	MUNSHIGANJ—(*contd.*)			
68	Tangibāri Mela	7 miles from Kamalāghat Steamer Station.	1 day during Rathjātra in June and 1 day during Dasahra.	300
69	Rāmgopālpur Mela.	2 miles from Kamalaghat Steamer Station.	1 day during Bāruni Mela in April.	300
70	Rāmpāl Mela ...	3 miles from Kamalāghat Steamer Station.	Ditto ...	300
71	Rekabi bāzār Mela.	Close to Steamer Station.	1 day during Bāruni Mela and 1 day during Dasahra.	500
	SRINAGAR.			
72	Srinagar Fair ...	7 miles from Kadirpur Steamer Ghat.	3 days during Rathjātra in June.	4,000
73	Bagra Fair ...	1½ miles N.-W. of Kadirpur Steamer Station.	7 days during Dipanwita in October and 1 day on 1st Baisākh.	500
74	Tāltala Galaya	Close to Tāltala Steamer Station.	1 day on 1st Baisākh.	2,000
75	Syam Sidhi Galaya.	7 miles from Kadirpur Steamer Station.	1 day on 2nd Baisākh.	500
76	Bhāgyakul Galaya	2 miles from Kadirpur Steamer Station.	1 day on 1st Baisākh	500
77	Kukutia Galaya	5 miles from Tārpāsa Steamer Station.	1 day on 7th Baisākh.	200
78	Rājānagar Galaya.	5 miles from Tārpāsa Steamer Station.	1 day on 1st Baisākh.	500

List of fairs and melas held in Dacca District—(concld.)

No.	Name of Mela or Fair.	Situation.	Duration of Fair.	Number of people attending.
	SRINAGAR—(*contd.*			
79	Baraikhali Galaya.	5 miles from Tārpāsa Steamer Station.	4 days from 2nd Baisākh	700 each day.
80	Shekharnagar Galaya	Ditto ...	1 day on Chaitra Sankrânti.	400
81	Sholaghar Galaya Fair.	...	1 day on Chaitra Sankrânti.	1,000
82	Kanyamara Galaya Fair.	...	Ditto ...	900
83	Maijpāra Galaya Fair.	...	1 day on 1st Baisākh.	400
84	Serajdigha Galaya Fair.	Close to Serajdigha Steamer Station.	Ditto	1,000
85	Kola Galaya Fair	...	1 day on 2nd Baisākh.	400
86	Ichhāpura Galaya Fair.	...	2 days on 1st and 2nd Baisākh.	300 each day
	LOHAJANG			
87	Jhulan Mela at Lohajang.	½ a mile north from Tārpāsa Steamer Station.	5 days in the month of August.	2,000
88	Gaodia Mela ...	3 miles north of Tārpāsa Steamer Station.	8 days in April from the beginning of the Bengali new year.	500
89	Nagerhāt Mela...	7 miles north of Tārpāsa Steamer Station.	7 days do. ...	500
90	Kanakshar Mela	5 miles do.	3 days do. ...	400
91	Kumarbhog Goila.	2 miles N.-E. of Mowa Steamer Station.	Ditto ...	400
	MANIKGANJ.			
92	Bethila Mela ...	½ a mile from Palora Steamer Station.	7 days in November during Rastjātra.	3,000

CHAPTER VIII.

NATURAL CALAMITIES.

The most serious natural calamities to which the district is exposed arise not from a deficiency but from an excess of water. The rice crop suffers no doubt from time to time from the want of rain at due seasons, but it is flood and not drought that is really dreaded by the inhabitants of Dacca.

The famine of 1769-70.

The first scarcity on record subsequent to the assumption of the *Diwāni* by the British occurred in 1769-70. The greater part of the rice crop was destroyed by a prolonged inundation in in 1769, and this was followed by a period of intense drought in the spring of 1770. Tanks and wells dried up and fires, arising from the friction of branches and bamboos, were of constant occurrence in the jungles and the neighbourhood of villages. The poorer classes were compelled to subsist largely on aquatic plants during the ensuing rainy season and many of them perished.*

The famine of 1784.

In 1784, there was again a famine which was due to a succession of bad crops coupled with a certain lack of caution amongst the cultivators. The water subsided early in 1783 and no grain formed in the ears of rice growing on higher land. High prices were at that time ruling in other parts of India and the inhabitants of the lower tracts somewhat recklessly sold their crops, relying on the harvest of the following year. But this harvest never came, for spring, summer, and autumn rice were alike destroyed by the ever rising floods. The price of food-grains mounted with great rapidity and in June rice was selling in the Baldā Khāl pargana at 17 seers to the rupee. This according to modern standards is far from dear, but it must be borne in mind that even twenty years later the wages of a boatman varied from eight annas to one rupee four annas a month so that at those prices he would only be earning from four and a half to eleven chhataks of rice a day.† The rich attempted to lay in a stock regardless of the price and the dealers held up their supplies, opening their shops only in the middle of the night and declining to sell more than one seer at a time to any person. The distress

* Taylor's Topography, p. 299.

† Taylor's Topography of Dacca, p. 306. These wages seem extraordinarily low, but as Taylor in his table of wages expressly states that coolies and Bhandaries receive diet in addition to their wages, it seems clear that the Manjhies and boatmen about whom he makes no such statement did not. The same authority states (Topography, p. 313) that in 1808 bearers at the commercial factory were paid Rs. 2-4 per mensem and that these were considered high wages, and the average earnings of a weaver in 1839 were put at Rs. 2-8 per mensem.

lasted on into the following year and in March 1785, the Collector reported that "though the price had fallen to 25 seers to the rupee thousands of unhappy wretches are now lying on the banks of the Brahmaputra some in the agonies of death and others emaciated by famine with hardly strength to crawl along imploring assistance from passengers." * The Collector arranged for the supply of boiled rice at suitable centres and took what steps he could to save the dying, but how grave was the distress can be judged from the fact that a brisk trade arose in children, who were sold by their starving parents to low caste Portuguese and shipped by them to Calcutta.

The famine of 1787-88.

Three years later a much more serious calamity overtook the district. The rains set in early in the month of March and in the middle of July the rivers rose to an unprecedented height. Boats could sail along the streets of Dacca and in the interior the villagers were compelled to leave their huts and live on rafts or bamboo platforms. The local rice crop was destroyed and the imports from outside were insufficient to feed the starving people. In many parts of the district the price of rice rose to four seers to the rupee and crowds of starving wretches came flocking into the city. Between nine and ten thousand persons were fed daily by public charity, but it was impossible to deal with all deserving cases and numbers perished. Some parganas are said to have lost three-fourths of their population by death or emigration and the total death roll was put down at 60,000, a large proportion of a population which was estimated at that time to be considerably under a million souls. "From the enquiries instituted by this gentleman (the Collector Mr. Day) to ascertain the loss of life by this direful calamity, he calculated that 60,000 persons perished during the inundation and the subsequent famine. 'No pergunnahs suffered in so dreadful a degree,' he observes, 'as Rajanaghur and Cartickpore.' The distress and misery to which the inhabitants were reduced is painful to the feeling mind to describe. The famine raged with such violence that some thousands miserably perished, while whole families forsook their habitations to avoid the most cruel of deaths, but so reduced and emaciated were many through sickness and hunger, that they ended their days in search of sustenance; others repaired to the town of Dacca in the hopes of finding some alleviation of their distresses and to such misery and wretchedness were mothers reduced by the griping hand of hunger, that forgetting all parental affection, they offered their children for a handful of rice. Although every assistance was offered, yet the numbers that flocked into the city, precluded the possibility of affording relief to all. Many thousand unhappy wretches consequently miserably perished in the city and environs." The loss of property occasioned by this famine appears to have been very

* Collector's letter dated March 2nd, 1785.

great. The zamindars were unable to pay their revenue, and subsequently, from the loss of ryotts and cattle, their lands remained uncultivated for a considerable time. Several of the pergunnahs were deprived of three-fourths of their industrious inhabitants, who died or emigrated and the lands were in consequence soon overrun with jungle, infested with tigers and hogs."* Dacca is, however, very little exposed to risk of famine and no such calamity occurred during the eighteenth century.

But at the beginning of 1906 high prices were ruling in Eastern Bengal, and in August they suddenly rose to what in less wealthy districts would have been famine rates. On Sunday, August 12th, rice was selling in Dacca city at Rs. 5-8 per maund, five days later the nominal rate was 8 per maund and as much as Rs. 10 per maund was paid. This sudden movement was probably due to a combination of the dealers but they only anticipated a rise which soon became general throughout the province. The flood in August was exceptionally high and in the lower parts of the district it was quite impossible to open anything in the shape of relief works. Relief works were in fact not needed, for so wealthy is the district that able-bodied persons experienced little inconvenience. The pinch was felt by beggars and the poorer families of the middle class who were reluctant to disclose their necessities. About Rs. 24,000 was distributed in doles to the poor and a workshop was opened in Dacca city to give employment to poor women who had no one to support them. A poor-house was also constructed but was fortunately not required. Large quantities of Rangoon rice were imported through Chittagong and did much to relieve the pressure on the local stocks. It is a significant indication of the change in the economic conditions of the district and in the value of money, that in 1785 thousands of people lay famine-stricken and dying with rice selling at 25 seers to the rupee and that in 1906 when rice was selling at between 4 and 5 seers to the rupee there was not a single death from starvation and only the very minimum of assistance was required. **The scarcity of 1906.**

On April 7th, 1888, the city of Dacca was struck by a tornado of exceptional violence. Dr. Crombie the Civil Surgeon who contributed an interesting account of this phenomenon to the Asiatic Society of Bengal [J.A., S.B., Vol. LVII, Pt. II, No. 2, 1888], is of opinion that the tornado originally formed in the higher strata of the atmosphere and that it first struck the earth at the south-west corner of the Municipality near the *Fakirna ka masjid*. From this point it travelled in a south-easterly direction levelling huts and uprooting trees but it was not till the Lāl Bāgh was reached that it had developed sufficient strength to demolish masonry buildings. Here, however, it knocked down a portion of the police barracks, killing one constable and severely wounding twelve others. It then crossed the river unroofing the **The tornado of 1888.**

* Taylor's Topography of Dacca, p. 304.

Commissioner's launch, the *Linnet*, and tearing the police launch *Marion* from its moorings and driving it up stream to founder in deep water. On reaching the southern bank of the Buri Ganga the storm ground to pieces a masonry house that had been recently constructed by one Abdul Bepari killing its owner and severely wounding three other persons. At this moment it seemed that the city was safe and that the village of Subadiya towards which the tornado was advancing was doomed. But suddenly it changed its course, swung back at right angles across the river and burst upon the Nawāb's palace, the *Ahsun Manzil*. From there it made its way to the Sankāri Bāzār where it appears to have mounted into the air to descend again near Rājābāri in the south of the Munshīganj subdivision. Here it crashed through six or seven villages and killed from 60 to 80 persons.

In the city it completely destroyed 9 masonry buildings and injured 148 more and it wrecked 3,518 native huts and 121 boats: 118 persons were known to have been killed and 1,200 severely wounded nearly 20 of them fatally. The damage done in the city was estimated at 6¾ lakhs of rupees. In no part of its course did the breadth of its path exceed 200 paces, and the very violence of the wind in some cases served to save its victims. The house in which a member of the Nawāb's family was standing was demolished and he was pinned below a heavy beam which fell upon his shoulder. But so great was the force of the wind that the beam instead of crushing him descended slowly and gently pressed him to the ground. The back wall of the office in which Mr. Kelsall was working was blown out but the beams remained supported by the wind long enough to admit of his escape. Many of the eye-witnesses declared that the cloud accompanying the whirlwind glowed with a dull glare, but none of the killed or injured were scorched in any way.

The tornado of 1902. In April 1902 Dacca was again visited by a tornado. It appears to have formed on the south bank of the Buri Ganga river and to have travelled northwards demolishing some jute godowns and damaging the Dolaiganj railway station. North and east of Dolaiganj there is a considerable expanse of open country and the tornado was next reported at Mijmiji about five miles north of Nārāyanganj. Here it crossed the Lakshya, razed the village of Sonāchora to the ground, and travelled eastwards striking Rānighi, Barpara and Nāngalband where it finally spent itself in the open country east of the old Brahmaputra river. The path of the storm varied from 100 to 400 yards in breadth, 88 persons were killed and 238 injured. About 2,000 huts were demolished.

Earthquakes. The slight tremblings of the earth which are so common in portions of Assam are seldom felt, but from time to time the district has suffered from earthquakes some of which have been of considerable severity. The following account of early visitations is taken from Taylor's Topography of Dacca*:—"In general, the shocks are slight but at times they have been productive of great loss of life and property. The earthquake in April 1762 proved very violent at this place and along the eastern bank of the Meghnā as far as Chittagong. At Dacca the rivers and *jhils* were agitated, and rose high above their usual levels, leaving, when they receded, their banks strewed with dead fish. The shocks were accompanied by subterranean hollow noises and were so severe that a number of houses were thrown down by which 500 persons, it is said, lost their lives. In 1775 and 1812 there were severe earthquakes. In the latter year violent shocks were experienced on the 10th of April and 11th of May which injured a number of houses and several buildings in the city and at Tezgong."

The great earthquake of 1897 did much damage in the city but luckily caused comparatively little loss of life. The Shaheen Medical Hall, a temple known as the *Nazirs Math*, the Shāhbāgh, and the house occupied by Mrs. Stansbury all collapsed and five persons were killed beneath the ruins, while nine other houses including the residences of the Commissioner, the Collector, the Judge, and the Civil Surgeon were rendered uninhabitable. It was estimated roughly that the cost of repairing Government buildings throughout the district would amount to about Rs. 1,50,000.

---

* P. 18.

CHAPTER IX.

MEANS OF COMMUNICATION.

RAILWAYS

The Dacca-Mymensingh railway runs through the district from Nārāyanganj, the southern terminus on the Lakshya, to Kaoraid. There are stations at—Chāsāra on the 1st mile, Dolaiganj (8th), Dacca (10th), Kurmitola (18th), Tangi (23rd), Jaydebpur (30th), Rājendrapur (37th), Sripur (44th) and Kaoraid (52nd).

The line is a single one on the metre gauge and was constructed in 1884.

A special peculiarity of the line is the unusually loud noise produced by a train when travelling over the metals. There is some uncertainty as to the cause of these 'roaring rails,' as they are called but it is suggested that it may be due to the action of the salt carried by the monsoon winds.

The waterways.

The most important means of communication in Dacca are, however, the waterways. The Padmā and the Meghnā which bound it on the south, east and west are open to steamer traffic at all seasons of the year. Express and slow passenger steamers ply daily between Nārāyanganj and Goalando, which is connected by the Eastern Bengal State Railway with Calcutta. Heavy cargo boats with their attendant flats go either to Goalando or through the Sundarbans to Calcutta. The journey to Goalando takes about six hours by despatch steamer and about fifteen hours by the slower boats which stop at the following stations after leaving Nārāyanganj:—(1) Kamala Ghāt, (2) Shatnol, (3) Bahar, (4) Sureshur, (5) Tārpasā (Lohājang), (6) Mowāh, (7) Kadirpur (Bhāgyakūl), (8) Narisa, (9) Moynot, (10) Jelaldi, (11) Kanehanpur, (12) Goalando.

The steamers along the Meghnā call at the following stations:—(1) Baidya Bāzār, (2) Baradi, (3) Srimadi, (4) Bishnundi, (5) Bhangarchur, (6) Narsinghdi, (7) Manipura, (8) Manicknagar, (9) Rāipura, (10) Lalpur, and take about seven hours to reach Bhairab Bāzār, a great trade centre situated just on the further side of the northern boundary of the Dacca district. During the rainy season cargo boats come up to Dacca city, and a service of light steamers plies up the Buri Ganga and Dhaleswari stopping at (1) Rājphulbāri, (2) Sābhār, (3) Singair hāt, (4) Aldongganj (Byra), (5) Mattaghāt, (6) Lalitganj, (7) Darogram. All these vessels are owned and managed by the India General Steam Navigation and the River Steam Navigation Company, but there is also a line of cargo boats plying to Nārāyanganj which belong to the East Bengal River Steam Service, Limited, a company which was founded in 1907 and is managed and largely financed by the Ray family of Bhāgyakūl.

When the rivers rise the whole of the lower part of the district goes under water and not only can boats proceed in every direction but they are practically the only means of transit for men and goods. In addition to the Lakshya, which is navigable by boats drawing 5 feet of water as far as Lakhpur Chur at all seasons of the year, the following rivers and water-courses become important routes for traffic. The Ichbāmati gives access to the interior of the Bikrampur pargana and a steam launch can go from Ghior past Balla, Jhitka, Harirāmpur, Joy Krishnapur, and Sheikernagar into the Dhaleswari. The Tāltala khāl enables boats to avoid the dangerous journey down the Dhaleswari to Rājābāri, while a branch of it gives direct access to Munshīganj town. The Buri Ganga and the Dhaleswari are open to steamer traffic even in their upper reaches and large boats and steam launches can ply on the Gazikhali, the Bansi and the Turāg, even over the bar at Kāliākoer which in the dry season prevents communication between the two latter rivers. The Turāg is joined to the Balu river by the Tangikhāl, though the railway bridge at Tangi will only admit of low boats passing under it, and the Dolaikhāl connects Dacca with Demra and saves travellers down the Lakshya a journey of 25 miles past Nārāyanganj and up the Buri Ganga. This canal was deepened and improved in 1864 and tolls are levied on all boats using it at the following rates:—On all boats above 50 maunds capacity, two annas per 100 maunds tonnage. On all boats under 50 maunds of tonnage six pies. Rafts of timber, bamboo or grass not exceeding 50 feet in length and 5 feet in breadth four annas per raft.

Steam launches can get up the Balu river as far as the Kāliganj road; and the Arialkhān and the old Brahmaputra are full of water. Every one travels by water and on a market day in the flooded tracts hundreds of boats will be met coming from and going to the bāzār. The vessels are of every shape and size, ranging from the earthenware pipkins in which children paddle themselves to school or from one house to another in the village, to the huge top-heavy country boats capable of holding 1,600 maunds of jute. *Ghasi* boats about 45 feet long ply on the rivers as *gaina* boats, or boats which call for passengers at fixed stations at stated times, and the well-to-do travel in 'green boats' or house boats built on the lines of an ordinary country boat, which cost as much as Rs. 3,500.

Roads. In 1839 there were only two roads in the district, one connecting Dacca with Nārāyanganj, the other ending at Tangi bridge. These are described by Taylor as 'made roads,'* but he states that there were still remains of the old military road beyond Tangi to Toke, and he recommended that this road

* Topography of Dacca, p. 118.

should be repaired as communication between Dacca and Mymensingh was almost impracticable during the dry season. This work was subsequently undertaken but it seems to have been considered a waste of public funds by the Europeans residing in the district. Mr. Forbes, the Secretary to the Local Planters Association, writes of it as follows:—"The road is utterly useless as scarcely a human being resides in the district through which its whole length, 40 miles, stretches. It is no sooner made during the cold weather than the jungle which covers it during the rains commences to grow. When the working season again comes round, this jungle, 10 and 12 feet in height and very thick, has to be cut down. The only time I ever went along it was on a tiger hunt, and we started two tigers from the very centre of the road about four miles from Dacca."* The re-opening of this road no doubt did much to assist in the development of the jungles of Bhowal, but the construction of the railway in 1884 diverted most of the traffic from it and it is now comparatively little used. There are the ruins of a fine masonry bridge over the Tangi river which is assigned to the period of Muhammadan rule. The centre arch is said to have been blown up by the District Magistrate at the time of the Mutiny and, though another bridge was subsequently constructed by the zamindār of Jaydebpur, that too was carried away by a high flood and the river is now crossed by a ferry. The total length of the road from Dacca to Toke is 52 miles.

The next land routes to be undertaken were the road to Aricha opposite Goalando and the embanked bridle-path from Munshīganj to Srīnagar. The latter had been constructed by 1873, but in that year the former had only reached a point seven miles west of Dacca. The Aricha or Goalando road is 36 miles in length, and cost Rs. 1,23,000 to construct, exclusive of the bridge which was thrown across the Turāg at Mirpur at a cost of Rs. 1,82,000. West of the Dhaleswari a considerable length of the road is still below flood level and is only open to traffic in the dry season. The Munshīganj-Srīnagar bridle-path runs through low country and the repairs have proved a heavy charge upon the finances of the District Board. In the Bikrampur pargana every one travels by boat in the rainy season and on foot in the dry weather, and it seems doubtful whether embanked roads are worth the heavy sums they cost. They are useless in the rains, unnecessary in the dry weather, and it is only in the intermediate period when the water is rising or falling, when it is too shallow to boat and too wet to travel on foot across the plain, that they serve any useful purpose.

Between 1887—1892 when Sir Lancelot Hare was Collector of Dacca, he realised the importance of constructing feeder roads to the railway through the high land of Bhowal, and nearly

* India Office Records, Vol. 572.

64 miles of road were built for the modest sum of Rs. 80,000. Starting at the north of the district a road runs from Mathajuri eastwards to Srīpur railway station (14¼ miles). Crossing the line it reaches Gosinga on the Lakshya river (4½ miles), turns south along the Lakshya to Kāpāsia (6 miles), then west again to Mirzapur on the Turāg (14½ miles), crossing the railway at Rājendrapur station. Another road fourteen miles long runs westwards from Jaydebpur through Kāsimpur to Simulea on the Turāg; while lower down a road from Tangi crosses the Lakshya at Kāliganj (11¾ miles) by a ferry and reaches Narsingdi on the Meghnā (23¼ miles). Further south a road runs from Hājiganj opposite Nārāyanganj to Baid Bāzār on the Meghnā (7¾ miles). Unembanked roads run from a point opposite the city of Dacca to Moynot on the Padmā and from Chur Sindur through Manohardi to Chalak Chur, and an embanked path connects Munshīganj and Rājābāri. Altogether there are outside municipal areas 8½ miles of metalled road, 313 miles of unmetalled road and 419 miles of village roads.

Sir William Hunter in his Statistical Account of the Dacca District states that it was believed that there was not a single cart in the rural parts of the district. This is true of the Munshīganj subdivision and almost true of Nārāyanganj where only 47 carts were found when a census was taken in 1906. In the Sadr subdivision there were 2,758 carts, no less than 1,476 being found in the Kāpāsia thāna alone. Even in the Mānikganj subdivision there were 267.

Postal service. The district enjoys a fairly complete postal service and in 1911 there were 256 post offices of various grades.

Ferries. No less than 73 ferries are maintained by the District Board on the rivers and khāls with which the district is intersected. The right to work these ferries is sold at public auction and yields from Rs. 30,000 to Rs. 35,000 annually to the Board. The maintenance charges of the steam ferry which plies between Nārāyanganj and Munshīganj are considerable, but elsewhere the receipts are almost entirely profits. The ferry boats are as a rule open country boats which are well adapted for the conveyance of foot passengers but are not convenient means of transport for horses and carriages. Steps have been taken to provide rafts of the Assam pattern on ferries where there is much wheeled traffic.

CHAPTER X.

GENERAL ADMINISTRATION.

STAFF AND ADMINISTRATIVE SUBDIVISIONS.

The district is in charge of a Magistrate-Collector under the Commissioner of the Dacca Division. It is divided into four subdivisions, the *sadr* subdivision and those of Munshīganj, Mānikganj, and Nārāyanganj. At Dacca the Collector is assisted by a staff of Deputy Magistrates and Sub-Deputy Collectors. The sanctioned staff of Deputy Magistrates is four first class Magistrates and two Magistrates of the second or third class. Sub-Deputy Collectors are allotted to the division as a whole and are posted by the Commissioner in accordance with the requirements of the different districts. In addition to this there is a Deputy Magistrate in charge of Excise and Income-tax, and another whose special duty it is to inspect the work of the Presidents of Panchayat. Dacca is also the head-quarters of the Commissioner, of a Superintending Engineer, and an Executive Engineer, of the Deputy Inspector-General of Police, of the Eastern Bengal Range, and of the Inspector of Schools of the Dacca Division.

The Munshīganj and Mānikganj subdivisions were opened in 1845, and the Nārāyanganj sub-division in 1882. In addition to the subdivisional officer, who, in Nārāyanganj is almost invariably a European covenanted Civilian, a second Magistrate is posted to each subdivision. Criminal work is particularly heavy at Munshīganj, and a third Magistrate is often needed there. A peculiarity of the district is the close proximity in which the city of Dacca and the subdivisional towns of Nārāyanganj and Munshīganj are situated to one another. Dacca being only ten miles from Nārāyanganj and Munshīganj but six miles farther on. This mileage gives, however, a very misleading idea of the real distance between the two latter places, for the waters of the Dhaleswari and the Lakshya interpose their barrier between them and though a steam ferry plies across these rivers, the accommodation of necessity is limited and the Bikrampur pargana could not conveniently be administered from Nārāyanganj. The latter place is undoubtedly very close to Dacca but it would not be easy to administer the two subdivisions as a single unit, for they have a population of over one and three-quarter million souls, and, given a Nārāyanganj sub-division, the head-quarters could hardly be fixed at any place other than the large and thriving town from which it takes its name. Prior to 1882 the Nārāyanganj thāna was included in the Munshīganj subdivision and Rāipura and Rūpganj in the *sadr*. Had this arrangement been left unmodified the population of the Munshīganj subdivision in 1911 would have been 880,168 and of the *sadr* 1,605,422, and a town which in the busy season has probably over 30,000 inhabitants would have been left without a resident Magistrate. The subdivisions are mainly centres for the administration of criminal and civil justice as the khas mahals are small and unimportant and the functions of the Local Boards are very limited.

Early system of administration.

In 1765 when the Company assumed charge of the *diwāni* of Bengal, they found the administration of the district divided into two departments—*huzuri* or revenue, and *nizamat* or criminal, and civil justice, with this admixture of revenue, however, that the officer in-charge collected that portion of the revenue assigned to him for his own maintenance. In 1769, a European supervisor, Mr. Kelsall, was appointed to have entire control over both branches of the administration. The district budget as finally passed by the representatives of the Company was Rs. 2,08,862. This in itself is not an unreasonable figure but the greater part of this modest total was allotted to more or less unremunerative expenditure, no less than Rs. 1,20,000 being absorbed by the salaries of the Indian officials and nearly Rs. 35,000 by pensions to State prisoners, so that only Rs. 54,000, or less than a quarter of the whole, remained for the actual work of Government. The Superintendent and his establishment, which consisted of three European covenanted servants, an English writer, three sherishtidars, eleven mohurrirs, three amins, a naib, and two munshis, was to cost Rs. 36,000 per annum.* In 1,771, a covenanted Civilian was added to supervise the collection of the sayer duties as they had become the source of serious abuses and an European officer was required to attend in court when important cases were in progress.

In the following year the Collector was made President of the Civil Court, and in 1776 the Provincial Council was constituted at Dacca. The first Chief was Mr. Barwell and Messrs. Purling, Thackeray, Shakespear and Holland were the members. European assistants held the following appointment :—Treasurer, Assistant in the Revenue Department, Sub-Export Warehouse-Keeper, Secretary, Accountant, Assistant for the Records of the *Diwāni Kachari*, Assistant to the Secretary, Assistant to the Chief, Persian Translator. The control of the criminal courts and the police was still left in the hands of the Muhammadan official who had been in charge in the days of Mughal rule, and six companies of militia were raised to afford the Council the military backing it required. The country was still full of those lawless bands which sally forth to prey upon their weaker neighbours when the power of the central authority is relaxed. The rivers were infested with dacoits who had agents in the city to warn them of any measures taken for their apprehension and even a European, Captain Holland, was murdered on his journey to

* Topography of Dacca, p. 211.

Calcutta. A large band of Sannyāsis also collected in the neighbourhood of Madhupur, plundered the country and compelled the inhabitants to leave their villages and take refuge in the jungle. In 1775, the germ of the subdivisional system may be found in the appointment of naibs to decide cases at the various *Aurangs* in which weavers were concerned. In 1781, the Council was abolished. Mr. Day was appointed Magistrate and Collector and Mr. Duncanson, Judge, though he seems to have combined executive with judicial functions as he was especially entrusted with the duty of apprehending the dacoits. The functions of Magistrate and Collector were subsequently held by different persons, but in 1859 were re-united and this arrangement has continued to the present day.

Changes in district boundaries.

Considerable changes have taken place in the boundaries of the district since first it came under British rule. At the time of the Permanent Settlement of 1793 the district of Bakarganj and the greater part of the present district of Faridpur were included in the Dacca Collectorate. Independent revenue courts were erected at Faridpur in 1811 and from that year must be dated the separate existence of that district but it was long before the district of Dacca took its present form. Part of the country lying between the Padmā and the Dhaleswari was for many years included in the Collectorate of Faridpur and it was not till about 1856 that the Mānikganj subdivision and a portion of the Nawābganj thāna were restored to Dacca. Bakarganj was formed into a separate revenue unit in 1817 and even before that date enjoyed a Judge and Magistrate of its own, but the criminal jurisdiction over thāna Mulfatganj south of the Padmā river was not transferred from Dacca till 1866. The last great change to take place was the removal of Faridpur from the civil jurisdiction of the Judge at Dacca in 1875.

Apart from changes such as these which are carried out by executive order, the area of the district is subject to continual modification. The huge rivers which flow along its borders are great alike as destroyers and as builders up and from time to time large slices of land are cut off from one section of their banks and large deposits of sand and fertile silt left as accretions to another. These are changes which take place without any administrative action, but in another way also the great Padmā, or Kirtinasa, modifies the districts through which it flows. The main channel of that great flood is taken as the district boundary for want of any better, and this main channel is situated some times on one side of the huge strath, sometimes on the other. When this takes place the islands and *chars* situated in the centre of the river, in the debatable water which is in some years to the left, in some years to the right of the main current, suffer a change of jurisdiction, and are transferred to the district from which they are separated by the less formidable waste of waters. The arrangement seems a cumbrous one but it is difficult to devise another. It can hardly be laid down that a *char* that has once formed in one district shall remain permanently in that district. For the *chars* are subject to alluvion and diluvion, and it might well be that a *char* which had originally formed in Dacca might be joined by accretion to a *char* which had formed subsequent to a change in the main channel of the river and therefore in Faridpur and the same *char* would then be situated in two different districts and great confusions of jurisdiction would ensue. Neither would it be convenient to take the main bank as the boundary and to allot the whole of the river to one district. Islands would be liable to be joined by accretion to the main bank and thus to change their district and in the rains it would not be easy to administer islands separated by the whole flood of the Padmā from their parent district. The present arrangement is thus likely to continue though it means that an island may be transferred two or three times from one district to another before it suffers what is usually its last fate and is finally washed away.

Revenue. Statistics for the principal heads of revenue will be found in the Statistical Appendix. The total reuenue in 1901-02 was Rs. 22,56,694 as compared with Rs. 19,11,157 ten years before. In round figures the increase amounted to Rs. 3,45,000, of which Rs. 2,01,001 occurred under the head of excise and opium, and Rs. 67,000 under the head of other sources of revenue. As the greater part of the district is permanently settled there is little fluctuation in the land revenue, and the increase under this head was less than Rs. 4,000. In 1901-02 it was about 22 per cent of the total revenue, while the receipts from stamps were 40 per cent. Stamps and excise are the most progressive heads of revenue and the land tax tends to form a constantly diminishing proportion of the total district receipts.

Excise. Few things could be sold without paying a tax in the days of Mughal rule but, strangely enough, intoxicating drugs and liquor seem to have been exempt. The vendor of such harmless things as milk, fish, vegetables or firewood had to pay his quota to the State, but if he wished to deal in ganja or country spirit he escaped scot-free. Liquor is, of course, forbidden to the followers of the Prophet and possibly the Muhammadan governors were influenced by scruples similar to those which affect that section of the English people which is opposed to anything in the form of State regulation of vice. But the English were not oppressed by any quasi-religious delusions in the matter, and as early as 1789 the right to distil liquor in the city was let out for Rs. 2,100. Taxation was only the preliminary to regulation and in 1790 the Collector, Mr. Douglas, submitted his proposals for the better management of the liquor trade. Briefly these were (1) to compel all stills to be of a uniform size, (2) to require distillers and vendors to take out licenses, the fee for the same being Rs. 10, (3) to compel the distiller to register the number of stills employed and to report any variation in this number, (4) that a tax of six *pans* per mensem should be levied on each still, (5) that a distiller who wished to dispose of liquor by retail vend should only be allowed to do so in a shop distinct and separate from his distillery, (6) that the distiller should submit accounts showing the amount of liquor distilled and the vendors to whom sold, (7) that the retailer should pay to Government a duty equivalent to 5 per cent of the sum paid by him to the distiller, (8) that the liquor shops should be closed at 10 p.m., that no gambling should be permitted and that, if Government would go so far, consumption on the premises should be prohibited.* It is difficult to believe that the vice of drinking was not to some extent checked and restricted by these regulations. In 1793, a duty of Rs. 2-4 per maund was imposed on all ganja imported into the city and a duty varying from two annas to one rupee per month was levied on the retail vendors. In 1795, the products of opium were taxed and in 1796 opium itself. The excise revenue, which in 1789 was only Rs. 2,100, had risen in 1837 to Rs. 40,765.

The expansion in the excise revenue has been steady, but the native of Eastern Bengal does not readily waste his money on these somewhat deleterious articles and the revenue raised in the district from excise during the year 1909-10 was less than 2 annas 8 pie per head of the population. In 1865-66 the excise revenue was Rs. 1,21,207, in 1892-93 it was Rs. 2,45,592 and in 1909-10 it was Rs. 4,51,070. In that year hemp drugs yielded over 48 per cent, country spirit over 40 per cent, and opium over 10 per cent of the total.

Country spirit used formerly to be manufactured on the out-still system, the right of manufacture and vend at a particular spot being put up to auction. In 1890, the central distillery system was introduced and approved persons are now allowed to erect stills and manufacture liquor in the central distillery at Dacca. The distillers erect their own stills, provide their own raw materials and conduct the whole process of distillation, but the distillery is under the charge of a Superintendent who is a member of the Excise Department. Duty which is levied at the rate of Rs. 4 per London proof gallon is paid when the liquor is removed from bond, and there are bonded warehouses not only at the distillery itself but at Munshīganj and Mānikganj.

Retail sale is carried on at duly licensed shops of which in 1909-10 there were 59. The right of vend at these shops is put up every year to auction. Liquor is generally sold 25 per cent under proof at from Re. 1-4 to Re. 1-12 a quart and is said to be of good quality. Persons under the influence of liquor are not often to be seen in streets or public places, but brawls and drunken quarrels sometimes occur in the brothels of the city.

---

* Collector's Letter dated May 22nd, 1790.

Licenses are issued for the wholesale and retail sale of foreign liquor, the former at a fixed fee, the latter at a price determined by public aution. Auction has not, however, invariably proved a satisfactory method of disposing of these licenses, and it is now proposed to settle the shops at fixed fees with vendors of approved character. The only places outside the towns of Dacca and Nārāyanganj where foreign liquor can be obtained are Munshīganj, Mānikganj, Jaydebpur and Lohajang.

Most of the juice drawn from the date-palm is converted into *gur* and no attempt is made to impose a tree tax, though licenses have to be taken out for the sale of the juice as a beverage, whether it is fresh or fermented. These *tari* licenses are issued at the rate of Rs. 5 for fresh and Rs. 43 for fermented *tari*, but few are taken out except in the towns of Nārāyanganj and Dacca.

Licenses for the brewing of rice beer for home consumption are issued at the rate of Re. 1-12 per house. These licenses are issued for the most part to aboriginal tribes inhabiting the jungles in the north of the district but they bring in little revenue.

Ganja is imported by wholesale dealers under bond who issue it to the retail vendor. The latter sells it at a licensed shop which he has bought at public auction. In 1909-10 there were 74 such shops in the district. Opium is issued from the treasury and sub-treasuries to retail vendors, of whom there were 29 in 1909-10. These persons pay Rs. 30 per *seer* for the drug and retail it at Rs. 50 per *seer*, but in 1909-10 they had to pay Rs. 18,000 as license fees. For the management of the excise revenue the Collector is assisted by a special Excise Deputy Collector and the following staff, 2 Deputy Inspectors, 4 Sub-Inspectors, 7 clerks, 1 jamadar and 23 peons. Country spirit, opium and ganja are generally all sold at the same shop which is regularly inspected and is free from any nuisance or impropriety. Drunkenness, at any rate in public, is rare, and breaches of the excise laws or public decency are not common.

Stamps. Stamps are the one head of revenue in which the district shows a steady and very great increase. In 1836-37 the receipts from stamps amounted to Rs. 83,265, in 1865-66 they were Rs. 2,15,536, by 1892-93 they had risen to Rs. 7,14,428 and in 1907-08 they were Rs. 11,72,411 of which Rs. 8,19,846 were received for judicial and the balance for non-judicial stamps. Growth of population, advance in material prosperity, increase in business transactions and increased resort to the courts in preference to private settlement of cases and village arbitration are assigned as the main reasons for the great increase in the judicial stamp revenue.

Cesses. Roads and public works cesses are levied at the usual rates of one anna in the rupee. A revaluation of the district was carried out in 1907-08, and it was ascertained that there were 19,471 estates with 147,886 tenures. The gross rental of the district was Rs. 41,36,674 as compared with Rs. 22,49,564 in 1872 when it was first valued for cess purposes.

Income-tax. The Excise Deputy Collector is in charge of income-tax and has an Assessor working under him. Assessments over Rs. 10,000 are made by the Collector, and appeals lie direct from the Excise Deputy Collector to the Commissioner. The conversion of Dacca into the capital of a province led to a great increase in the receipts under this head.

Registration. In 1910 there were 18 Registration Offices in the district. Registration is apparently growing in popularity and the volume of business has largely increased of recent years. The great bulk of the documents registered are mortgages and sale of movable property. Statistical details will be found in the Statistical Appendix. It was originally the practice to pay the rural sub-registrars by commission and to leave them to make arrangements for their offices. The sub-registrars have now become salaried officials, and as many of the existing offices are ramshackle untidy buildings, arrangements are being made to replace them by suitable structures erected by Government.

Civil justice. Litigation in Dacca is very heavy and the staff employed is proportionately large. In 1909 in addition to the District Judge there were three subordinate judges, one small cause Court judge, with powers of a subordinate judge, and 17 munsifs. An additional judge who has been posted to Dacca, Sylhet and Tippera also sits in Dacca for about four months in the year. Dacca is, of course, the centre of the civil administration but there are munsifs stationed at each of the subdivisional head-quarters. Some idea of the volume of work can be gathered from the fact that in 1906 43,056 original civil cases and 1,051 appeals were decided, but for further statistical information reference should be made to the Statistical Appendix. The great majority of the civil suits are for arrears of rent or mortgage suits and the value as a rule is small.

Criminal justice. The District Judge also acts as Sessions Judge and there were in the district in 1910 18 stipendiary and 33 honorary magistrates. There are usually three stipendiary magistrates at Munshīganj and two both at Nārāyanganj and Mānikganj. The remainder were stationed at Dacca itself but many of them are junior officers under training or, though members of the provincial service, employed for the most part on executive and not judicial work. There are single sitting honorary magistrates at Dacca and each of the subdivisional head-quarters, at Balla and at Teota in Mānikganj, and at Srīnagar in Munshīganj. There are benches of Magistrates at Dacca, Mānikganj, Munshīganj, Teota and Srīnagar. Honorary Magistrates dispose of a considerable number of petty cases but they are very apt to be dilatory in their procedure and it is doubtful whether they are popular with the people.

Crime. As in the rest of Eastern Bengal serious crime is by no means uncommon. This is the result partly of the character of the people themselves, partly of the conditions under which they live; more perhaps of the latter, as character is largely dependant on environment. For centuries the hand of government has been weaker in Eastern Bengal than it has been in other parts of India. In the days of Muhammadan rule it was a frontier province and exposed to the raids of Maghs, Arakanese and Ahoms. It was situated far from the seat of central government and the rulers of Eastern Bengal not infrequently repudiated their allegiance and set up as independent chieftains. These two facts in themselves tended to creat a feeling of instability in the minds of the inhabitants and an indifference, bred of long usage, to turmoil and confusion. But even when the government is firmly established administration in these water districts must of necessity be less efficient than in drier country. Elsewhere it is not so easy for a person who is wanted by the authorities to abscond. A man who travels by land is likely to be seen by villagers who live along the route he takes, and if he wishes to carry property with him he is tied to a few high roads and to a slowly moving cart. But in the flooded tracts a person who is wanted by the police can at a moment's notice disappear. He has only to step into a boat with his belongings and in five minutes he is swallowed up into that waste of waters, leaving no tracks behind him, no traces of his movements, for there will be nothing in his little craft to attract the attention of those who pass him on his way. Or if the criminal is well-to-do and the police officer is venal he has merely to offer him a bribe to say that the man is missing, and the policeman can return assured that it will be quite impossible to test the accuracy of his statement. On land it is not so easy to escape from justice, the criminal can be followed and tracked down, but amidst these gigantic rivers, with their network of minor channels and huge swamps, he vanishes from mortal ken and none, even if they wished to do so, can say where he is gone. Added to this the district and local units of administration have always been too large for efficient management and control. The population was no doubt originally turbulent and for centuries it has lived under conditions in which Government was not sufficiently strong to compel general obedience to the law and thus create a more pacific and law-abiding disposition.

There is another factor which has a prejudicial effect upon the character of the people. Any dispute with regard to land is always in agricultural communities attended with exceptional bitterness and violence. Disputes as to land titles are the bitterest of all and there are two causes which tend to make such disputes exceedingly common in East Bengal. The minute subdivision of estates under the Hindu joint family system and the absence of a reliable survey promotes the growth of boundary disputes even where the land is a fixed factor in the case. But in the neighbourhood of the great rivers the matter is much aggravated. Islands are formed and there is often reasonable doubt as to the particular estate within whose boundaries they have arisen. The disputing parties generally endeavour to take forcible possession and bloody fights from time to time occur. The relations between one co-sharer and another and between landlord and tenant have for many years been vague and indeterminate. A powerful and ambitious co-sharer would often attempt to seize and take under his immediate control a larger share of the joint property than was his by right, and landlords would attempt to extort from their tenants more than the law allowed. At times, too, tenants would combine to resist demands which were not unreasonable or to set up claims opposed to equity and right. Sometimes these disputes would be fought out in the law courts but not infrequently they would be settled with the bludgeon of the lathial or the sharp fishing spear of the raiyat. These are the bigger cases where landlord fights direct with landlord or with tenant but smaller frays occur between contending tenants. At the present day when there is a question of title in dispute the rival landlords both grant leases for the same plot of land to different men. Both then attempt to plough it, each relying on a *primâ facie* title, and not unfrequently, the soil is fertilised with the life-blood of the weaker. In conditions such as these human life has lost much of its sanctity and value.

Police. For the purposes of police protection the district is divided into the following thānas and independent outposts:—*Sadr* subdivision—Dacca city (Kotwali), Keraniganj. Kāpāsia, Sābhār, Kāliākoer and Nawābganj; Nārāyanganj subdivision—Nārāyanganj, Rūpganj, Rāipura and Manohardi; Munshīganj subdivision—Munshīganj, Srīnagar, Rājābāri and Lohajang; Mānikganj subdivision—Mānikganj, Sealo Aricha, Ghior, and Harirāmpur. In 1910 the sanctioned force consisted of two Superintendents, (one temporary) one Assistant Superintendent, two Deputy Superintendents, 7 Inspectors, 69 Sub-Inspectors, 67 Head Constables, and 724 Constables. There was one police constable to every 3·1 square miles of area and to every 3,393 persons in the district. The force has been largely strengthened since the creation of the new province but work continues to be heavy. In 1910 there were 102 cognizable cases under investigation for every Sub-Inspector employed on the prevention and detection of crime. The police are further supported by the village chaukidars of whom in 1910 there were 4,208. But these men are poor and stupid and in many cases old, and they cannot be regarded as in any way an efficient force. In 1905 the experiment was tried of requiring the chaukidar to report crime not to the thāna but to the President of his Union, but in practice it was found to be so unsatisfactory that it had to be abandoned.

Dacca is the head-quarters of a military police battalion with a total strength of 784 officers and men. Strong detachments from this battalion are however stationed at Bakarganj, Silchar and in the Garo Hills.

There is an interesting letter in the records of the Magistracy describing the arrangements made in 1814 for watch and ward in the city. In addition to the regular police the Magistrate recruited a force of 759 chaukidars who were paid by a levy of about two annas per house per mensem. He very properly considered that a newly raised body of men composed of such materials as this suddenly let loose upon the community might be productive of greater evils than those it was intended to redress unless under the guidance of a system of vigilant inspection and control. "For between a spirit of activity and inquiry so ardent as to be absolutely irritating to the people and a degree of apathy and indifference so extreme as to render the establishment altogether nugatory, it is no easy matter for persons of this class to discriminate."

The Magistrate accordingly appointed daffadars and divided the chaukidars into three sections. One section was stationed as fixed guards at the various outlets or passes generally termed *ghats* or *nakas*. These men remained on duty all night. Of the other two sections one patrolled at the same time as the 'zamadar' but in the opposite direction, the other at the same time as the thānadār. Thus about 500 chaukidars were on duty the whole night through. It is no matter for surprise that with this large force continually on its rounds at night the professional burglar was not encouraged to pursue his trade. The Magistrate also seems to have considered that the arrangement had the advantage of providing comfortably for potential malefactors, as he assumes that many of his chaukidars were "either formerly rogues, or maintained a precarious livelihood by that mixture of alternate labour, indolence and dishonesty so common among the lower class of natives."

There must have been a jail of considerable size at Dacca even in the days of Muhammadan rule, and in 1775 there were 110 prisoners, of whom 87 were dacoits, 15 were confined for murder and 8 for theft. Of the above number 95 were at work on the road and in irons, whose guilt had never been established before a court of judicature and many of them had been so circumstanced for nine years.* The supervision exercised over the extra-mural labour was, however, very lax, and in 1811 the Magistrate reported that he had seen a gang of prisoners in chains looting a *mudi's* shop before his very eyes and that he had previously received complaints of similar occurrences. Matters had doubtless improved by 1824 when Bishop Heber visited Dacca for he describes the jail as being very well arranged with roomy wards and dry and airy apartments.† In 1837 the criminal jail had accommodation for 800 prisoners and a daily average population of 526. At the present day the jail premises cover an area of nearly 30 acres. They are enclosed by a high brick wall within which stand the sleeping wards, working sheds, hospitals and offices. Jails.

* Topography of Dacca, p. 217.
† Heber's Journals, Vol. 1, p. 152.

The wards are two or three stories high and are lofty, cool, and well ventilated, they provide accommodation for 1,171 male and 17 female prisoners.

More than half the total number of prisoners are employed on manufactures which include printing, weaving, tailoring, carpentry, canework, wheat-grinding and oil-pressing, and the manufacture of carpets. The total cost of the jail at present stands in the books of the P. W. D. at Rs. 4,84,000. It is in charge of a whole time officer of the Indian Medical Service.

At Nārāyanganj and Mānikganj there are subsidiary jails, built of brick, which can accommodate 35 and 22 prisoners respectively. The jail at Nārāyanganj was built in 1900 at a cost of Rs. 14,500 and the jail at Mānikganj in 1891 at a cost of Rs. 13,800. The Munshīganj jail is situated in a corner of the old Muhammadan fort and is built of bamboo and thatch ; it can accommodate 16 prisoners and as Munshīganj is a criminal subdivision in which there are often a large number of under-trial prisoners in confinement the jail is not infrequently overcrowded. Only prisoners with sentences of 14 days or less are kept at these jails convicts with longer terms being despatched to Dacca.

CHAPTER XI.

LAND REVENUE ADMINISTRATION.

Land revenue system in days of native rule.

Little is known of the system of land revenue administration that prevailed under the Hindus prior to the conquest of Bengal by the Muhammadans in the thirteenth century. It is said that the revenue was collected and remitted by the village headmen and that the zamindār, who was merely an official tax gatherer removable at will, was a Muhammadan creation, but it would be dangerous to attach too great importance to these legends of a golden age. Tradition has it that Sikandar Shāh (1359—68) made a survey of at least a part of Dacca district with a large standard of measurement still known as the Sikandari *gaj*, but the first settlement of which any record remains is that made by Rājā Todar Mal, Akbar's great finance minister, in 1558. The province of Dacca, which included the Dacca division with Tippera and Noakhali, was divided into two *sarkars*, Bajuha which included Dacca city, and Sonārgāon. Bajuha was assessed at Rs. 9,87,921 and Sonārgāon at Rs. 2,58,283.* The revenue administration was revised by Jafir Khān in 1722 and again by his successor Suja Khān, but the details of their arrangements are of little practical interest as the unit with which they were concerned was so much larger than the Dacca district.

Under the Mughals it was the practice to allot almost a third of the total area as grants for the maintenance of the great services of State. The principal grants were the *nawara* for the support of a fleet (which in Akbar's time is said to have consisted of 3,000 boats) to defend the country against the Maghs and Assamese, the *ahsham* for the maintenance of artillery, the *sarkar ali* for the expenses of the Nawāb, the *faujderani* for the expenses of the Naib (a grant which was valued at over a lakh of rupees per annum) and the *jaghir* of the Commander-in-Chief of the Empire from which he could maintain 2,650 horse.

Abwābs.

In addition to the land revenue or *mahal* other taxes called *abwābs* were collected by the Muhammadan rulers. The principal *abwābs* were (1) *Khasnavisi*, a fee exacted from the zamindārs at the renewal of their leases, (2) *Nazirāna Mokurra* to cover the cost of the presents sent to the Imperial Court, (3) *Zer mathout*, a cess of 1½ per cent on the original land revenue, (4) *Faujdāri abwāb*, a tax imposed by the Naib and retained by him, (5) *Chauth Marhatta* levied to defray the cost of the Marhatta tribute. This does not however exhaust the list of

* Topography of Dacca, p. 192.

abwābs and considerable sums were realised under the heads *Keffyat* and *Tanfir* which seem to have been in theory collections to make good sums improperly omitted from the revenue demand.

Sayer.

Another large source of income was the *sayer* or duty levied on professions and trades and most articles in ordinary use. These taxes were collected at gauges, ghāts, and bāzārs and were generally let out to farmers who extorted as much as they could realise. The following were the principal *sayer* duties :—

Mhir tari.—A tax on the building of boats varying from 8 annas to Re. 1-4 per vessel. This in itself was not a serious matter, but every boat arriving at or leaving the city was taxed according to the length of the intended voyage, *e.g.*, boats leaving for Calcutta paid 10 annas an oar and boats arriving from that place a lump sum of Rs. 2. This tax gradually spread to the mofussil and survives in the shape of ghāt dues at the present day.

Chauk nikass.—A tax on all articles sold in the market place. Vendors of copper utensils, cutlery, hookahs, etc., paid at the rate of one anna in the rupee. In addition to this there were specific taxes on the sellers of grass, wood, vegetables, vermilion, paper, salt and dried fish. There was a general tax on all traders, and specific taxes for goldsmiths, shell-cutters, firework makers, musicians, snake charmers and others. The monopoly of the sale of betel leaf in the city was let out and in 1773 realised over Rs. 18,000. Evil customs die hard and in spite of the abolition of the *sayer* duties in 1790 such monopolies of vend in their markets are still sold by zamindārs at the present day.

This however does not exhaust the list of taxes. The officers charged with the supervision of the weights and measures used in the market were allowed to levy a duty of ½ per cent on all merchandise exposed for sale, while money was realised from dealers at the different marts in Bikrampur. There was a tax too of one anna in the rupee on all money taken out of the district, while natives of the district who had earned money in service in other parts of the country had to surrender a quota of it on their return home. According to the accounts submitted at the time of the transfer of the *diwāni* to the Company duties were levied at 556 markets in the Dacca province, which yielded an annual revenue of nearly Rs. 69,000.

Land revenue under the Company.

After the assumption of the *diwāni* by the Company in 1765 settlements were first made for short periods. The members of Council at Dacca remarked with much justice that "the collecting of the revenues of so large a district is an important business which we are not much acquainted with,"* and they very prudently confirmed the existing officers in their appointments. The correspondence of the first Collectors of Dacca is chiefly concerned with these settlements and with the difficulties experienced

* India Office Records.

in inducing the zamindārs to take settlement at a *jamma* which seemed suitable, difficulties which were accentuated by the floods and famines with which the district was afflicted at the close of the eighteenth century.

In 1765 the net revenue of the province of Dacca, which was a very much larger area than the present Dacca district, after deducting the allowances made for the cost of collection was Rs. 16,13,203.* This was, as was only natural, a far from complete account of all the sums rightly due to Government and the corresponding figure for 1772 was Rs. 26,93,041. In 1777 the net revenue was fixed at Rs. 28,49,110 and in 1783 the province was settled for a period of ten years for Rs. 28,09,998 or nearly Rs. 40,000 less than at the preceding settlement, a reduction which was by no means unreasonable in view of the losses which it had sustained in the famine of 1784. The settlement of 1793 was made permanent, the amount of revenue assessed on Dacca and Bakarganj, which at that time formed the unit of administration, being 12½ lakhs of rupees.

Position of the zamindārs.

Mr. Sen in his Agricultural Report of the Dacca district (p. 61) remarks that whatever may have been the case elsewhere there can be no doubt that the zamindārs of the Dacca district had no proprietary rights in the land, that they were tahsildārs of the Government revenue with more or less local influence and that it was the permanent settlement which converted persons who had formerly been mere rent collectors into proprietors. A reference to the earlier records tends to confirm this view. The Collector writing to the Board of Revenue in 1790 states that it was the difficulty of collecting revenue through tahsildārs and the inconvenience of requiring every petty taluqdār to pay at Sadr that induced the Muhammadan rulers to settle with the zamindārs, who were comparatively few in number and persons of some respectability. From this letter it would appear that these persons had no more property in their estates than the expectation of a resettlement, provided that they accepted the proposed revenue and that their conduct continued to be satisfactory, and that their position was entirely different from that of a free holder.

In 1792, against the advice of the Collector, the inferior talukdārs were made independent and allowed to pay their revenue direct into the treasury instead of through the zamindār. The Collector opposed this change on the ground that it would very much lower the position of the zamindār, who derived some pecuniary advantage and additional consequence from the management of these taluqs. He was of opinion that tahsildārs were just as likely to prove oppressive as zamindārs and that it would be very inconvenient for the petty taluqdārs to pay their few annas of revenue at *sadr*. His objections were, however, overruled and tahsildārs were appointed, but they were soon abolished

* Topography of Dacca, p. 206.

and the system of payment at *sadr* introduced. This system is still in force and the whole of the land revenue is paid direct at Dacca, with the exception of the amounts realised from the khas mahals where Government stands itself in the position of the zamindār and collects direct from the cultivators through tahsildārs.

Different classes of estates.

The following different classes of estates and tenures are found within the district:—

I. Estates in chief—

(1) Estates the unalienated property of Government.

Khas Mahals:
- (a) Resumed lakhirāj.
- (b) Purchased estates.
- (c) Alluvial accretions.
- (d) Islands.
- (e) Other khas mahals.

(2) Settled estates paying revenue to Government.

(a) Permanently settled—zamindāri, kharija, hazāri taluq.

(b) Temporarily settled—khās ijāra.

(3) Revenue-free estates.

(a) Redeemed.

(b) Religious foundation (Debottar).

(c) Charitable foundation (Brahmottar).

(d) Service estates (Lakhirāj).

II. Subordinate tenures—

(1) Held direct from the zamindār.

(a) Hereditary and transferable.

At a fixed rent—*samilat, patni, sikimi, mirash, mukhasi.*

At a rent liable to enhancement—*haola.*

(b) Hereditary but not transferable.

At a fixed rent—*bandobasti, kayemi.*

(c) Temporary but transferable—*ijara.*

(2) Held from a tenure-holder under the zamindār.

(a) Hereditary and transferable at a fixed rent—*dar-patni, dar mirash.*

At a rent liable to enhancement—*nim haola.*

(b) Temporary—*dar ijara.*

III. Rent-free tenures.

(1) Religious foundation.

Hindu—Debottar, Brahmottar.

Muhammadan—Chiragan.

(2) Charitable.

Hindu—Bhagattar.

(3) Service.

(a) Held by zamindārs' servants—*paikan.*

(b) Held by personal servants—*naffaran, chakran, mahatran.*

The permanently settled estates.

The following abstract shows the number and nature of the different classes of estates in 1910-11 :—

Permanently settled estates.			Temporarily settled estates.			Estates held in direct management.		
Number.	Area in acres.	Revenue.	Number.	Area in acres.	Revenue.	Number.	Area in acres.	Revenue.
		Rs.			Rs.			Rs.
10,184	1,690,661	4,23,706	464	69,679	60,618	236	10,986	30,935

The greater number of the permanently settled estates are very small. The highest revenue paid by any estate is Rs. 14,133. There are only 3 estates which pay above Rs. 10,000, 6 estates which pay between Rs. 5,000 and Rs. 10,000, and 52 which pay between Rs. 1,000 and Rs. 5,000. Turning to the other end of the scale there are 947 estates which pay less than a rupee and 4,554 which pay from one to ten rupees. The average revenue paid by an estate is Rs. 41.

Temporarily settled estates.

The temporarily settled estates are estates which were settled after the permanent settlement. The settlement holder has a permanent, heritable and transferable title subject to the payment of the revenue assessed.

Estates held in direct management.

The khas mahals of Dacca are neither numerous nor important. They fall into the following main classes—island *churs* thrown up in the beds of rivers outside the boundaries of any permanently settled estate—lands resumed as invalid lakhirāj, service lands and lands bought in at revenue sales. The estates are small and scattered and efficient management is far from easy. The revenue assessed by Government is generally light and ranges from Rs. 2 to Rs. 3 per acre of culturable land. Eleven of these estates are situated in Dacca city.

Subordinate tenures.

Reference has already been made to the small size of the average estates and this perhaps is the reason why there has been no very elaborate development of under-tenures in Dacca. A large number of raiyats hold direct from the zamindār and tenures below the second degree are very rare.

The following are the principal forms of tenures in existence in the district:—A *kharija* or *huzuri taluq* is a *taluq* or estate excluded from a zamindāri and paying revenue direct to the treasury. There is practically no difference between such a *taluq* and a *zamindāri*. In a *samilat taluq* the revenue is permanently settled, but is paid to the Zamindar and by him to Government.

The following paragraphs are extracted from a letter written by the Collector of Dacca in 1790 to the Board of Revenue at

Fort William and are interesting as showing the relative positions of zamindārs and taluqdars at that time:—

"The first question that occurs is what is a Talookdar and what the essentials that constitute him an actual proprietor of the soil. As I was not satisfatorily informed on this subject I referred to the most authentic evidence written or verbal within my reach and I find that they are in this district of four kinds besides a similar description of renter called a Kawaladar, as follows.

1*st. Jungleboory.*—Previous to the division of the country into pergannahs and Tuppahs and fixing what is called the Tuxeembundy many persons undertook to cultivate jungle and waste lands and when the Tuxeembundy was made these new cultivated lands were constituted Talooks and included in the Jummabundy of the nearest zamindār by the Government of that time and if any increase or remission was granted the zamindār a proportional part fell to the Talookdars. If the zamindār withheld from the Talookdar any part of this he was at liberty to complain to the Government who compelled the zamindār to allow the Talookdar his proportion of the remission. If the Talookdar died leaving heirs they got possession of the lands in the same manner as their predecessor and the zamindār had nothing to do with them but receive his Mulgujari agreeably to Kistbundy, but if there happened to be no heirs the zamindār was the manager for the behalf of Government.

2*nd. Zur Khereed.*—The Talookdars under this denomination were at liberty to sell their Talooks by bid of sale with or without the permission of the zamindār, and on failure of heirs the zamindār could take possession and sell the lands or keep them, as he might be inclined. These Talookdars were subject to increase or entitled to remissions proportionately with their zamindārs agreeably to their respective jummas.

3*rd. Pottah Talookdar.*—The zamindars and Chaudries could grant hereditary Talookdary Pattahs to any person for lands belonging to themselves called their neej, whether cultivated or uncultivated, in which pattah it was stipulated that the Talookdars should have possession of the whole lands agreed upon, and that the management should descend to his heirs for ever: but this Talookdar could neither sell nor make over by deed of gift the lands of his Talook neither could the zamindār dispose of it but on failure of issue it reverted to the zamindār. Pattah Talookdars were subject to increases and remissions along with the zamindārs.

4*th. Wassut Talookdar* or Talookdār within Talookdar is the same in respect to a Talookdār that a *Zur Khereed* Talookdar is to a zamindār.

5*th. Howlladar.*—In the pargunnah of Bikrampur a custom prevails that if any Talookdar sell any part of his Talook to another person upon receiving the purchase price, he calls him a Howlladar of so much land who pays his rents to the Talookdār, but if any dispute arises between the Talookdar and Howlladar he can get his Howlladar separated from this Talookdar and included in some other Talookdary. The land is subject to increase and decrease of revenue along with the other renters and the property is hereditary and transferable.

The above is as accurate a definition of the different Talookdars of this district as I have been able to procure, and it remains with the Board to decide what description of them or whether the whole are to be considered as having an actual property in the soil and to be separated from the zamindārs.

The number of Talookdars in this district are computed to be upwards of 20,000. Many pergunnahs are already a Talookdary settlement, zamindārs standing between them and Government in the light of Tasseeldārs.

I am authorised by the resolutions of the Governor-General in Council to appoint Tasseeldārs in these pergunnahs where the Talooks are too numerous to receive the revenues immediately from the Talookdars. This mode I must consequently adopt in many pergunnahs—but in doing this zamindārs will murmur as long custom and possession have given them a sort of hereditary claim to the management from which they derive pecuniary advantages as well as influence and consequence. The new Tasseeldars it is true can for some time to come have no hereditary claim, though there is no doubt but possession may at some future period give them a handle to set up pleas of the same kind: thus then a new set of men will be set up who may claim property to which they have no title, at the expense of those, who are already admitted to possess or supposed to have a right in the soil.

In the mehal Keteraboe, the zamindārs have not a foot of ground, all Talookdary, yet they claim a right to the lands and are allowed the usual Russum. May we not suppose them to have been originally only Tasseeldārs and from long possession have set up hereditary claims, and may we not also from thence infer that our Tasseeldārs may have a sense of their own interests sufficient at least to attempt a similar claim.

I beg to subjoin a list of some of the principal zamindārs of this district, showing the Talukdary jumma, the neej jumma, the neej jumma of the zamindārs and the number of Talookdars in each zamindāry:—

	Own land.	Talookdar's jumma.	Total jumma.	Number of Talookdars.
Pergunnah Jalalpur ...	11,000	76,001	87,001	2,148
Do. Chunderdeep ...	17,000	72 725	89,725	400
Do. Bikrampur ...	2,010	25,642	27,652	268
Do. Ranjinagar ...	92,555	2,01,118	2,93,673	400
Tappa. Mysurdee ...	4,000	14,004	18,004	5,661
Pergunnah Essakabad...	1,700	2,000	3,700	200
Tuppah. Hydrabad ...	1,237	750	1,985	200

From the above comparative view of the property of the Talookdars and Zemindars it appears that the latter possess but little real property of their own and that a separation of the Talookdars would reduce many of them from affluent circumstances to a state of indigence, and the titles of Raja and Zemindars which they are allowed to enjoy will become a mere empty name."

A *sikimi* tenure dates from the permanent settlement, is hereditary and transferable, and the rent is as a rule fixed in perpetuity by the deed granting the tenure. There are, however, a few cases in which there is nothing in the terms of the deed to prohibit enhancement, but the custom of the district is against it. A *mirash* does not date back to the permanent settlement but otherwise does not differ materially from a *sikimi*. A *haola* is a *taluq* created for the reclamation of jungle land, it is heritable and transferable but the rent may be enhanced. *Mushkasi* is a tenure held immediately under the zamindar at a fixed rent: it is hereditary but not transferable by sale or gift. *Bandobasti* is a tenure which is generally created when a person wants to build a house or dig a tank or to reclaim jungle land. It can be inherited but not transferred by sale or gift.

Tenants.

The great majority of tenants are occupancy raiyats, but there are many ways of eluding the provisions of the Bengal Tenancy Act and the occupancy raiyat does not invariably enjoy all the privileges to which he is entitled. The custom with regard to the transfer of land by sale or gift or the right to cut down fruit or timber trees is not clearly settled, but the right of transfer is generally recognised on payment of *salami*. The *utbandi* raiyats or tenants-at-will are generally to be found in newly formed *churs* and islands and in the jungles north of Dacca. In Munshiganj there are a few tenants at fixed rates but they are a small proportion of the whole. On the whole, however, the relations between landlords and tenants are not unsatisfactory. Rents are generally moderate and the benevolences levied in addition to the rent are seldom excessive.

CHAPTER XII.

LOCAL SELF-GOVERNMENT.

DISTRICT BOARDS.

Outside the municipalities of Dacca and Nārāyanganj local affairs are managed by a District Board, which was constituted in 1885 under the Bengal Local Self-Government Act, superseding the District Road Committee which had been constituted under the Cess Act of 1880.

The principal functions entrusted to the District Board are the construction and maintenance of roads and bridges, the provision and management of ferries and rest-houses, the management of pounds, the inspection and financial aid of educational institutions and dispensaries, the provision of veterinary assistance and of wholesome drinking water, the improvement of the lesser waterways and of the sanitary surroundings of villages and towns, and the development of industries. In each subdivision there is also a Local Board to which certain of the functions of the District Board are delegated.

The District Board is composed of 29 members, of whom 8 hold office ex-officio, 7 are nominated and the remaining 14 are elected by the Local Boards. About five-sixths of the members are natives of India. The Collector is the Chairman, but the Vice-Chairman is a non-official Indian gentleman. The total income of the Board in 1909-10, excluding the opening balance, was in round numbers Rs. 2,36,000, the three principal heads being Provincial Rates (Rs. 1,09,000), Ferry Receipts (Rs. 35,000) and Provincial Grant (Rs. 72,000). The incidence of taxation is very low and only amounted to 8 pies per head of the population. The total expenditure chargeable to current income was Rs. 2,56,000, the principal heads being Education, Rs. 78,000 and Public Works Rs. 1,42,000. For further financial details reference should be made to the Statistical Appendix.

In 1907-08 the District Board maintained 8½ miles of metalled, 312 miles of unmetalled, and 418 miles of village road, the cost of maintenance per mile being Rs. 1,641, Rs. 80 and Rs. 50 respectively. It also kept in repair five major bridges, and controlled 73 ferries. Only five rest-houses are maintained, but comparatively few people travel by land and staging bungalows are not as necessary as in other parts of India. The provision of wholesome drinking water is a matter that is constantly engaging the Board's attention and no less than 198 masonry wells have been constructed and 49 tanks have been excavated and are kept in proper repair. There are, however, few objects on which money can be better spent and the number of wells increases every year. Something has also been done for the improvement of the sanitary surroundings of certain villages—but this is a matter which must largely be left to the action of the villagers themselves.

The Board maintains ten dispensaries and gives grants in aid to six more. In 1909-10 it gave grants in aid amounting to Rs. 44,700 to 1,377 schools. Attempts have been made to introduce the cultivation of eri silk, and improved methods of weaving, but up to date they have met with little success. The opening of a model weaving school at Dacca is, however, in contemplation. An itinerating veterinary assistant is engaged by the Board to tour in the interior and treat the cattle of the villagers and a contribution is made to the support of a second man stationed at Dacca. The executive staff of the Board consists of a European engineer on a pay of Rs. 600—25—800, three overseers on pay ranging from Rs. 60—Rs. 100, and six sub-overseers. In the education department the Board employs three deputy inspectors and 11 sub-inspectors of schools.

LOCAL BOARDS.

Local Boards are constituted in each subdivision and administer allotments ranging from Rs. 9,000 to Rs. 12,000 which are made over to them by the District Board. They have no independent sources of income and they are only entrusted with the duty of repairing village roads and providing to some extent for village water-supply. The Boards consist of from 9 to 16 members, the majority of whom are elected. They are only required to deal with petty local matters and discharge their functions as well as could reasonably be expected of them. There is, however, hardly room for a subdivisional Local Board under the District Board, and the standard of efficiency is consequently low. The following abstract shows the number of wells and bridges and the mileage of village roads kept up by these Boards :—

	Number of wells and tanks.	Mileage of village roads.
Sadr	45	135
Munshīganj	19	94
Nārāyanganj	74	123
Mānikganj	50	65

MUNICIPALITIES. Dacca.

The germ of municipal administration in the district is to be found in the arrangement made in 1776 when the nuzzurs received by the Provincial Council at the Puneah or day of annual settlement with the zamindārs were made over to defray the expense of repairing the roads in Dacca.* Prisoners were also employed for the same purpose and for many years the care of the

* Topography of Dacca, p. 218.

city remained directly in the hands of Government. In 1864, the District Municipal Improvement Act was introduced into Dacca and the affairs of the city have been administered by Commissioners since that date. At the present day they are 21 in number, two-thirds of whom are elected. Only four of the Commissioners in 1910 were Europeans and the chairman was a non-official Indian gentleman, so that the Dacca Municipality may be regarded as an example of representative institutions subjected to the minimum of official interference. The total area of the Municipality was 6·05 square miles and the population residing within municipal limits in 1911 was 108,551. The principal sources of direct income are a tax on holdings levied at the rate of 10 per cent of the annual value, latrine rates, tolls on roads and ferries, and a tax on animals and vehicles.

Few cities offer more serious obstacles to successful municipal administration than Dacca and few Commissioners have received freer or more generous aid in their struggle with their difficulties. For the proper understanding of the situation it is necessary to briefly summarise the many drawbacks of the town. The streets are extraordinarily narrow and congested and, as the cost of stone is very high, they have been metalled with broken brick which wears into holes and is ground by traffic into a peculiarly irritating dust. Before the construction of the water-works the only sources of water-supply were the river and wells sunk in soil contaminated with every species of impurity. Even at the present day about 5,000 latrines cannot be reached by the conservancy sweepers and the removal of night-soil from the ones that are accessible is a process attended with considerable public inconvenience. There is no system of surface drainage and the cost of ordinary road clearing is extremely heavy. There are hardly any open spaces in the city and the surroundings of the market places are far from sanitary. On the other hand Dacca has benefited from the generosity of the family of the Nawāb and, since 1905, from the grants which Government has made with the object of removing some of the more glaring sanitary disabilities under which it laboured. The water-works have been remodelled, a conservancy tramway conveys night-soil to a point outside the city, and the more important roads have been metalled with stone. For further details see article on Dacca city.

Nārāyanganj was constituted a muncipality in 1876. The area within municipal limits is 4½ square miles and the population in 1911 was 27,876. There are twelve Commissioners, four of whom are nominated and eight elected; four of the Commissioners are Europeans but none are Government servants. The European jute merchants have large interests in the town, one of their number has always served as chairman, and it is possibly owing to the predominance of western interests that Nārāyanganj Nārāyanganj.

has been described as being more of a western than an eastern town, and as the model municipality of Bengal. The roads are always clean and in excellent repair, the town is well drained, rubbish is nowhere to be seen, the municipal market is admirably arranged and all is neatness and order. The municipality have recently erected water-works at a cost of two lakhs of rupees, the water being drawn from the river Lakshya, passed through a 'jewel' filter, and distributed over the town in pipes. The principal sources of income are a tax on holdings, conservancy and water rates, and tolls on roads and ferries.

CHAPTER XIII.

EDUCATION.

EARLY HISTORY OF EDUCATION

Public education was not entirely neglected in the Dacca district even in the days of native rule, though then as now it would appear to have been of too literary a character and to have failed to pay adequate attention to the proper training of the recipient for the active work of life. The Mughal Government paid a salary of Rs. 60 per mensem to a professor who lectured on the Arabic language, logic, metaphysics, and law, but on his death in 1751 his place was not refilled.* For Hindus there were numerous Sanskrit schools and in 1838 there were no less than 125 of these institutions. The course of instruction was, however, far from practical; the study of Sanskrit grammar occupied ten years, the Vedas eight, and the art of reasoning no less than twelve years. It is not, therefore, matter for surprise that only 828 scholars were attracted to these institutions. Astronomy and medicine were also studied in Bikrampur. The bias towards medicine still persists for, even at the present day, the number of medical practitioners in that portion of the district is unusually large. The old paternal relation was maintained between the master and his pupils, who were not only taught, but fed, clothed, and lodged by him, the master looking for his support to the donations of the charitable. In Dacca city there were in 1838, 11 Hindu schools with 302 scholars and 9 schools for Muhammadans with 115 scholars. In the Hindu schools children paid fees amounting to two annas a month; education in the Muhammadan schools was free.† The course of instruction was simple but practical and consisted of reading, writing, ciphering, and the keeping of commercial and agricultural accounts. Muhammadans also studied grammar, literature and religion.

Education on European methods.

The first schools to be opened under European supervision were those started by the Rev. O. Leonard, a Baptist Missionary, in 1817. They were seven in number, five imparting instruction in Bengali, one in Persian, and one in English. Five years later the number of schools had risen to 23 and of scholars to 1,300, and in 1825 separate schools were opened for women and girls. Funds, however, were not forthcoming in sufficient quantities and in 1837 the number of mission schools had sunk to 11 with 529 male and 99 female pupils. An English school had, however, been opened by Government in 1835 and met at once with warm support, Mr. Taylor writing of it as follows :—

* Taylor's Topography of Dacca, p. 274.
† Taylor's Topography of Dacca, p. 271.

"The natives of this part of the country have evinced great eagerness to acquire a knowledge of the English language, and accordingly the school which has lately been established in the city by Government is well attended, and altogether is in a most flourishing and promising condition. The institution is admirably conducted, and under the able tuition of the present masters the pupils have made great proficiency not only in reading, writing, and arithmetic but in the higher branches of education as geography, history, and geometry." *

Education continued to make steady progress and in 1867 there were 169 boys' schools in the district with 8,213 pupils on the rolls, while there were 452 girls at school in 26 institutions. The principle of making grants in aid had been introduced and 147 of the boys' schools fell into the category of aided schools. There were also the Dacca College which was opened in 1841 and the Collegiate school attached to it, while two normal schools provided for the instruction of teachers. These were in addition to the *madrasas* and *tols* in which instruction was imparted on the old traditional lines. The attitude of the people is thus described by Mr. Clay, the Collector, in 1867:—

"The natives, especially the Hindus, as a rule evince a most laudable desire to obtain an English education, and will often pinch and screw and almost starve themselves in order to be able to pay their school or college fees. They are actuated by the strongest of all motives—self-interest, knowing as they do that a knowledge of English is now made almost a *sine quâ non* in the distribution of the best appointments under Government which every native covets. As regards vernacular education the vernacular scholarships offered a strong stimulus. There is still a strong feeling of opposition to the spread of female education." †

Progress of education. That there has been a great advance in education, especially in English education, during the past fifty years is a matter of common knowledge, but the mere citation of figures taken from official papers might induce impressions regarding the actual spread of knowledge which would be misleading. The absence or presence of a state-aided village pundit does not make all the difference between light and darkness that writers such as Sir William Hunter would sometimes have us think and though the introduction of reforms, such as those initiated by Sir George Campbell, produce an enormous increase in the number of pupils of whom cognisance is taken in blue-books, the immediate change is very much less than the figures would suggest. An aided school generally develops into something more efficient than one which does not receive assistance from the State, but the fact that a number of schools and scholars appear for the first time in the

* Topography of Dacca, p. 274.

† Principal Heads of the History and Statistics of the Dacca Division, Calcutta, 1868.

books of the department must not be assumed to imply that they have only just been called into existence.

The following figures showing the number of scholars must be read with the reservation that in the earlier years of the period there were students of whom the Government had no official knowledge. In 1856-57 there were 1,449 recognized pupils; in 1860-61, 2,003; in 1870-71, 7,155; in 1872-73, after Sir George Campbell's reforms had been put into effect, 18,086; in 1892-93, 78,834; and in 1909-10, 86,586.

Distribution of Literates.

It is not easy to trace in the census tables the growth of literacy, *i.e.*, of the capacity to read and write, as prior to 1901 persons under instruction were returned as such whether they could read and write or not. In 1901, 12·1 per cent of the male population of Dacca were literate, the percentage for Bengal as a whole being 10·4. Table XXV of the Statistical Tables shows the distribution of literacy by thānas and religion in 1901 and is interesting reading. Education has made considerable progress amongst Hindus and in that year 24·23 per cent of their males could read and write. Amongst Muhammadans the percentage was only 4·9. Taking Hindu males as the measure of value the proportion of literates was highest in Dacca city (48·8 per cent), Munshīganj (32·6 per cent), and Srinagar (27·3); lowest in Kāpāsia and Keraniganj (12 and 15 per cent). Dacca city (18·3 per cent) was the only place where the proportion of Muhammadan literates exceeded 7 per cent. Female education is still in its infancy. In the district as a whole 990 females out of every thousand were illiterate, and even in Dacca city only 8·2 per cent of Hindu females could read and write.

COLLEGIATE EDUCATION. The Dacca College.

There are two colleges in the district, both of which are located in the city. The first Government English school was opened in 1835 and in 1841 was converted into a college in which students could read for the degree of Bachelor of Arts. In the same year the foundation-stone was laid of the substantial premises near the Judge's cutcherry in which the college remained for over sixty years. In 1908 the college was transferred to the buildings near the Ramna field which have been erected at a cost of nearly 14 lakhs of rupees and which include hostel accommodation for 200 students and residences for four of the staff. Everything has been designed upon the most approved lines, no expense has been spared, and the institution can justly be described as a residential college of the best kind. The college has a very complete scientific equipment and claims to have some of the best laboratories in India. It contains a library of 8,000 volumes, which is rapidly growing in size, as there is an annual allotment of Rs. 1,000 for its maintenance and extension. The staff consists of a Principal and sixteen Professors and Lecturers, none of whom receive a salary of less than Rs. 100 per mensem. The college is affiliated to the Calcutta University and is, after the Presidency College, the largest first grade college under the control of that body. It also maintains law classes in which students can read for the degree of B.L.

The Jagannath College.

The Jagannath College was founded as a proprietary college in 1883 but in 1908 was transferred to a Board of Trustees on which the teaching staff is represented. Prior to that date it was located in poor buildings in a congested portion of the city, but it has recently been moved to more suitable quarters. The stock of apparatus is sufficient for the First Arts standard under the existing regulations, and there is a small library containing 800 volumes. The staff consists of ten Masters of Arts and four assistants. The advantages offered by this institution are much inferior to those of the Government College, but the fees charged are considerably lower and this is a consideration with needy students. Government has recently made a capital grant of Rs. 90,000 and a recurring annual grant of Rs. 15,000 for the purpose of improving the administration of this college.

High or Entrance Schools.

A special feature of education in the Dacca district is the large number of schools which aspire to send up students to matriculate at the Calcutta University and which are known as High or Entrance schools. In 1872-73 there were six of these schools, twenty years later there were 19, and in 1908-09 there were 45. Of these 2 were supported and managed by the Education Department, 9 were aided, and 34* were entirely unaided. The statement appended to this chapter, which gives particulars as to the location of these schools, shows what a very large proportion of them are situated in the Munshiganj subdivision. Out of the total of 45 no less than 23 are to be found in Munshiganj. The Government schools are well staffed and well equipped, but the same cannot be said of many of the aided and most of the unaided schools. The buildings and appliances are often quite inadequate, the staff is miserably paid, the instruction given poor, and the whole tone of the institution far from satisfactory. Some of the schools are opened by generous individuals who have a laudable desire to advance education in their native villages, but who do not realise that the cause they have at heart would be better served if they were to combine with some other person to found a really efficient central school instead of starting an institution which can never thrive on the amount they are able to allocate for its support. Other schools owe their origin to those feuds which are so common in rural Bengal, and which are thus described by a Bengali gentleman who is an Inspector of the Education Department:

"The high school as a rule has a committee and the committee is often a hotbed of quarrel. And the quarrel arises sometimes on trivial grounds such as the promotion or transfer of a boy. The rival school is started in most cases with insufficient or no funds. The teachers engaged, therefore, cannot be men of high qualifications for want of proper remuneration."

---

* Including 8 schools not recognised by the University.

It is hardly to be expected that an institution that comes into existence amongst such circumstances and surroundings can do good work and there can be little doubt that the cause of education would be advanced by a process of consolidation. This principle has at last been accepted by the Calcutta University, and in 1907-08 a survey of high schools was carried out under its instruction. The result of the survey was that recognition, *i.e.*, the right of sending up pupils to the Matriculation Examination of the University, was withdrawn from four schools and warnings were issued to several others.

Middle schools. Middle schools are classed as middle English and middle Vernacular, but in practice there is little difference as English is freely taught even in the vernacular schools. Middle schools are as a rule poorly housed and poorly equipped and the staff is poorly paid, with the inevitable result that the education given is also poor. Parents prefer to send their sons whenever possible to read the middle course at a high school and the number of middle schools does not increase. They are supported partly by fees, partly by subscriptions, partly by grants made to them by the District Board which vary from Rs. 10 to Rs. 20 a month. In 1908-09 there were 58 middle English schools of which 33 were aided by the District Board, 3 by the Education Department, and 22 were unaided. Of the 75 middle vernacular schools, 67 including 53 departmental circle schools were aided and 8 unaided. The number of pupils in middle English schools was 4,882 and that attending middle vernacular schools was 4,219. A statement showing the distribution of the middle English schools is appended to this chapter.

Primary schools. Primary schools are divided into upper and lower. In 1908-09 there were 254 of the former with 12,782 pupils and 1,091 of the latter with 38,332 pupils. The course of instruction in a lower primary school consists of (1), Science Primers, standards I and II, writing and reading; (2), Arithmetic including mental arithmetic; (3), Drawing; (4) object lessons; (5) drill. Upper primary schools add to this course a history reader and a literature book, geography, and elementary geometry and mensuration.

Most of these schools are housed in very humble quarters and their equipment and apparatus are simplicity itself. Many schools sit in a verandah or outbuilding belonging to the richest man in the village and those that rise to the dignity of a separate house can seldom boast of anything more pretentious than a hut with earthen floor, bamboo walls and roof of thatch. The apparatus usually consists of nothing more than the boys' own books and slates, and even the latter are occasionally dispensed with and the children learn to write on palm leaves. But simple though their quarters are, they satisfy the desires of those that use them. The Bengali has in his heart a certain contempt for material luxury; he prefers to sit in spacious leisure to expending time and sweat on the improvement of his dwelling and he is not too exacting in his requirements when his children's school-house is in question. In 1906 Government made a grant of Rs. 27,600 for the erection of primary school buildings subject to the proviso that where possible one-fourth of the sum should be raised from the villages in which the schoolhouses were built. But this liberality evoked little enthusiasm, and though 50 houses were ultimately erected the people evidently thought the whole matter something of a bore. In the flooded tracts the children have to come by water in the rains, and the collection of craft outside the door is quaint to a degree. Many paddle themselves to school in big earthen pipkins, others come on rafts of plantain trunks, and it is seldom that anyone rises to anything so elaborate as even the humblest skiff.

Instruction in teaching.

There is a fine school in Dacca city for the training of teachers and head pandits of middle schools, and lower pandits of high schools. The school possesses a good library of over 5,000 volumes and is well equipped in every way. There are six teachers on the staff, three of whom are Masters of Arts, and in 1907 there were 84 pupils on the rolls, exclusive of pandits under training. For the training of lower primary teachers there are schools at Munshīganj, Mānikganj, Rāipura, and Agla.

"The characteristic guru training school of Eastern Bengal has nothing attractive or insirping about it. A somewhat dishevelled mat or mud hut divided into two halves, an ill-qualified instructor; in place of an intelligent display of the methods of instruction, a string of lugubrious complaints from the gurus, how their stipends and their pay are inadequate, how they have to yield up the fees and salary of their school for two years to a substitute, and how the chances are that when they return home they will find themselves permanently displaced by that very substitute, and left, as a result of their training, without even their former scanty means of livelihood. The arrangement for training of teachers is admitted on all hands to be unsuccessful. ....This lamentable state of affairs can only be remedied by the erection of hostels, by the reduction of the length of the course, by the improvement of the condition of the gurus during the period under training, and, above all, by the increase of the grant to those of them who undergo the prescribed course of instruction."

These remarks which are taken from the Report on the Progress of Education in Eastern Bengal and Assam during the years 1901-02—1906-07 applied in all their entirety to the Dacca district. Hostels for the accommodation of the gurus have, however, now been erected and decent houses provided for most of the schools.

Special instruction.

The Ahsanulla School of Engineering attached to the Dacca College was originally founded in 1876 as a survey school. In 1902 it was decided to convert the institution into a school of Engineering, the requisite funds being obtained from a grant of Rs. 60,000 from Government and a donation of Rs. 1,12,000 from the late Nawāb of Dacca. Fine buildings have been erected which include a hostel with accommodation for 100 students in close proximity to the Dacca College, and the necessary workshops have been fitted up. The course comprises the four overseer classes and pupils presenting themselves at the Sibpur College examination are eligible for Overseer Certificates. Arrangments have been made for the final 18 months of practical training which leads up to the Foreman Mechanic's Certificate and an artizan class has been opened. The original Survey School still continues in the shape of Amin and Survey classes, but their popularity has been to some extent affected by the transfer of work which used formerly to be done by Civil Court Amins to junior pleaders with a knowledge of survey. The school has a European head master and a European foreman and has proved extremely popular. In 1901-02 there were 140 pupils on the rolls, and in 1908-09 there were no less than 373.

The Dacca Medical school.

The medical school which is attached to the Mitford Hospital was founded in 1875. The present building was erected in 1889 at a cost of Rs. 64,000, which was raised by private subscription, and contains two lecture rooms, two separate dissecting rooms for males and females, a laboratory, a library and a museum. Administrative sanction has been accorded to the erection of an examination hall, a laboratory, a gymnasium and a hostel. The Civil Surgeon of Dacca acts as Superintendent and the teaching staff consists of five teachers, two demonstrators, one chemical and one anatomical assistant. The course extends to four years and practical instruction is given in the wards of the Mitford Hospital. Twenty-four scholarships and as many free studentships are annually awarded to successful students. The number of pupils on the rolls in 1908-09 was 205.

Muhammadan education.

The importance attached by Muhammadans to the acquisition of a proper knowledge of the faith of Islām has led to the development of a special class of educational institutions for their community, *i.e.*, madrasas, maktabs, and Koran schools. The course taught in madrasas is known as the Nezamiah course, and purports to be based on the system of instruction followed in the Nezamiah College of Bagdad which was founded in 1065 A.D. and was for two centuries the great centre of Muhammadan learning. The pupils are divided into two divisions. The senior division comprises four classes and the subjects taught are Arabic and Persian literature, rhetoric, Muhammadan jurisprudence, logic, science of controversy, philosophy, scholastic theology, arithmetic, geometry and history. The junior division has from four to seven classes and the course generally consists of Arabic and Persian literature, grammar, elementary logic, arithmetic and Muhammadan law. The premier madrasa of the province is the Dacca Madrasa, which was founded in 1872. The institution owes its origin to the liberality of a pious gentleman, Haji Muhammad

Muhsin, a resident of Hugli district, who died in 1806, and left an estate which yielded an income of about Rs. 45,000 per annum to be devoted to charitable purposes. The madrasa is divided into two departments, the Anglo-Persian department which is simply a high school teaching up to the matriculation examination, and the Arabic department in which English can be taken as an optional subject. The staff consists of 21 maulvis and masters in addition to the Superintendent and the institution receives an annual grant of Rs. 2,400 from provincial funds. There is a fine hostel attached which was erected in 1905 at a cost of Rs. 45,500, two-thirds of which were contributed by private persons and the rest by Government. Other senior institutions are the Ahsaniah and Hammadiah madrasas in Dacca city.

Outside the city there are 19 smaller madrasas which can hardly be regarded as very satisfactory institutions. They have little or no organisation, and are insufficiently staffed and poorly equipped. They do not in all cases follow the full course of studies prescribed for the corresponding classes in the larger madrasas and the education they impart is never such as will help a pupil in practical life. It is said that many of the students after receiving a very imperfect education return to their homes and endeavour to obtain a living as religious instructors, but as the supply is considerably in excess of the demand, there is often unseemly competition between rival maulvis. There are four recognised middle madrasas which are virtually middle English schools with the addition of Urdu in standards I to IV and Persian in standard VI. They also have Arabic departments in which instruction is supposed to be given up to a sufficiently high standard. Maktabs are Koran schools which have developed into lower primary schools, and which receive aid from local funds if they reach the requisite standard of efficiency. In 1908-09 the number of these institutions was 167. Koran schools, as their name implies, impart purely religious instruction; their number in 1908-09 was 945 with 15,214 pupils.

The figures of literacy quoted in the preceding pages have already indicated the extraordinary difference between the educational attainments of Hindus and Muhammadans. This difference is partly due to the conservative tendencies of Islām, but to a much greater degree to differences in social position. The great majority of the manual workers are Muhammadans and it is rather qua manual worker than qua Muhammadan that they are illiterate. But even in the villages the Muhammadan is ceasing to be content with his position of educational inferiority and of recent years there has been a great increase of Muhammadan students. In 1904-05 the pupils in public institutions numbered 26,260 but in 1908-09 they were no less than 40,081 as compared with 45,731 Hindu pupils.

Female education. Female education has made some progress of recent years but the progress continues to be slow. There is one high school for girls, the Eden female school, which was opened as a middle vernacular school in 1878, one middle and 548 primary schools. In addition to this, arrangements have been made for zenana classes in the city and a certain number of girls read in boys' schools. The total number of females under instruction in public institutions in 1908-09 was 13,776, of whom the immense majority were in the primary stages. The percentage of girls of school-going age who were actually at school was less than 7. In addition to the children who come within the purview of the Education Department, there are a certain number of girls belonging to prosperous Hindu families who receive some measure of instruction in their own homes, but the figures of the census of 1901 showed conclusively how much leeway has still to be made up.

European and special schools. St. Gregory's School at Dacca, a high school managed by the Roman Catholic Mission, was founded in 1889 and offers instruction to Eurasian scholars. There are also four commercial schools under private management in the city at which type-writing and shorthand are taught.

Administrative staff. For the purposes of departmental control the district falls in the charge of the Inspector of Schools for the Dacca division. The staff employed in 1909 consisted of 5 deputy inspectors, 11 sub-inspectors, 2 assistant sub-inspectors and 15 inspecting pandits.

List of High Schools.

Name of School.	Name of Thāna.
Sadar Subdivision.	
Dacca Collegiate	Dacca City.
„ Eden Female	Do.
„ Armanitola	Do.
K. L. Jubilee	Do.
Pogose	Do.
Imperial Seminary	Do.
Ukils Institution	Do.
Teghoria	Keraniganj.
Jaydebpur	Do.
Kāliganj	Kāpāsia.
Nawābganj	Nawābganj.
Govindapur	Do.
Roail	Sābhār.
Nārāyanganj Subdivision.	
Nārāyanganj	Nārāyanganj.
Baradi	Do.
Sonākānda	Do.
Sonārgaon	Do.
Rāipura	Rāipura.
Araihazar	Rūpganj.
Murapāra	Do.
Satirpāra	Narsingdi.

Munshīganj Subdivision.

Name of School.	Name of Thāna.
Munshīganj	Munshīganj.
Bajrajugini	Do.
Abdullapur	Do.
Paikpāra	Do.
Sonāraug	Do.
Autshai	Do.
Kalma	Do.
Svarnagram Radhanath	Do.
Kathadia Simulia	Do.
Ronthbhog	Do.
Malkhānagar	Srīnagar.
Ichāpura	Do.
Hasara	Do.
Beltali	Do.
Bhagyakul	Do.
Solaghar	Do.
Brahmangaon	Do.
Lohajang	Do.
Kukutia	Do.
Kazirpagla	Do.
Sidhesvari	Rājābāri.
Bānari	Do.
Telirbag	Do.

Mānikganj Subdivision.

Name of School.	Name of Thāna.
Mānikganj	Mānikganj.
Teota Academy	Sealo Aricha.

List of Middle English Schools.

Name of School.	Postal address.
Sadar Subdivision.	
Amligola	Dacca.
Konda	Konda.
Balia	Paralia.
Khash Haola	Do.
Salim's	Dacca.
Tetuljhora	Tetuljhora.
Nannar	Nannar.
Suapur	Suapur.
Debinagar	Debinagar.
Kusumhati	Manudpur.
Nārāyanganj Subdivision.	
Gopaldi	Meratali.
Duptara	Duptara.
Amdia	Panchdona.

Nārāyanganj Subdivision—(*contd.*)

Name of School.	Postal address.
Panchrukhi	Duptara.
Barpāra	Nāngalbanda Barpāra.
Manipur	Amirabadlapur.
Sarrabād	Belaba.
Govindapur	Do.
Lakshipura	Do.
Gotasia	Gotasia.
Lakhpur Simulia	Lakhpur.
Sadhar Char	Paralia.

Munshīganj Subdivision.

Name of School.	Postal address.
Gaodia	Gaodia.
Bejgāon	Bejgāon.
Rarikhal	Maijpāra.
Abirpāra	Serajdigha.
Solaghar	Solaghar.
Sekhernagar	Sekhernagar.
Baraparaldia	Malkhanagar.
Sridarkhola	Sekhernagar.
Feringi Bāzār	Munshīganj.

Mānikganj Subdivision.

Name of School.	Postal address.
Baliati	Baliati.
Chandair	Garpāra.
Dhankora	Dhankora.
Daragram	Saturia.
Tilli	Tilli.
Jianpurchaklaradhia	Khalsi.
Kustia	Ghior.
Mahādebpur	Mahādebpur.
Betila	Betila.
Jhitka	Jhitka.
Krishnapur	Kanchonpur.
Lotakhola	Lotakhola.
Diabari	Jhitka.
Rājkhara	Rājkhara.
Kāliharnagar	Chandahar.
Bakihaty	Joykrishnapur.

CHAPTER XIV.

GAZETTEER.

Baidya Bazar.—Large bazār situated in 23·39 N. and 90·37 E. on the right bank of the Meghnā river. Baidya Bāzār is connected by road with Nārāyanganj and has an unfavourable reputation as being not unfrequently the scene of river dacoities.

Bajrajogini.—Large village in the Munshīganj subdivision situated in 23·32 N. and 90·29 E. which is best known as being the home of a very large number of Government servants.

Baliati.—Village situated in 24·0 N. and 90·2 E. in the north of the Mānikganj subdivision. A considerable trade in jute is done in the bāzār, but the village is best known as the home of the Bāliati Babus. From a distance their house stands up above the level plain, an imposing mass of masonry which recalls a Georgian country house in England. A closer inspection shows that it is not one fine house, but a terrace of five very ordinary ones.

The founder of the family was one Gobinda Ram Shāha who was a big salt merchant in the middle of the 18th century. He left four sons: Dadhi Ram, Ananda Ram, Pandit Ram and Golap Ram. Dadhi Ram left two sons whose descendants now form the "east" and "west" houses as they are called. Pandit Ram's family forms the "middle house" and Golap Ram's the "north house," while Ananda Ram's descendants are known as the "Golābāri." The Jagannāth College in Dacca was founded and endowed by a member of the Bāliati family, Babu Kishori Lāl Ray Chaudhri, in memory of his father.

Barmi.—Large bāzār situated in 23·42 N. and 90·31 E. population, 1911, 276. The place is a collecting centre in the north of the district for jute, which is then despatched down the Lakshya to Nārāyanganj. The ruins of an old indigo factory are situated close by.

Baradi.—Village situated in 23·42 N. and 90·38 E., in the Nārāyanganj subdivision, the residence of the Nags of Bāradi. Population, 1911, 1,189. The Nag family originally came from Bakarganj and their fortunes were founded by one Nayananda Nag, an eminent and learned man at the court of Nawāb of Murshīdābād, who was rewarded with a large *jagir* of land for his skill in deciphering a letter which came from Constantinople. The family estates are situated at Nagabād in the Tippera district immediately opposite to Bāradi, and are divided into three shares or *hisyas*, the eastern, the western, and the middle or *panch hisya*

Situated as they are on the banks of the Meghnā, whose changing current gives rise to many land disputes, the Nag family has always been noted for the capable and courageous manner in which they have defended their own interests and for the skill they have displayed in fishing in troubled waters. Various members of the family have been efficient Government servants, others have lent their undoubted abilities to less worthy leaders. In the words of the member of the family who supplied the account of its history. "In the dark days of the sepoy mutiny they stood by the side of Government without seeking to attract notice by ostentatious operations."

Bhagyakhul.—Village situated on the banks of the Padmā river in the south-west corner of the Munshīganj subdivision. It is the family home of the wealthy Bhāgyakul Babus, but as it is exposed to the erosive action of the river, they have abandoned the attempt to erect masonry buildings and their present quarters are of the most primitive description. There is a prosperous market at Bhāgyakul and a charitable dispensary maintained by the family. The Bhāgyakhul Babus have made their fortunes in trade and the principal members of the family live in Calcutta.

Dacca.—The city of Dacca is situated in 23·43 N. and 90·24 E., on the north bank of the Buri Ganga river, eight miles above its junction with the Dhaleswari and 254 miles distant from Calcutta by rail and river, *viâ* Nārāyanganj, and Goalando. The Dacca-Mymensingh branch of the Eastern Bengal State Railway runs through the town, and in addition to its communication by rail it is connected by road with Mymensingh and with the port of Nārāyanganj. The latter road is nine miles long and is metalled. The Buri Ganga is open for steamer traffic in the rains but will only carry native boats of light draught in the dry season.

It has been suggested by Taylor that Dacca may be identical with Bengala, a large and wealthy city to which reference is often made by European travellers in the sixteenth and seventeenth centuries. This view receives some confirmation from the fact that Dacca and Bengala are never both mentioned by the same author. Methold describes Rājmahāl and Bengala as being "faire cities" while Herbert and Mandelso who travelled about the same time refer to Dacca and Rājmahāl, but make no mention of Bengala. Rennell states that Bengala was near the eastern mouth of the Ganges and that its site had probably been diluviated by that river, but Taylor points out that though the natives have traditions regarding the destruction of Seripur and Kolesar, they have never even heard of Bengala.* Whether Dacca and Bengala were identical it would be hard to say, but there can be little doubt that the town was a place of some importance even before it became the scene of the Provincial Government in 1608.

* Topography of Dacca, p. 92.

Rājā Mān Singh, Akbar's famous general, administered the country from this spot for some years, and in 1608 Islām Khān moved his capital here from Rājmahāl. Three explanations are given of the origin of the city's name: one that it is derived from the *dhak* (butea frondosa), a tree which is said to have been common there in ancient times; another that it took its name from Dhakeswari, 'the concealed goddess,' whose temple is said to have been first erected by Ballāl Sen; while a third story has it that Islām Khān fixed the boundaries of the city at those points north, east and west where the sound of the drums (*dhak*) beaten on the river banks ceased to be audible. From 1608 to 1639 Dacca continued to be the capital of Bengal, but in the latter year the Government was retransferred to Rājmahāl where it remained for one and twenty years. In 1660 Mīr Jumla again made Dacca the capital and it continued to enjoy this proud position till 1704 when the court was moved to Murshidābād. It is said that when the city was at the height of its glory it extended from Jāfarabād on the west to Postgola on the east, a distance of ten miles, and on the north nearly fifteen miles to the Tangi river, and that the population was close upon 900,000 persons.* A large proportion of these people were no doubt hangers-on of the court and the military forces and much of the city doubtless was of the nature of a camp.

Tavernier visited Dacca in 1666 and described it in terms which are sufficiently modest but are in fair accord with the Dacca of the present day.

"Dacca is a great town that extends itself only in length; every one coveting to have a house by the Ganges side. The length of this town is above two leagues. And indeed from the last brick bridge, which I mentioned, to Dacca there is but one continued row of houses separated one from the other. inhabited for the most part by carpenters that build galleys and other small vessels. These houses are properly no more than paltry huts built up with bamboo and daubed over with fat earth. Those of Dacca are not much better built. The Governor's palace is a place enclosed with high walls, in the midst whereof is a pitiful house built only of wood. He generally lodges in tents which he causes to be set up in the great court of that enclosure. The Hollanders finding that their goods were not safe in the ordinary houses of Dacca have built them a very fair house and the English have another which is reasonably handsome. The church of the Austin Friars is all of brick and is a very comely pile." †

It is strange that Tavernier makes no reference to the two *katras* which had been built before the date of his visit, as the *burra katra* at any rate is an imposing building.

Tavernier's description agrees with that given by an Italian called Manucci who visited it a few years earlier. According to

* Rahman Ali's Tarikh-i-Dhaka, MSS., p. 35.

† Tavernier, Travels in India, Part II, Book I, p. 55.

him "The city of Dacca without being strong or large has many inhabitants, most of its houses are made of straw. At this period there were two factories, one English and the other Dutch: there were many Christians, white and black Portuguese, with a church served by a friar called Afostinho." During the ten years that followed Tavernier's visit the city seems to have grown for a certain Captain Bowrey who came there about 1678 writes of it as follows:—

"The Citty of Dacca is a very large spacious one, but standeth upon low swampy ground and the water thereof very brackish, which is the only inconvenience it hath, but it hath some very fine conveniences that maketh amends, havinge a fine and large river that runneth close by the walls thereof, navigable for ships of 5 or 600 tunns in burthen, and the water of the river beinge an arme of the Ganges is extraordinary good, but it is a great way to be fetched by some of this citty, for it is not lesse in circuit than 40 English miles.

"An admirable citty for its greatnesse, for it's magnificent buildings, and multitude of inhabitants. A very great and potent army is here in constant sallary and readinesse, as alsoe many large, stronge and stately elephants, trained up for a warlike service, which are kept continually neare to the Pallace.

"Many elephants, both for warre and state, are here kept by several rich men, and therefore by consequence a very great soldiary, for noe man in the kingdome is admitted to ride an elephant in state, unlesse he continually keep 500 horse to be ready at the Prince's service."

In 1713 the city was visited by a Jesuit priest who refers to it in by no mean favourable terms. "Pour ce qui est de la ville rien de plus sale et de plus mal-propre." He stated that the streets were full of dirt and ordure which s'y rassemblent after the slightest shower, and these are characteristics which have unhappily survived down to the present day.*

The actual area of the city within municipal limits is 6·05 square miles, and the new civil station to the north covers an area of ·77 of a square mile. A traveller approaching the town from Nārāyanganj first meets with small huts similar to the ones referred to by Tavernier, and the garden-houses of wealthy merchants, but shops and masonry buildings appear a few hundred yards to the east of the Dolai Khāl. This creek is crossed by a fine suspension bridge erected by public subscription during the magistracy of Mr. Walter in 1830. Shortly after passing the bridge the Sutrapur Bāzār, a great centre for the grain trade, stretches away towards the north but the main road keeps near the river through Farāshganj, a small tract of land which belongs to the French Government and which is now a centre for the lime trade.

* Principal Heads of the History and Statistics of the Dacca Division, p. 80.

From the Northbrook Hall a fine embankment, known as the Buckland Bund, stretches along the river to the end of the Nawāb's Palace. It is this river frontage which has earned for Dacca the title of the Venice of the East, and which undoubtedly, when the stream is descending in full flood, affords a view that contains some elements both of the stately and the picturesque. At the eastern end of the embankment is the magnificent dwelling of two bankers, Babus Rup Lal Das and Raghu Lal Das, and at the western end the Ahsun Munzil or palace of the Nawāb. Between them are the residences of the Commissioner, the Collector, the Civil Surgeon, and one or two European and Indian gentlemen. The Buckland Bund is about three-quarters of a mile in length but its appearance as a promenade is to some extent marred by the fact that it is liable to be overtopped by high floods and by the difficulty experienced in entirely prohibiting its use as a place of disembarkment for passengers and goods. When the embankment finishes the river is fringed by houses, some of which are both dignified and picturesque, conspicuous amongst which stand out the two fine old Muhammadan ruins, the Bara and Chota Katra.

Back from the river the effect, unfortunately, is very much less pleasing. Leaving the Buckland Bund the road turns inland and runs parallel with the river, but three or four hundred yards away from it, through Patuatuli, Islāmpur, Babu Bāzār, and Mogultuli to the Chauk or Market Place, and thence to the Lāl Bāgh, where the city proper may be said to end, though the municipal boundary is some distance farther on. The road is very narrow, and for a distance of 1,500 yards its width from house to house varies from 20 to 25 feet and in places is only 18 feet. This totally inadequate channel for the commerce of the city is packed with foot passengers, through whom lumbering bullock carts and ramshackle ticka gharis with difficulty make their way and on either side is bordered by mean and dirty looking shops. The chauk is a large square which is crowded with stalls and surrounded by unassuming shops and other buildings. The jail and lunatic asylum lie at the back of the chauk, while the Mitford Hospital is situated on the river front a little farther on. Beyond the hospital population and traffic become less congested and at the Lāl Bāgh we reach the suburban quarters of the town.

The other main thoroughfare is known as the Nawābpur road and runs from the Buckland Bund northwards to the railway. This road is in places of a reasonable breadth and is not so mean and squalid as the one which runs westward to the chauk. Between the Buckland Bund and the place where it crosses the Dolai Khāl it passes the old European Club, the Bank, the cutcherries of the Collector and the Judge, the church and the office of the District Board. At the Dolai creek bridge it becomes inconveniently contracted and from here to the railway line there are a number of small shops interspersed with dwelling houses of very moderate appearance.

These two roads are the main arteries of the city but they are connected with a great number of lesser roads and lanes. The chief markets for the supply of food are situated at Sutrapur and the Rai Saheb's Bāzār and their surroundings from the sanitary point of view are far from satisfactory. The great centre for the jute trade is Postgola, for the grain trade Sutrapur, and for lime Farāshganj. Most of the timber trade is done in the village of Keraniganj immediately opposite Dacca, but there is a large business in bamboos and canework in Bangshal Bāzār. The residential quarters most favoured by Indian gentlemen are Wari, Nawābpur, Tanti Bāzār, Bangla Bāzār, Sutrapur, Lakshi Bāzār, and Armenitola. Some of the houses are of considerable size, especially in the Bangla Bāzār, where many wealthy Shāhas live; but after the sites along the river's bank, the most attractive residential quarter of the town is the suburb of Wari. This is a Khas Mahal which in 1888 was laid out for building by the Collector who subsequently as Sir Lancelot Hare became Lieutenant-Governor of the province. It is intersected by wide roads, each house is surrounded by a pleasant garden and additional buildings cannot be erected without the Collector's sanction.

Nothing, in fact, could well be greater than the contrast between the amenities of Wari, and the squalid discomfort of the remainder of the town. For Dacca suffers from all the manifold drawbacks of an old Eastern city. The streets and lanes are extraordinarily narrow; there are neither sidewalks nor room for them, and as the foot passengers wander at will all over the roadway, continual shouting or the ringing of a bell are required to clear a passage for a wheeled vehicle. In the absence of stone the roads have been metalled with burnt brick which is unable to stand the heavy traffic, so that the surface is worn into holes and in all but the wettest weather is intolerably dusty. There is no system of drainage either for the removal of sewage or of surface water and filth and garbage accumulate in all the lanes. The city is intersected by the Dolai Khāl and its dependant creeks, and though these channels are well enough when full of water in the rains, in the dry weather many of them contract into small pools filled with mud and every form of abomination. Many of the houses have been so built that it is impossible to obtain access to their back premises, and it is calculated that there are no less than 5,000 latrines in the city which are never cleaned. Many improvements have however been effected or taken into consideration since Dacca became the capital of the Province. The Nawābpur road has been metalled with stone, the water-works have been enlarged, the conservancy arrangements have been remodelled and a drainage scheme is under consideration.

One of the most crowded parts of the city is the Sānkhāri Bāzār, the quarter of the workers in shells. The houses here have a very narrow frontage with a quite disproportionate depth. The most extreme instance of a characteristic which is common in a greater or a less degree to all the houses in this bāzār is to be found in a well built masonry dwelling which in 1909 was inhabited by a family of eight persons. This extraordinary structure had a depth of 55½ feet and a uniform breadth of *3 feet 4 inches only.* Another curious house is 60 feet deep, 27 feet high and only 6 feet wide. These houses are well built and kept in excellent repair but very little light or air can penetrate into the curious little cave-like chambers of which they are composed.

Public buildings.

The principal public buildings in Dacca are the Secretariat and Government House, the jail, the lunatic asylum, the Mitford Hospital, the college, and the madrasa, the four Christian churches, Greek, Armenian, Protestant and Roman Catholic; the cutcherries of the Judge and the Collector-Magistrate, the offices of the Municipality and the District Board and the Northbrook Hall. The cutcherries of the Magistrate-Collector and District Judge were completed in 1865. Prior to this the Collector held his office in the building which till 1905 was the Collegiate High School. In a letter written in 1857 he complains bitterly of his cramped quarters and describes how the Tauzinavis had to work in the kitchen and the Nāzir to transact his business in the open air. The Magistrate held his court in what was afterwards the European Club, and the Civil Judge sat in the house which in 1907 was assigned as an office and residence to the Executive Engineer.

The old buildings of Dacca.

The following account of the old buildings in Dacca has been for the most part condensed from Notes on the Antiquities of Dacca by Khān Bahādur Saiyid Aulad Husain, (Dacca, 1904). Of the European factories in Dacca no traces now remain. The English factory stood on the site of what till recently was the Dacca College. Even in 1837 the only part of the building still existing was the outer wall. The site of the French factory is now covered by the women's apartments in the Palace of the Nawāb, the Ahsun Munzil, and the Dutch factory stood at the south-west corner of the compound of the Mitford Hospital.

The Lāl Bāgh fort was commenced in 1678 by Prince Muhammad Azam, but it was never completed by his successor, Shaista Khān. The enclosure is 2,000 feet long by 8,000 feet broad, but there are walls only along two sides and the gateways though very lofty and impressive are falling into ruins. From the architectural point of view the most interesting building in the fort is the tomb of Bībī Peri, daughter of Shaista Khān, a great niece of Nūr Jahān, who died in 1684 A.D. The tomb is thus described by Colonel Cunningham: "The tomb is built entirely of stone, of black basalt from Gaya, grey sandstone from Chunar and white marble from Jaypur. It consists of nine rooms, the central one being 19 feet 3 inches square. ....The walls of the central room are of white marble, panelled with black lines, and the floor is laid out in a small pattern of the same material. The walls of the four central side rooms are also white marble, but the walls of the corner rooms are decorated with glazed tiles. The colours of the panels are dark blue, orange, green and purple, on a yellow ground, with borders of orange and blue flowers on a green ground. But the most curious part of the tomb is its roof, which is built throughout in the old Hindu fashion of overlapping layers. The summit of the roof is 19 feet 11 inches from the ground and on the top of the pyramid is a small dome, about ten feet in diameter covered with copper plates. The sarcophagus in the central room is of white marble." * There are a *hammam* and the ruins of a mosque in the fort, but the principal mosque in this quarter is one just outside the southern wall, measuring 164 feet by 54 feet. It was built by the Prince who afterwards became the Emperor Farrukh Sīyar at the beginning of the eighteenth century and is still in use.

The Katras. The Bara Katra was built in 1664 by Mīr Abul Kasim. It offers a noble front to the river with its lofty and imposing central gateway which is flanked by smaller entrances and by two octagonal towers but was formerly used as a caravan serai. Much of the building is now in a very dilapidated state. On the south bank of the Buri Ganga opposite to the Bara Katra are a tower and a few ruined chambers which are the sole remains of the Zanjira Palace, which was built by Ibrahim Khān about 1620. It is said that the palace was connected with the north bank of the river by a wooden bridge, though at the present day it is difficult to imagine the Buri Ganga being spanned so easily.

The Chota Katra is situated about one hundred yards to the east of the Bara Katra, and was built by Shaista Khān in 1663. The plan is similar to that of the Bara Katra but the style of architecture is similar to that which is known as Shaistakhāni. It is now used as a warehouse.

The Husaini Dalan. The Husaini Dalan is a large two-storied building in the north of the city which was built by Mīr Murād, Superintendent of the Fleet, in 1642. The Muharram is celebrated here and a grant for the purpose which was made by the Nawāb has been continued by the British Government. The building was badly damaged by the earthquake of 1897 and was restored by the late Nawāb Sir Ahsanullah Bahādur, K.C.I.E., at a cost of nearly a lakh of rupees.

Other mosques. The following are some of the most interesting mosques in the city. The mosque on the west side of the Chauk was built by Shaista Khān in 1676. It measures 50 feet by 25 feet and is kept in a state of very good repair. Khān Muhammad Mirdhā's mosque is situated a little to the north-west of the Lāl Bāgh and was built in 1706. It stands on a platform measuring 125 feet by 100 feet and, as the mosque is very poorly endowed, the rooms below the platform are let to the Municipality as a stable for their bullocks. The oldest mosque in the city is Binat Bībi's

* Archæological Survey of Bengal, Vol. 15, p. 131.

mosque at Narandia which was built in A.D. 1456, but it has nothing but its age to recommend it. Other old mosques are the one in Ashik Jamadār's lane which is ascribed to Islām Khān, who made Dacca his capital in 1608 and the one in Naswala Gulli which was built in 1458. The Churihatta mosque is situated about a quarter of a mile west of the Chauk and the interior measures 30 feet by 15. Tradition has it that a Hindu official was ordered to build a mosque at the spot but built a temple instead, but that this was converted into a mosque in 1649 A.D. The mosque and mausoleum near the southwest corner of the Ramna race-course must have been originally handsome buildings but they are now in a very dilapidated state. They were built by Hāji Khwāja Shāhbāz in 1679 A.D. The mosque measures 68 by 26 feet and is surmounted by three domes. The mausoleum is 26 feet square and has one dome only.

On the Mymensingh road just north of the railway crossing, beyond the new civil station, is the mosque of Khwaja Ambar which was built in 1680 A.D. The building is surmounted by three handsome domes, but is now in a very dilapidated state. A deep well dug by the pious founder in the compound still yields particularly good water, and the brick bridge built by him across the Iskatan Khāl where it crosses the Mymensingh road is still in use. Khwāja Ambar is said to have been the head eunuch of Shaista Khān. West of the city, about two miles beyond the municipal boundary, is the Satgambaz Mosque, which measures 58 by 27 feet. The main building is surmounted by three domes and there are domes on the towers that flank each of the four corners. This mosque originally stood on the banks of the Buri Ganga but the river has now receded fully a mile towards the south. Tradition has it that it was built by Shaista Khān and that the mausoleum close by covers the tombs of two of the daughters of that great Nawāb. The mosque in Babu Bāzār was also built by Shaista Khān, and in his residence close by on the site of what is now the Mitford Hospital, he is said to have met Tavernier. Not far away, about a mile to the north-west of the pilkhana, is the mausoleum of Dara Begam. The inner apartment is 27½ feet square, the walls are 7 feet thick and the dome which crowns the whole is the largest in the city, having a diameter of 25 feet. At Azimpura there is a mosque owned by the descendants of a famous saint. The head of the family for the time being, following the example of his pious ancestor, never leaves the precincts of his mosque and compound. The Pagla bridge is an interesting old relic on the Nārāyanganj road. It is said to have been built by Mir Jumla about 1660, though Bishop Heber states that the natives told him that the architect was a Frenchman. The bridge is now in ruins but two towers are still standing and the general effect is rather picturesque.

Hindu temples.

The most celebrated temple in Dacca is the Dhākeswari which is situated in the north-west corner of the town. The temple is said to have been originally founded by Ballāl Sen in gratitude for assistance rendered to his mother when she was banished here with her infant after her intrigue with the river Brahmaputra had been discovered. Rājā Mān Singh, Akbar's famous general, is said to have rebuilt the shrine, but all traces of these ancient temples have disappeared and the present building is ascribed to the piety of an employé of the Company who lived about two hundred years ago. In the Nawābpur road is the shrine of Lakshi Nārāyan who is an object of special reverence to the Basāks inhabiting this quarter. One of the exterior stones of the temple abutting on the road is worn smooth by the foreheads of devout Hindus saluting the deity within. The Shivbāri and the Kālibāri near the Ramna race-course have also recently attracted many worshippers.

Trade and Commerce.

The history of Dacca as a trade centre is virtually the history of the district, and will be found discussed in detail in Chapter VII. At the present day it is to some extent hampered as a trade centre by the deterioration of the Buri Ganga. During the rains that river is open to steamer traffic along its whole length, but in the dry weather only the smallest country boats can enter its western mouth and even steam launches cannot get up to the city from the east. Dacca collects jute and oil-seeds for export, but is not so large an emporium as Nārāyanganj, and it has a fair export business in hides. The principal imports are grain, salt, oil, piece-goods, lime, stationery, umbrellas, drugs, ready-made clothing, and the miscellaneous articles which an American would describe as 'notions.' There are few weavers of fine muslin left, but a few looms still are worked in Wari. There is, however, a considerable manufacture of *jhappans* and *kasidas* which are exported to Turkey and Arabia. Other industries are shell cutting, which has its centre in the Sankhāri Bāzār, brass and metal work in the Tatari Bāzār, gold and silver work in the Tanti Bāzār and Nawābpur, soap-making and boat-building. The Bank of Bengal at Dacca is the financial centre not only of the district but of much of Eastern Bengal and there are a certain number of wealthy money-lenders in the Bāzār.

Water works.

The water-works of Dacca took their origin in gift of Rs. 50,000 made by Nawāb Sir Abdul Gani, K.C.S.I., in 1871 to commemorate the recovery of King Edward VII, then Prince of Wales, from a serious illness. This gift was subsequently doubled by the generous donor and another half lakh was given by his son Nawāb Sir Ahsanullah, K.C.I.E., to form the nucleus of a maintenance fund. The works were completed in January 1878 at a cost of Rs. 1,95,000, the amount in excess of the gift of one lakh being paid by Government. The water was drawn from the Buri Ganga, passed through settling tanks and filtering beds, and distributed through 4½ miles of pipes fitted with 25 street stand-posts. The daily supply of filtered water available was 200,000 gallons. This supply was far from meeting the requirements of the city and the system was extended from time to time, Rs. 25,000 being provided for the purpose by the Nawāb and Rs. 1,25,000 by the Municipality. Ultimately there were nearly 16 miles of piping with 142 street hydrants. In 1893, the great disturbers of Eastern Bengal began to make their influence felt. The main stream of the Buri Ganga receded and a *chur* began to form in front of the intake pipe. The length of the pipe was extended and a channel was dug through the *chur* in the dry season. But these expedients proved of no avail in face of the constantly increasing size of the *chur*, and ultimately a new pumping station had to be erected on the further edge to drive the water across it through an open conduit into a pool from which it could be drawn by the main suction pipe. It was then felt that the time had come to remodel the whole system. The population had outgrown the available supply of water, the engines were old and expensive in their working and the supply of the unfiltered water precarious and unsatisfactory. It was at first suggested that four wells each 26 feet in diameter should be sunk in the *chur* and the water pumped direct from them into the mains but this scheme was rejected, as, apart from other objections, it was considered doubtful whether the wells would yield the requisite supply of water. Ultimately administrative sanction was accorded to a scheme estimated to cost Rs. 5,00,000, of which Rs. 3,00,000 were given as a grant by Government and the remainder as a loan to the Municipality repayable in twenty years. Under this scheme two new engines have been provided each capable of pumping 100,000 gallons per hour and the two old Worthington pumps which can deliver 40,000 gallons an hour are retained as a reserve. The water is drawn direct from the river through a suction pipe 1,600 feet long, is filtered in six jewel filters, and is finally distributed thoughout the city. Much credit is due to the Chairman of the Municipality Nawāb Khwāja Muhammad Yusuf Khān Bahādur, for the tact and ability shown by him in bringing to a conclusion a scheme that was beset with many difficulties. A note recorded by him in 1908 on the water-works remodelling scheme contains much useful information.

Cemeteries. The Anglican cemetery is situated in the north-east corner of the city and was consecrated by Bishop Heber in 1824. It is described by that prelate as being about a mile distant from the inhabited portion of the city and as surrounded by a wilderness of jungle.

"Some fine elephants with their mahouts were browsing on the trees and bushes round the walls and amid the neighbouring ruins. Indian cattle occupied the little grassy glades which intersected what would else have been a trackless forest and the whole had so wild and characteristic an appearance that I regretted that I had no time to make a drawing." *

* Heber's Journal, Vol. I, p. 151.

Since the development of the Khas Mahal of Wari the cemetery has had adjoining it on the west a really charming suburb and Heber's description is of interest from the contrast it affords to the present day surroundings. The cemetery has still plenty of vacant space and is tastefully laid out with avenues of casuarina trees and beds of flowers. The most conspicuous object is a Moorish gateway which now stands near the centre of the enclosure and thus indicates that the original cemetry must have been considerably enlarged.

The Baptist Mission has a cemetery close by but it contains no tombs of special interest. The Greek cemetery is to the west of the race-course and is in a very neglected state. Cemeteries for Muhammadans have been opened by the municipality, but Muhammadan graves are to be found on almost any piece of waste land in the suburbs and afford a far from pleasing spectacle. A framework of bamboo is placed above the body and the earth heaped upon it. When the bamboos rot the earth falls in and the grave is left as an empty hole two or three feet deep. A piece of land closely pitted with these holes has a most melancholy appearance.

The New Civil Station.

The European residences in old Dacca were not uncomfortable houses and had the advantage of being situated near the river. They were, however, surrounded by the most densely crowded portions of the city which had to be traversed before either walking or driving could be enjoyed in comfort. The new station has been located to the east and west of the Ramna race-course stretching away towards the Mirpur road. The site is an open one and beyond it the country has some claims to beauty, so that in time to come, new Dacca may be a not unpleasant place of residence. The Ramna race-course was first cleared by Mr. Dawes, the Magistrate, in 1825, who threw up the mound at the northern end now known as Dawes' folly.

The family of the Nawāb of Dacca.

The city of Dacca is so intimately associated with its Nawābs that no account of it would be complete without some reference to the history of the family of the present Nawāb of Dacca. This family has no connection with the old Muhammadan rulers of the province but is descended from Khwāja Abdul Hakim who was governor of Kashmīr during the reign of the Emperor Muhammad Shāh. Abdul Hakim was at Delhi when the city was sacked by Nadir Shāh and fled to Bengal with the remnants of his fortune. He settled in Sylhet but on his death his two brothers moved to Dacca, where one of them, Maulvi Abdullah, was the founder of the present family. This gentleman was succeeded by Maulvi Ahsanullah, the great-great-grandfather of the present Nawāb, who died soon afterwards when on a pilgrimage to Mecca. Up to this time the family had been engaged in trading in gold dust and skins, but the next head, Maulvi Hafizullah, brother of Ahsanullah, began to invest the property in land. He was succeeded by Maulvi Abdūl Kāfur, who was followed by Khwāja Alimullah, great-grandfather, Nawāb Sir

Abdul Gani grandfather, and Nawāb Sir Ahsanullah, father of Sir Salimullah, G.C.I.E., the present Nawāb Bahādur of Dacca.

Maulvi Hafizullah and Khwāja Alimullah accumulated a magnificent estate, and though its dignity and importance has been diminished by the Muhammadan law of inheritance which allocates it to numerous shareholders it is still a splendid property. The Nawābs of Dacca have now for several generations maintained the traditions and position of great nobles, and their influence over the Muhammadan community was and is immense. The Ahsun Munzil, which was built in 1872, is a stately residence whose public apartments are furnished in the best European style and their garden houses at Dilkusha, Shāh Bāg, and Bāgāubāri give evidence of equally good taste. The Nawābs offered a splendid hospitality alike to Europeans and to Indians and to the poor of the city they were an ever present help in trouble. Even at the present day when the resources of the estate have been to some extent dissipated by their distribution into so many channels no less than Rs. 65,000 are annually spent on religious and charitable purposes and the liberality of the Nawābs in the past has been phenomenal. They gave 4½ lakhs of rupees to provide Dacca with electric light, 2½ lakhs for water-works, a lakh for the Dacca relief fund and another lakh for the Dacca plague fund, but these are only the more conspicuous of their many benevolences. The present Nawāb Sir Salimullah was created a K.C.S.I. in 1908 and a G.C.I.E. in 1911 and has served on the legislative council of the Viceroy. He takes a keen interest in everything affecting the Muhammadan community and was a staunch supporter of the Government during the agitation that followed the partition of Bengal. He is not, however, the only distinguished member of his family for his uncle, Nawāb Muhammad Yusuf, has for many years done exceptionally meritorious work as Chairman of the Municipality and Vice-Chairman of the District Board.

Dasora.—Head-quarters village of the Mānikganj Subdivision situated in 23° 53′ N. and 96° 2′ E. The village and bāzār stand on a fine grass Maidan on the banks of a khāl which in the rains is connected with the Dhaleswari river. The public offices include the cutcherries of the Subdivisional Officer and of the three Munsifs stationed here, a brick built sub-jail with accommodation for 22 prisoners, a charitable dispensary with eight beds, an entrance school, a bonded liquor warehouse and the office of the Sub-Registrar. The police station is situated on the banks of the Dhaleswari river about two miles away. Dāsora like the rest of the Mānikganj subdivision is a feverish locality and the District Board have recently spent a large sum of money in digging tanks and using the earth obtained from them to fill up the insanitary ditches and hollows which surrounded most of the habitations in the centre of the town.

Dhamrai.—A large village situated on the Bansi river in 23° 55′ N. and 90° 13′ E.; population, 1911, 635. Dhāmrāi is built upon a low hill of laterite, which is an outlyer from the high land of Bhowal, standing up amidst the swamps that lie to the north of the Dhaleswari. Dhāmrāi is much more of a town than most of the villages of Dacca. Many of the houses are built of masonry and the laterite soil discourages that luxuriant growth of vegetable life which is so characteristic of a Bengali village. A broad road runs through the place, in which stands a colossal car adorned with rough carvings, some of which depict the workings of the reproductive instinct in its most abandoned forms. This car is used in the Rathjatra festival in June-July when Dhāmrāi is crowded with pilgrims. There is a large mosque in the village to which is attached a Muhammadan school.

Dhankora.—Village situated in the Mānikganj thāna, which is the seat of the Dhānkora zamindārs. The founder of the family was Rām Narasingha Ray, the great-great-grandfather of the present zamindārs who was a legal practitioner and shop-owner at Mymensingh. The estate pays a revenue of Rs. 10,483. The present owners of the property are two cousins Babus Hem Chandra Ray Chaudhuri and Babu Dinesh Chandra Ray Chaudhuri.

Durduria.—Ruins of a fort on the banks of the Lakshya river in 24° 7′ N and 90° 34′ E., nearly opposite the village of Kāpāsia. The fort is in the form of a crescent resting on the river, the outer wall, which is surrounded by a moat, being about two miles in circumference. Within this there is a second earth-work and in the centre of all there are the ruins of the citadel, which seems to have been built of brick. On the opposite bank of the Lakshya there are mounds and scattered bricks which suggest that the place was once the site of a city of considerable size. According to Taylor, who describes the places at length (Topography of Dacca, p. 113), the fort is said to have been erected by Rāni Babani who was probably the last of the Bunea Rājās at the time of the Muhammadan invasion in 1204 A.D. The fort was twice besieged by the Emperor of Delhi in the latter half of the fourteenth century but on both occasions unsuccessfully. The fort at Durduria is sometimes spoken of as the Ekdala fort, the name having been transferred from the fort at Ekdala, eight miles lower down the river.

Jaydebpur.—Village situated in 24° 0′ N. and 90° 25′ E. Jaydebpur is the family seat of the zamindārs of Bhowal who are generally considered to be the leading family of Hindu landlords in the district. They have been in possession of their estates for upwards of ten generations; their property has not been dissipated amongst a multitude of co-sharers, and much of it lies in a compact block, surrounded by a ring fence. It has always been the tradition of the family to do things in the grand style. They gave, for instance, the land required for the railway and for roads through Bhowal free of charge and for several generations they have maintained a fine establishment at Jaydebpur. The first chief of Bhowal was Fazl Ghazi, one of the followers of Isā Khān, whose descendant Bahādur received a jagir of 22 parganas in Eastern Bengal from the great Emperor Akbar. The estate remained in the family of the Ghazis, who settled at Kāliganj, till the time of one Daulat Ghazi, who received a fresh settlement in 1645 A.D. Daulat Ghazi failed to exercise proper supervision over his affairs or his employés, his revenue was not paid up with punctuality and it is alleged that the Mughal authorities deprived him of the zamindāri and settled it with three of his Hindu servants, Bala Rām, Krishna Rām Chaudhari of Gacha aud Balsanna Ghosh. Bala Rām was succeeded by his son Srikrishna and the sanad dated 1683 A.D. confirming him in the zamindāri is still preserved amongst the family archives. The new zamindārs at first made some arrangement for the support of their former masters but these allowances were withdrawn, and though the Ghazis contested their title, both by force of arms and in the law courts, they met with no success in either field and their claims were finally rejected in a judgment delivered in 1704 A.D. The present Jaydebpur family traces its descent to Keshab, a learned pandit of Bajrajogini in Munshīganj. Fourth in descent from him was Bala Rām, who was the *diwān* of Daulat Ghazi and succeeded in ousting his master and obtaining settlement in his place in the latter half of the seventeenth century. Sixth in descent from Bala Rām was Lakshi Nārāyan, who held the zamindāri in 1763 when the Company first assumed the *diwāni* of Bengal. Lakshi Nārāyan was a strong man but died when his son Golack Nārāyan was but three years old and the widow and orphan were driven from their home by the wife of a member of a collateral branch. The widow subsequently succeeded in regaining her estates but Golack preferred a life of religious meditation to one of action and declined to take any interest in the affairs of this life. His son, Kāli Nārāyan Ray Chaudhari, was of a very different temper. The Gacha zamindārs had sold a portion of their estates in Bhowal to Mr. Wise, the famous indigo planter of Dacca, who thus became a co-sharer in Bhowal. Quarrels soon sprang up between the partners and after several murderous riots Mr. Wise decided that there was not room for two rulers in Bhowal and in 1851 he sold his share of the zamindāri to Kāli Nārāyan for Rs. 4,46,000. Kāli Nārāyan also purchased the zamindāri of Phulbaria and played a leading part in the social life of the district both amongst Europeans and Indians. He was a keen sportsman and a charitable and enlightened landlord and was the first gentleman in Eastern Bengal to receive from Government the title of Rājā Bahādur. Kāli Nārāyan died in 1878, and was succeeded by his son Rājā Rājendra Nārāyan Deb Bahādur. During his incumbency the income of the property was much enlarged and the son well sustained the excellent reputation bequeathed him by his father. He died in 1901 and since that date the estate has passed through some vicissitudes. Frequent changes of managers did not prove conducive to good administration, and though Bhowal is still a fine property, some years of careful management will be required if it is to attain to the position of eminence it enjoyed a quarter of a century ago. Rājā Rājendra Nārāyan left three sons Ravendra, Ramendra, and Rabendra Nārāyan. The two eldest did not long survive their father and left no issue and the youngest son is now the sole male representative of the direct family line. The family possesses a fine house at Jaydebpur and the roads in the immediate vicinity have been well laid out. The estate maintains an entrance school and a charitable dispensary and there is a large market in the village.

Kaliganj.—Important bāzār on the west bank of the Lakshya river, population in 1911, 347. There is an entrance school at this place maintained by the zamindār of Jaydebpur, who has a cutcherry here, and a registration office.

Kapasia—Bāzār on the west bank of the Lakshya in 24° 7′ N. and 90° 34′ E. The zamindārs of Jaydebpur have a cutcherry here and a charitable dispensary, and there is a police station. The banks of the river Lakshya at this point rise to a height of thirty or forty feet above the water, and the surroundings of the village with their fine umbrageous trees and bamboo groves are really beautiful.

Kasimpur.—Village situated in 23° 59′ N. and 90° 20′ E., on the west bank of the Turāg river, the home of the zamindārs of Kāsimpur. The family was originally domiciled in Barisal, but one Trailokya Nath Guha, eleventh in ascent from the present zamindār, settled at Kāsimpur and married the daughter and only child of the local talukdār, whose property in due time passed to his grandson. The estate was increased by Bhabani Prasad Guha, sixth in descent from Trailokyanath, who was a man of considerable ability and enterprise and maintained a band of armed retainers. During the stormy times that preceded the downfall of the Muhammadan administration he succeeded in taking possession of a considerable tract of land. The estate was permanently settled in 1793 with Babu Gouri Prasad Ray Chaudhuri, grandfather of the late Shyama Prasad Ray Chaudhuri, who lived till 1907. The property has generally been in possession of a single individual, but the present zamindār, Babu Sarada Prasad Ray, has no less than five co-sharers, the sons of his dead brothers. Kāsimpur is situated in one of the prettiest quarters of the district and is one of the few places where a little shooting can be had. Deer and pig are plentiful in the surrounding jungles, but tiger and leopard, though occasionally to be found, are very scarce.

Lohajang.—Large bāzār situated on the banks of the Padmā river, in 23° 25′ N. and 90° 19′ E.; population in 1911, 935. The bāzār is situated on either side of a khāl flowing into the Padmā, and is a great centre for the trade in jute, timber, oil, and salt. Messrs. Turner Morrison and Co. have a salt godown here and there is a large depôt for oil; there are also a sub-registrar's office, and an independent police outpost. At the present day Lohajang is a very busy little place but its existence is threatened by the Padmā river, and it is possible that before long much of it will have been washed away.

Mirkadim.—Large bāzār situated on the south bank of the Dhaleswari river in 23° 34′ N. and 90° 30′ E., about one and a half miles north-east of Munshiganj. Population in 1911, 292.

Mirpur.—Large trading village situated 8½ miles west of Dacca, on the banks of the Turāg, in 23° 67′ N. and 90° 20′ E.; population in 1911, 818. The village is rather picturesque as it is situated on several low hills intersected by the various channels of the Turāg. Two large madrasas are maintained here and in the neighbourhood is the shrine of Hazrat Shāh Ali, which is visited every year by thousands of pilgrims. The mosque in which he is buried was erected in 1480 A.D., but the saint did not die till 1577. It is stated that he shut himself up in the mosque after requesting that he might not be disturbed in any way for forty days. On the thirty-ninth day the disciples heard a noise as of boiling liquid inside the mosque and in their alarm decided that the door must be burst open. On entering the mosque all that they found was a pool of boiling blood upon the floor, while a voice from heaven, which they recognised as being that of the saint, ordered them to bury the blood where it lay.

Manohardi.—Bāzār situated in the north of the Nārāyanganj subdivision in 23° 47′ N. and 90° 37′ E. There is a charitable dispensary and independent police outpost here.

Munshiganj.—The head-quarters of the Munshīganj subdivision, situated in 23° 33′ N. and 90° 32′ E., population in 1911, 883. The bāzār is built on the banks of a branch of the Taltala Khāl, which in the rains affords a safe and direct route from the Dhaleswari to the Padmā. In the cold weather it is too shallow for navigation and the question of deepening it is under the consideration of the District Board. Both criminal and civil work are very heavy here and the ordinary staff consists of three magistrates and five munsifs. The public buildings include a a sub-jail with accommodation for 17 prisoners, a dispensary, the office of a sub-registrar, an entrance school, a bonded liquor warehouse and a public library presented by Babu Harendra Lal Ray of Baghyakul. A jewel filter for the supply of filtered water with a pipe installation was presented to the station by Babu Sita Nath Ray of the same family in 1909. The Subdivisional Officer's residence is situated in the Idrakpur fort which was erected by Mir Jumla about 1660 A.D. The enclosure walls and five bastions, all built of red sandstone, are still in very fair condition. From December to February a large fair, the Kartic

Baruni *mela*, is held on the banks of the Dhaleswari at a distance of about half a mile from Munshīganj. This fair used formerly to be a great centre of trade, and though with the development of steamer communication it has declined considerably in importance, a large business is still done in timber, pottery, and brass ware.

Nangalband.—Village situated in 23° 39′ N. and 90° 33′ E. on the banks of the old Brahmaputra in the Nārāyanganj subdivision. The village is only of importance on the occasion of the great bathing festival which takes place on the eighth day of the moon in Chait. Tradition has it that Parasurām after killing his mother was unable to free his hand from the axe with which he did the horrid deed till he bathed in the waters of the Brahmakund amongst the Mishmi Hills. Anxious to convey these healing waters to mankind he converted the accursed axe into a plough and cut a passage through the hills down which the lake poured into the Assam Valley. He continued to carve a channel for the river till his plough stuck fast at Nāngalband. Satisfied that his labours had at last come to an end he went on pilgrimage but was enraged on his return to find that the Brahmaputra had broken through the barrier that stayed it and mingled its waters with the Lakshya river. In his wrath he cursed it and declared that the river should only enjoy its peculiarly purifying powers for one day in the year.

On this occasion the village is visited by thousands of pilgrims anxious to purge their souls of sin. Cholera used at one time to be a serious menace for Nāngalband is no longer situated on the main stream of the Brahmaputra but on a dying channel which contains little water save in the rains. The District Board has accordingly taken over the management of the *mela*; tube wells have been sunk and temporary hospitals established.

Narayanganj.—Nārāyanganj stands on the banks of the Lakshya in 23° 37′ N. and 90° 30′ E., in a position that is admirably suited for all purposes of trade. Unlike most of the rivers of East Bengal the Lakshya flows between high banks so that Nārāyanganj has escaped the fate that befalls most of the delta towns and has neither been washed away nor left high and dry a mile or more from a navigable river. The Lakshya at this point falls into the Dhaleswari and the Dhaleswari, after uniting its waters with the Meghnā, joins the Padmā a few miles lower down. Nārāyanganj is thus in touch with all the trade of Tippera and the Surma valley, with Calcutta, *viâ* Goalando and even with the sea. It is in fact the port of Dacca from which it is separated by nine miles of road or railway and by about twenty miles of water. In the height of the rains, when the Kumaria Bhanga Khāl is full, the distance by river is reduced by two or three miles.

Nārāyanganj is mentioned in some of the earliest records in the Collectorate. There is a petition dated 1790 in which the petitioner, an old servant of the Company, alleges that he has built the ganj for upwards of thirty years, "for the purpose of defraying the expenses of the thakur, for feeding the poor, and for my own support." In 1814, the Collector stated that the place was well known to Government as a great salt emporium and the residence of one of their salt agencies. It was said to be about a third of the size but more populous and opulent in proportion than the city of Dacca. This estimate of size was clearly incorrect and Hamilton writing in 1820 puts the population at 15,000 souls. The inhabitants carried on a great trade in salt, grain, tobacco, and lime and the town exhibited a scene of commercial bustle and activity seldom seen in a community entirely composed of Hindus. Most of the principal merchants were, however, foreigners.* In 1838, when Mr. Taylor wrote, the population only amounted to 6,252, but he states that the place had been declining for about 30 years, having suffered from the competition of Sirajganj. About 5,00,000 maunds of salt were imported from Chittagong and Bulwah and no less than 160 sloops were engaged in the trade. Mughs and people from the eastern coast below Arracan, including a few Chinese, also visited Nārāyanganj in the north-east monsoon, exchanging catechu, cotton, arsenic, pepper, and bullion, for betel-nut, sugar, tobacco and manufactured goods.† In 1867, the trade in jute which has made Nārāyanganj what it now is was beginning to assume importance. The estimated annual exports amounted to four lakhs of maunds of jute and the trade in oilseeds was increasing. The population in 1872 was 11,377. The next nine years witnessed little growth and in 1881 it was only 12,508 : in 1891 it was 17,785, in 1901 24,472 and in 1911, 27,876. The census is taken at the beginning of the year, before the commencement of the jute season, and in August, when the river is packed with shipping and the mills with coolies, there are probably 35,000 people in the place.

On the right bank of the Lakshya the town is divided into the following quarters, starting up stream—Hajiganj, Bhagwanganj, Tan Bāzār, Nitaiganj and Sitalakshya. On the left bank the names of the quarters are Nabiganj, Bandar, Sonākānda, and Madanganj The total area within municipal limits is four square miles. Much of the land lies well below flood level and has to be artificially raised before it can be used for building but the municipality, on which the European jute merchants are strongly represented, is probably the most efficient in Bengal and the town has been well laid out and is admirably managed. The river frontage is for the most part occupied with jute factories. The fibre is pressed into bales, *cutcha* if only intended for Calcutta,

* A Geographical, Satistical, and Historical Description of Hindustan and the Adjacent Countries by Walter Hamilton, London, 1820.

† Topography of Dacca, p. 99.

and *pucka* or more tightly pressed if destined for Europe. The principal jute firms are Messrs. David and Co., Ralli Brothers, Messrs Sarkies and Co., R. Sim and Co. and the Sonākānda Bailing Company. An account of the jute industry will be found in Chapter VII. Boats bringing jute frequently load up on their return to the interior with a cargo of other goods, and the town has thus become a great distributing centre. There are three bonded warehouses for the sale of salt and upwards of 300,000 maunds were cleared in 1910. Oil is a great article of commerce and Messrs. Shaw Wallace and Co. have established an installation for the storage of oil in bulk. There is also a large market for grain, cotton, piece-goods, tobacco, sugar and miscellaneous articles. Oil seeds and cotton are exported as well as jute.

Apart from the jute factories, some of which are of imposing size, the town contains no modern buildings of interest, and nearly all the shops are built of nothing more permanent than timber and corrugated iron. There are the ruins of forts at Sonākánda and Hajiganj which are said to have been erected by Mīr Jumla to act as a barrier against the incursions of the Maghs. At Hajiganj there is a large mosque and mausoleum attributed to Shaista Khān and at Nabiganj there is the shrine of Qadam Rasul in which is deposited a stone slab which bears the impress of the Prophet's foot. The building was originally erected by Manwar Khān in the earlier half of the seventeenth century and rebuilt by Ghulam Nabi in 1642. Tradition has it that when Manwar Khān was travelling to Dacca he found an old man sitting in the jungle at the spot where the shrine now stands burning incense before the slab. He was at first inclined to doubt whether the relic was a genuine one, but was convinced, when he found that, as a result of his prayers before the sacred object, he was treated kindly at Dacca, though his revenue was heavily in arrears, while his pen, which he had locked in a box, put forth young leaves. The public buildings include the courts of the Subdivisional Officer and of the Munsifs, a sub-jail with accommodation for 36 prisoners and a hospital with 30 beds. The Bank of Bengal has an office here and there are two entrance schools. The town is supplied with filtered water, an installation which serves about 20,000 people having been erected in 1908 at a cost of Rs. 1,80,000.

Narsinghdi.—Village situated in 23° 56′ N. and 90° 44′ E., on the banks of the Meghnā; population, 1911, 382. The bāzār is a considerable centre of trade and contains an independent police outpost, a dispensary and an entrance school.

Nayan Bazar.—Large bāzār situated in 24° 16′ N. and 90° 39′ E., on the banks of the Lakshya river; population in 1911, 288. The bāzār is a centre of the jute and timber trade. The remains of the capital of Sissu Pal are situated a few miles from this place.

Raipura.—Bāzār situated in 23° 59′ N. and 91° 53′ E., on the banks of the Meghnā. The bāzār contains a police station, sub-registrar's office, entrance school and Guru training school.

Rajabari.—Village situated in 23° 29′ N. and 90° 30′ E., containing an independent police outpost and the office of a sub-registrar. About two miles to the south-west is the Rājābāri *mat*, which forms a conspicuous landmark for all voyagers upon the Padmā. The *mat* is a tower 80 feet high and 30 feet square at the base which is said to have been built by Chand Ray and Kedar Ray about the middle of the fifteenth century.

Rampal.—Village in the Munshiganj subdivision situated in 23° 33′ N. and 90° 30′ E.; population in 1911, 787. The site of the old capital of Bikrampur is pointed out near the large tank called Rāmpāl *dighi*, which is three-quarters of a mile long by a quarter of a mile broad. To the north of this tank is the Ballāl *bāri* or palace of Ballāl Sen, the remains of which consist of a quadrangular mound of earth 3,000 square feet in area surrounded by a moat 200 feet wide. Foundations and remains of other buildings are found for miles around and, early in the nineteenth century, a cultivator ploughed up in the neighbourhood a diamond worth Rs. 70,000. Inside the Ballāl *bāri* is a deep excavation called Agnikunda, where tradition says that the last prince of Bikrampur and his family burned themselves at the approach of the Musalmans. Close to Ballāl *bāri* stands a much venerated tomb of one Baba Adam or Adam Shāhid. The masjid of Baba Adam is 43 feet long by 36 feet broad, the walls are 6½ feet thick and the roof is adorned with six domes; it was erected in 1483 A.D. There are various legends with regard to Baba Adam, but they agree in describing him as a saint who came from Mecca to avenge a gross piece of injustice inflicted on a Muhammadan by a a Hindu Rājā. He was killed by the Rājā but his death was almost immediately followed by the Rājā's downfall.

Rekabi Bazar.—Large bāzār situated on the south bank of the Dhaleswari river about three miles from Munshiganj town in 23° 34′ N. and 98° 29′ E. The bāzār is chiefly inhabited by Muhammadan traders and contains a mosque 36 feet by 34 in outside measurement, which was built in 1569 A.D.

Rupganj.—Village situated in 23° 47′ N. and 90° 31′ E., on the west bank of the Lakshya river. There is a police station at Rūpganj and on the opposite bank is the bāzār of Murāpāra and the fine brick-built residence of the Murāpāra zamindārs. The founder of this family was one Rām Ratan Banarji, who towards the end of the eighteenth century, was appointed treasurer of Nator, then the head-quarters of the Rājshāhi district, by Mr. Douglas, formerly Collector of Dacca. In the early days of the permanent settlement estates were sold more frequently than at the present day and Rām Ratan acquired considerable wealth by paying in the revenue for zamindārs who were late in their remittances, a service for which he was handsomely rewarded, and by purchasing estates knocked down to him at auction at prices much below their actual value. The family property was augmented by Ishan Chandra and Pratap Chandra, the grandsons of Rām Ratan, and the gross rental now amounts to about 2½ lakhs of rupees. The Murāpāra Babus have continued faithful to the treasury department and the last three treasurers of the Bank of Bengal at Dacca have all been members of this family. The estates are at the present moment vested in the following persons: Dinesh Chandra, Tarak Chandra and Keshab Chandra, descendants of Rām Ratan's eldest son, each hold one-ninth; Jagodish Chandra and Ashutosh, the minor sons of Bejoy Babu, who was descended from Rām Ratan's younger son, hold one-third between them; Rajendra and Gyanendra hold three-sixteenths; while Birendra, Brajendra and Nripendra hold seven-forty-eighths between them: these five persons are the descendants of Rām Ratan's brother.

Sabhar.—Village situated in 23° 51′ N. and 90° 15′ E., on the left bank of the Dhaleswari river. Sābhār is a considerable trade centre and, many of the houses being built of dried mud and some of brick, it is more like a small town than the usual Bengali village. Immediately to the north of Sābhār are the ruins of an old Bhuiya chief named Harish Chandra. All that now remains are earthworks encircled with ditches, which are full of jungle, old tanks, and the foundations of what must once have been a tower.

Sealo Aricha.—Large bāzār situated on the east bank of the Padmā river, in 23° 49′ N. and 89° 47′ E., nearly opposite Goalando. Sealo is the head-quarters of a police station and is a mart through which grain coming down the Ganges enters the western part of the district. It is also a port of ingress for pilgrims and labourers coming from the west.

Sonargaon.—A tract of country about forty-eight miles in length and twenty in breadth, bounded on the east by the Meghnā and the Arialkhān rivers, on the west by the Banar and Lakshya rivers, on the south by the Lakshya, the old Brahmaputra and the Dhaleswari rivers and on the north by the old Brahmaputra and certain villages.* Under Muhammadan rule any place where the king resided was known as Balda Sonārgāon, and though Sonārgāon is shown as a large town in the half inch map of Dacca published in 1885, there is not even a village of that name in existence at the present day. Painam is a place which was formerly of considerable importance and which is said by Dr. Taylor to have been the ancient city of Sonārgāon. At the present day it is buried in a dense jungle of bamboos and other trees. There are the remains of earthworks and moats and, about a mile to the south, at Khasnagar there is a tank 400 yards in length and 200 yards in breadth. Mograpāra contains a tomb which is said to cover the remains of Ghiyas-ud-dīn Azram Shāh, the rebellious son of Sikandar Shāh, who ruled Bengal from 1368 to 1373 A.D. The sarcophagus is a single block of hard black basalt and was once surrounded by a pillared enclosure. About a quarter of a mile away to the west are five brick tombs which are said by the villagers to be the tombs of the Panch Pirs. Nothing is known of the persons who lie beneath but the graves are considered to be of peculiar sanctity. The oldest mosque at Sonārgāon is one at Goaldi, built in 1519 A.D. which, though small, is possessed of some architectural merit. Other places of interest are the tomb of Manna Shāh Darwesh in Mograpāra and a little to the north is the tomb of Poukai Diwāna, who sat for twelve years in the forest in meditation and had to be dug out from the mound that white-ants had raised around him. At Habibpur to the east is the tomb of the Pagla Sahib who is said to have been a great thief-catcher and to have nailed the heads of his victims to the wall. For a fuller account of Sonārgāon reference may be made to Cunningham, Archæological Survey of India Reports, XV, p. 137, and to a paper by Dr. Wise, J.A.S.B., Vol. XLIII.

Srinagar.—Bāzār situated in 23° 33′ N. and 90° 17′ E., in the centre of the Munshīganj subdivision. There is a police station and sub-registrar's office in the village which is also the home of the Srīnagar zamindār.

INDEX.

S

T

V

W